MW01100736

Making It
in
Japan

Work, Life, Leisure
and
Beyond

by
Mark Gauthier

SANSEIDO

Making It in Japan
Work, Life, Leisure
and Beyond

Copyright © 1993 by Mark Gauthier

First printed on October 1, 1993
ISBN 4-385-35476-6
Printed in Japan

Published by Sanseido Co., Ltd.
2-22-14, Misaki-cho, Chiyoda-ku, Tokyo

The author and publisher thoroughly reviewed and checked this book numerous times to produce what we feel is a most accurate display of useful, pertinent information on the Japan of today. Any misprint or change in addresses or phone numbers are truly regrettable and unavoidable. We accept no responsibility for forces out of our control and sincerely hope our facts are completely accurate. Please understand that a great deal of work went into preparing this book to make it as exact as possible and we hope that you will make us aware of any errors by letter so that we may include the corrections in our next edition.

INTRODUCTION

I have worked very hard in writing and compiling information for this book while in Japan. My partner, Forbes Benning, in Canada, has also worked long hours editing and filing all the data. Any errors in information are terribly regrettable and we would appreciate any corrections you may have in the future.

Places change, people move, and even buildings disappear in Tokyo. Prices usually go up, but what else is new?

Enjoy the book and we hope it will answer all of your questions or direct you to the proper channels during your stay in wonderful Japan.

Send in your thoughts, comments, gripes, successes, highs or lows about Japan and we'll have a Feedback Section in our next edition with your name beside it.

Send in as much info as you want. We'll read every letter! If this book has helped you in any way, try to help others in the future; you'll be glad you did! You'll find our address at the back of the book in the Book Order Section.

Thank you,

Mark Gauthier,
Tokyo, 1993.

BOOK DEDICATION

I know this list appears long, but it took me a long time to write a quality book and I had a lot of help. I dedicate this book to my beautiful wife, Rhonda, who consistently supported me in my goal to write a practical guide book for newly arrived foreigners. Rhonda, I can't believe we'll be parents soon, but I know it will certainly be an adventure that we'll tackle together just like everything else we've done ensemble the last six years. I also must thank my computer expert, **Forbes Benning**, who stayed up many a late night transforming my chicken scratches into the coherent pages you see before you. A big thanks to his wife Sofia Benning for tolerating all the late night faxes and phone calls.

In addition, mention must be made to my employer, TOP English School, its owner Yoshikawasan and her helpful secretaries; Tanisan, Emikosan, Hayashian, Kondosan and Murabayashisan. I was treated with respect and allowed to pursue my business interests while working for this school.

To my friends Washiyamasan, Akio Nakano, Takagisan and Sugimotosan, one big "Thank you" for everything you've done during our stay in Japan.

To Kazuo Morimoto who one day will translate this book into Japanese, I wish you all the best in Chicago–the future is yours to decide.

To the boys at Idemitsu Oil Company Noriyuki, Harunobu, Yasunori #1 and #2, Tatsuo, Tetsunori, Tomomi, Masahisa, Takechan, Tomoo, Fumio, Naotoshi, Norihito, Keiichi, Makoto, Masayuki and the other guys who serenaded me with all those wonderful Japanese love songs. Guys, don't quit your day jobs.

To my first two students in Japan, Hiromi and Keiko, and all those who followed who made a contribution: Kyoko, Nobuko, Kazuyuki, Rumi and Kurumi, Akinobu Tanso (for all his great and free legal advice) and all my students at Plady House during my first year in Japan.

To Hiro, Kyoko, Noriko who have helped me to learn Japanese, many thanks. I am positive you will be a great teacher Kyoko in your new job. If you can teach me, everyone else will be a breeze.

To Linda who typed this manual till she knew more about Japan than anyone of us, thank you very much.

To the Canadian Embassy Commercial Officers; Mr. Matsunaga, Mr. Kaneko, Paul Brunet and Ezio DiEmmanuel. They have been instrumental in helping me develop my Import business which promotes Canadian products in the Japanese Marketplace. Also, many thanks to Mr. Kimura at the Canada Trade Center for his unlimited energy selling my products.

To Chris Evans, Jane Withey, and Yeri Coyner at the Canadian Chamber of Commerce in Japan. Thank you for helping a pushy guy like me make use of the Chamber.

To Robert and Thelma Gunn who came to Japan and allowed us to take over their spacious apartment when they left, thanks a lot.

To Uncle Gerald who spent many a hard earned buck calling his nephew half–way around the world and for sending a huge Canadian sausage by mail!

Lastly, to my family back home in Canada: Mom, Dad, Paula, Mark, and dearly departed Gonzo. Thank you all for writing letters sending faxes, and doing countless errands. Without all of you, I don't think Rhonda and I would succeed as much as we do. Thank you Paula especially for taping all our favourite "Cosby", "Cheers" and "Home Improvement" shows, and good luck with baby Natalie in 1994. I hope everyone enjoyed their visit to Japan in October 1992 and will visit us again. We miss you and love you all. We will all be together soon.

WHY

HOME

ARRIVAL

JOB HUNTING

HOUSING

LIVING IN JAPAN

RECREATION

EXPLORE JAPANESE CULTURE

SHOPPING

TRAVEL

ORDERING JAPANESE BOOKS

GLOSSARY

Baiku-Bin	Motorcycle delivery service
Beya	Sumo stable housing the wrestlers
Bonenkai	Year-end drinking party
Chanko Nabe	Sumo wrestler's main diet
Chuko	Second hand store
Demae	Home delivery service for take out food
Diskauntoshoppu	Discount shop
Dojo	Drill hall used for karate and so on
Fudosan	Real estate agent
Gaijin	Foreigner
Gaijin House	A guest house of sorts for foreigners in Tokyo
Golden Week	One week of National Holidays at the beginning of May
Gomi	Garbage area
Hakama	Split skirt Kendo, Kyudo, and Aikido wear
Izakaya	A Japanese pub or bar that is really lively and cheap
JR	Japan railways, the largest private railway company in Japan
Judogi	Judo wear
Jujitsu	Judo
Juku	A system of schools where kids cram in extra work at the end of regular school
Kaisuken	11 train tickets for the price of 10
Kanji	Chinese writing characters which form the bulk of the Japanese written Language
Karatedo	Karate
Karoshi	Death from overwork
Katana	Sword used by ancient Samurai Warriors
Kenko Inryo	Health drinks
Key Money	A gift of 2 months rent to the landlord upon moving into your new apartment
Ki	Combination of force, energy, spirit, and power
Kiseru	Train fare cheating
Koban	A Japanese police box where people ask for directions
Kokugikan	National Sumo hall located in Tokyo
Kokuho	National health insurance program
Kyu Or Yumi	Bow used for Japanese archery
Mahjong	Kind of like Dominoes, but much more complicated. Sometimes called the Chinese Game of Four Winds.

Manshon	The Japanese word for mansion which means condominium in English
Natto	Fermented beans
Obi	Belt used when women wear traditional Japanese Kimono
Obon	One week in the middle of August when most Salarymen take their summer holidays
Ochugen	Summer gift giving period
Oden	A unique Japanese 'stew' made with vegetables, fish-paste cakes, fried foods etc boiled in a pot
Oseibo	Winter gift giving period
Real Estate Agent's Fee	Money you pay to the guy who finds your apartment for you
Returnee	A Japanese school kid who has studied abroad and returned to Japan
Ryokan	A Japanese hotel or inn
Salaryman	A Japanese businessman who works long hours and sacrifices all for the good of his company
Sashimi	Raw fish
Seriken	Sequentially numbered coupons used for buying concert tickets
Shaken	Road maintenance insurance
Shichiya	Pawnshop
Shinai	Bamboo sword used in Kendo
Shiyakusho	City Hall
Shogatsu	New year's festival
Tabe Hodai	All you can eat food in a restaurant
Tanimachi	Sumo wrestler supporters
Teiki	Commuter train pass
Tsuyoi	Strong (used in the same sense as English with one extra meaning for strong drinkers, those who can hold their liquor)
Yabusame	Horseback archery
Yakuza	Japanese Mafia
Yowai	Weak (used like in English and for weak drinkers, those who can't hold their drinks)
Zazen	Zen meditation

Noh Play

Kabuki

Bunraku

Tea Ceremony

Judo

Kokugikan Hall

Sumo Wrestling

Sanja Festival, Tokyo

Sanja Festival, Tokyo

Shinto Wedding

Yakitori Bar

Beer Hall

Bus

Dish Replicas

Dish Replicas

Taxi in Tokyo

Automatic Ticketing
Machine

JR Ticketing Counter

Commuters at Station

Tokaido Super Express
Train

World Map Showing
Japan

Tokyo Stock Exchange

Chiba Marine Stadium

Harajuku
Takenoko-zoku

Tennis Court

Mitsukoshi Department Store

Mt. Fuji & Oshino

Inside Department Store

A Beach in Okinawa

WHY

WHY I WROTE THIS BOOK

I am not a writer as anyone who knows me will tell you. This is my first piece, and maybe my last. I started very innocently and have since devoted countless hours researching, writing and rewriting this book. People used to come to me to get info about events, places to go, and where to look for work. I guess I'm a pack–rat when it comes to keeping pamphlets, schedules, and any tourist brochures, so I always seemed to have the answers they were looking for.

Then one day I got a crazy idea to start keeping files and jotting down some of my thoughts. Almost two years later, I finally was satisfied with the product and had it published. I feel my book has a lot of helpful hints that I didn't find in the bookstores when I first arrived in Japan. Read on and let me know with a postcard, letter or fax. Send any comments to the address mentioned at the end.

A systematic approach to the job hunt in Tokyo will leave you well ahead of the unprepared traveler who heard from a friend of a friend that there was money to be made in Japan. In addition, you have the opportunity to purchase my extensive jobs listing manual, ***1001 Teaching, Modeling, Editing and Hostessing Jobs in Japan***, to give you an idea what the going rate is; and to give actual leads that will be valuable today. See at the very end of this book for info on how to order this book and others. I have listed over 1000 actual leads from various sources.

My main goal is to provide the purchaser of this book with all the information available in English to start making money and live comfortably in Japan. I want you to be able to move in, set up shop as quickly as possible and start earning Yen. I was very frightened and nervous at first. What if everything had changed by the time I got there? What if I couldn't teach? This book will enable you to handle all these apprehensions and prepare your assault on the land of opportunity.

What annoys me most about several guide books on Japan is that they bore you with wads of useless information. I seriously believe the authors feel their books must have a certain number of pages to really be called a book. I mean, telling me how to open and close a door as one book did is a waste of my reading time and the publisher's paper. Why not talk about tricks of the trade, how to get private students who pay high fees, where all the really good English services are when you need them etc... This is the type of info I hope to give you here.

Before I left Canada to come to Japan, I scoured every book store in Ontario, Quebec and British Columbia during my summer travels, and what I found on the shelves was usually the same standard fare: general travel books, history of Japan and picture books on various Japanese culture and traditions. Amongst these books were a few "How to Live in Japan" books which came close but still did not encompass all the things a foreign worker really needs to know in order to have a successful experience.

Having bought every one of these "How to" guides, and having followed their suggestions to the last detail, I felt sufficiently prepared to embark on my adventure. And you know, I was prepared, but only for the immediate future. What so many of these books lacked was vision, a long term view of work, study, leisure, travel and basic day–to–day living.

What I wanted was something that was going to clue me in on living quarters, food, actual jobs, and generally what to expect in a sincere, but frank way–no embellishment. I wanted a book to tell me what to bring, where to go, and how to get there. It had to tell me where I could get a job, how should I get it, what did I need to get it, and finally, how to teach English to the Japanese once I got it. I strongly feel that I can inform you to the utmost on these subjects and a lot more in my book.

What I have compiled here has taken many phone calls, letters, personal visits and inquiries about all my needs and several ideas during my three–year working career as an English teacher in Japan. Soon after my wife and I arrived in Tokyo we had an apartment, found several jobs, and had started to build up the necessary comfort items for our apartment: pillows, futon, towels, etc. It seemed that we had more information from what little resources we found in Canada than most travelers, however, much information was still lacking. I want to share all the tricks I've learned with you because Japan is really a neat adventure, and one you will never forget. I want everyone to have a great experience like I am and make big money as a reward for taking a risk in coming in the first place. After all not everyone can boast a year or two of prosperous living in Tokyo, Japan.

I was surprised at the lack of information for the permanent resident of two or three years. Places to go, events, and phone numbers were scattered all over the place and difficult to uncover. I dug all the while I was in Japan to put together all the tips, advice and suggestions you see before you.

I think that *Jobs in Japan* by John Wharton was good seven years ago when Japan was unknown, but now, a more sophisticated, well–organized, planned attack is needed to maximize both your earning potential and your cultural experience. Everything in this book can give you that extra employable edge. I want to prepare you for the nuts and bolts of teaching English in Japan and beyond.

Often people who write books forget their first days, weeks, even months and think everyone who reads their book will be at their same level of comprehension. Or worse, they simplify info for the two day visitor to Tokyo. Plus, other teachers come and go quite often after one year taking all their hard earned experience with them without ever passing it on to someone else. Many are even reluctant to do so when asked directly, preferring you to go through the same blunders they went through to prove to themselves that they are not so stupid as they thought after all. I hope my book will be useful to the newly arrived traveler as well as the hardened veteran.

One final note on the job situation in Japan. Government attitudes regarding work visas and foreign workers has changed. Before Japan wanted as many foreigners as possible to fill the gap, but now with the economies of most countries suffering, they don't need all these people. As a result, teachers are staying longer in Japan because there is nothing to go back to in their host country. Therefore those ultra high salary jobs are no longer that easy to find due to a lower turnover rate. Yes, you will find a job, and yes, your pay will be substantial, but the speed in which you find a job and the quality of it will depend on the presentation of yourself. As I've stated, one of my main focuses in this book is to make you, the reader, extremely marketable and too valuable to pass up. Remember there is not any magic here, just plain hard work.

SHOULD YOU DO IT?

Yes! I hope that this book will lay to rest the opinion that Japan, especially Tokyo, is the most expensive city in the world to live in. I also hope my book can demystify Japan and its unique culture, living and working situations. I know once you get here, you'll see what I mean for yourself, but I want this book to teach you how easy it will be before you come.

There's money to be made here, and after the initial set up fee, there's no easier work to be had. You'll get into a groove, set your own working limit (something you could never do at home) and start making some *real* money. You could choose to party it up every night, travel anywhere in the world, save for a new stereo, car, or even a house. It's all within reach teaching English in Japan. I recommend being as prepared as possible, so there will be no surprises and you won't be caught short of cash or stuck in some job you don't like. Do a little homework and you'll easily save yourself a good US$1,000 a month and be so far ahead of the game you'll be laughing. Send away for the books listed at the back, call a travel agent and start planning your assault.

Anyone can make Japan a reality and have a lifetime experience you'll never forget. And that's no lie.

Top 10 Things I've Seen in Japan

1. A whole train car full of sleeping, druken salarymen on their way home from massive drinking parites, hostess bars and pubs.
2. Cherry Blossom Festival celebrations in April at Ueno Park, Tokyo. Singing, dancing, and drinking under the falling pedals.
3. Subway workers wearing white gloves literally pushing commuters into the trains like sardines.
4. Harajuku, Tokyo on Sundays. Live bands perform Elvis, Punk, Rock and everything else for free.
5. Mt. Fuji up close on a clear day.
6. Kinkakuji (The Golden Pavillion), Kyoto. A huge shrine made of gold built beside a beautiful pond.
7. Mt. Unzen in Nagasaki Prefecture erupt in 1991 and wipe out an entire village. Massive lava and ash blanketed everything in its path.

8.   Late night Japanese television. Virtual porn show for free.
9.   A farmer's field smack dab in the middle of Narita International Airport's #2 runway. The Farmer's Associaton refuses to sell this last piece to the government and occassionally throws bombs at riot police!
10. Anything for sale in The Ginza, Tokyo.
     For example: $4,000 suits
                     $2,000 stuffed toy elephants
                     $3,000 woman's Gucci handbags
                     $1,000 shoes
                     $250 neckties
                     $2,000 vases
                     $10,000 watches.

Top 10 Things I've Experienced in Japan

1.   Earthquakes! They're exciting every time and I kind of look forward to them as good conversation pieces in class.
2.   Typhoons. One particular typhoon caught my wife and I half way up our attempt to climb, Mt. Fuji! The weather was fine at the bottom, but at the 5th Stage (out of 10 Stages) unbelievably strong wind gusts and driving rain made the rest of the journey out of the question.
3.   Downtown Tokyo, in August, outside, in the sun, at 5pm. You wouldn't believe the intensity of the humidity. I lived in Africa for 5 months and I never felt this bad. First of all, there's no wind as the tall buildings stifle that. Secondly, every building in Tokyo is equipped with air-conditioning. The air-conditioners pour out the used hot air trapping it in the city. Temperatures soar to above 45° C!
4.   Standing at the Epicenter of where the world's first Nuclear Bomb destroyed Hiroshima and wiped out over 80,000 people in seconds. It was an eerie feeling.
5.   Zooming along at 280kmph across the Japanese countryside in a Bullet Train and feeling like we were doing 40kmph.
6.   Going to Disneyland December 31st, 1990, waiting 3 hours outside to get in and then having to wait at least an hour and a half per ride. Never again!
7.   Finding a post office, a laundromat, a barber, and a convenience store nearby our new apartment. I guess I had a little culture shock when I arrived and the first couple of days were full of these minor triumphs.
8.   Finding our first apartment. I remember thinking, "Here we are, in Japan!"
9.   Receiving my first pay. You will be paid monthly and I'll never forget taking the envelope from the secretary and going into another room to count the crisp ¥10,000 bills. Most companies deposit your salary automatically into your bank account, but my owner does things the old fashioned way and pays cash.
10. Being the center of attention at most times during the day every day. Whether it's on the subway, in a mall, teaching a class, or going out at

night with friends it seems that I am always a guest and treated kindly. There's discrimination here against foreigners no doubt, but I feel lucky to have been on the positive end of most Japanese people's fascination with us Gaijin.

EXPERIENCE NECESSARY?

I feel that no experience is necessary to land a teaching job in Japan. A university degree is essential, however, and is a requirement by the Japanese Immigration Department. There may be ways around this such as making a fake copy of a degree, but I don't know too much about this, and I refuse to write about it. People can and will forge anything, but beware of Japanese morality. If they catch you in the act, it is most definitely grounds for immediate dismissal. In one particular case I know of, a teacher was deported and refused re–entry into Japan for a period of one year due to diploma trouble.

I feel that there are more jobs than teachers. I was offered several teaching jobs and always work two or three jobs at a time. It's basically a numbers game–call enough schools, set up several interviews and you will have maybe five jobs offered to you and two or three good ones to choose from. Of course, things are tighter now for below average individuals due to more people coming over. If you are not presentable back home and can't find a job, chances are you won't get lucky here either.

NO JAPANESE REQUIRED

I started a part–time course on Mondays and Wednesdays from 10 to 11:30am for six months which cost me ¥60,000. I didn't need any Japanese at work, but it made me feel better being able to order in a restaurant, ask "How much" and understand the answer. Japanese people will appreciate any effort on your part, because they feel their language is impossible to learn.

Most subways and trains have English translations. There are several good English daily newspapers and magazines, bilingual television (English and Japanese news broadcasts simultaneously translated), movies, an English radio station for the American Armed Forces called FEN 880 A.M. and many more signs, posters and pamphlets you'll discover along the way to make you feel at home. Japanese is not needed unless you want to impress the boss, the secretaries and a few friends and students along the way, or move to a real career in finance, advertising, sales, or marketing.

TEACHING IN JAPAN

Teaching may not be the right word for what you'll do in Japan. Casual conversation is more accurate. Sure, I had textbooks for every class (which lasted from 45 to 90 minutes depending upon the school) but usually before starting the material I ask "What's new?" to get the ball rolling. The responses are always interesting. I have anywhere from 1 to 8 students at a time. I basically just read a dialogue, ask questions, and explain any expressions or vocabulary they do not understand.

I also ask about their trips abroad or what they did on the weekend and to bring in any pictures to be explained to me and the class–in English of course! Everyone is going on group tours these days and while three days in Paris is not what I call enough to understand French culture, the Japanese are quite satisfied and eager to talk about their vacations.

I also recommend putting together a small photo album of your family, friends, trips, and any interesting things you've done. Students will always be fascinated with your pictures and stories. Some pictures of your house or of a nearby park or of snow are great, and it's a great way to cure a bout of homesickness too. Those pictures got me through many a slow afternoon.

Top 10 Teaching Tips

1. Never arrive late for class as you'll lose student's respect.
2. Don't give your sutdents nicknames like *Lucy* and *Rolland*. It's old and stupid. Would you like to be called *Yukiko* or *Hiroyuki?*
3. Always prepare an extra handout for the lesson you are teaching that day. In case you run out of material you'll have that spare ace in the hole to fall back on.
4. End your lessons on time. Students have trains to catch and you've got the next class to get to.
5. Don't use Japanese in class.
6. Bring a Japanese/English dictionary to class in case your students forget.
7. **Always** write on the whiteboard. (Black to you and me, but white to the Japanese. You use magic markers that erase with a brush.) This gives students visual reinforcement as well as verbal and written.
8. Allow for a warm up. Ask them "What's new?", or "What did you do this week?".
9. Bring pictures from home to show and ask students to do the same for their family.
10. Bring maps and brochures of your home town. Travel abroad has really picked up after the Gulf War and you'll get a lot of mileage out of this one.

TEACHING INSTRUCTION

It is definitely to your advantage if you've had any teaching experience before coming to Japan. Check the universities in your area for a Teaching English as a Foreign Language Course (TEFL). If after your arrival you want to take a TEFL course, the Japan Times offers an introductory course several times a year. It is held on four consecutive Saturdays from 9:30am to 4:45pm and costs ¥64,000 for 36 hours of study and workshops. For a course outline and registration form contact:

The Japan Times..3453–0121
   fax 3452–1313
   Educational Projects Department
   7th Floor, 5–4 Shibaura 4–Chome,

Minato–ku, Tokyo 108.
Near JR Tamachi/Mita Stations.
Osaka also offers a one week intensive Monday to Friday for the same fee.

The Japan Times .... (06) 445–0881
    fax .... (06) 445–0887
Educational Projects Department
Edobori KN Bldg. 3F
1–25–29 Edobori
Nishiku, Osaka 550.

I feel these courses are great to give you extra confidence if you're a little nervous about never having taught before, or if you just need some new, fresh ideas. Even for the teaching veteran, it could improve your promotion possibilities or salary. Especially if you work for a big company or change to a new company and are looking for a raise, it never hurts to show interest in your profession with an extra course paid for out of your own pocket. I feel these courses are a good investment in your future for only ¥64,000.

Teaching Materials

Bring as much stuff with you as possible or have it sent by seamail. Coloring books, connect the dots or letters for kids, flash cards, easy crossword puzzles, monopoly, scrabble, Uno, and grammar fill in the blanks.
    If after a year or two you run out of ideas like I did, there are several places to turn to. English language Bookstores in Japan are good for textbooks, teaching techniques and games. Kinokuniya bookstore in Shinjuku is good, but personally, I found Maruzen in Nihombashi to be the best. There are also two mail–order companies offering excellent stuff for all ages listed below.

The English Resource 0427–44–8898
    fax 0427–44–8897
2–3–2 Sagamidai, Sagamihara–Shi, Kanagawa 228.
Contact: David Harrington. He's got flash cards, games, videos and books from over 50 different publishers all dealing with TEFL.

Little American Book Store .... (092) 521–8826
    fax .... (092) 521–2288
3–9–22 Heiwa, Chuo–ku, Fukuoka 810. Contact: Helene Uchida. Over 6,000 members have joined. You'll receive a buyer's catalogue full of educational teaching materials for students of all ages.

Top 10 Teaching Games for Kids

1.   Uno. You can buy this practically in any 7-11 for ¥1,200.
2.   Concentration. Use a deck of cards. Spread them out face down on the table. Kids turn over two at a time until they find a match. They have to say the pair in English.

3.   Bingo. Numbers or words from their textbooks.
4.   Fish. As in "Do you have any eights? No. Go fish!"
5.   Junior Scrabble.
6.   20 Questions.
7.   Hangman.
8.   "I see a .... At least 30 different things in any classroom to see.
9.   Last letter game. Teacher starts with for example DO**G**. Next kid has to say a word that starts with **G**, GIR**L**. LIO**N**, N**O**, and so on until somebody loses.
10.   "I packed my Grandmother's trunk and in it I put.... You start off with a hammer or something and the next kid has to repeat everything and add one of his own. You'll hear some pretty wierd things. If it's a lower level class, which is usually the case, just start off with "I have....""

TEACHERS OF ENGLISH IN JAPAN

Teachers in Japan are a very special breed. Everyone has a different reason for coming and different motives for staying.

Each teacher you meet is unique, vibrant, and alive with a story to tell about some amusing incident in Japan. I'm not saying you'll like everyone here, but everyone has made the same decision as you have to come to Japan and try their luck for a while. Some of them forget this fact and start to take on a superior air or attitude towards other newly arrived foreigners because they know it all now. They think they have seen and done it all and generally treat you, the newly arrived, with contempt. I've seen it many times and it never ceases to amaze me.

Why an ordinary guy back home becomes a star here is simple. A normal looking guy or girl suddenly becomes a celebrity in Japan, because he or she is 'international' and speaks English, the preferred foreign language. I think that's why many people stay; they get lots of attention that they wouldn't normally get at home. It makes them feel like a somebody!

Anyway, you'll feel a certain kinship with them because we're all in the same boat.

WHY THE JAPANESE DON'T LEARN ENGLISH

After Japan was forced to open up to the West in 1869, translation was the only method of language instruction available. Reading through translation was the only way to contact outside ideas.

Most foreign material was forbidden and during the period of Japanese aggression, close association with the enemy (America) was banned. Therefore, English study was relegated underground.

After the occupation, the American system of education was adopted. However, anyone fluent in English or well traveled was regarded with suspicion and suspect. Even to this day, many Japanese regard practical English as shallow and unnecessary. Plus, the well–known fact that Japanese people are nervous around foreigners and don't particularly like dealing with them at any level further begs the question, "So why do they bother with English at all?" Several reasons make English study indispensable and, therefore, profitable for you and me:

1.   Job promotion
2.   Travel abroad
3.   Intensive English study is needed to beat 'Examination Hell,' thus securing a place at a top university and consequently lifetime employment
4.   Contact with foreigners (even though sometimes we're unpredictable, rude, and generally inferior)
5.   Escape from boredom (usually housewives)
6.   Children who are forced to study by their mothers who want an hour of free time to relax or go shopping
7.   Employees who are provided free lessons by their company which are more or less compulsory to 'internationalize'.
8.   Love of study
9.   If it's foreign, it's gotta be good!

So why can't the Japanese after six to ten years of weekly English instruction tell you where the train station is or what they had for breakfast? Again, several factors inhibit fluent conversation:

1.   Students just want their credits like you and I did in high school French or Spanish.
2.   Show offs. Returnees (students who have lived abroad and speak fairly well due to their father's transfer to the U.S.) are suppressed by their peers either physically or by excluding them mentally from the group. "*The nail that sticks out gets hammered down* " goes the old Japanese proverb.
3.   Seventy–five percent of the time Japanese High School Teachers can't speak English naturally and only have a limited interest in conversation and probably have poor pronunciation skills.
4.   Universities reward scholarship, not teaching skills. Thus, teachers spend most of their time researching and doing other academic related tasks. Developing one's teaching prowess takes a back seat to easier book reading and translation activities.
5.   Students don't have the time, between cram schools, sports, other clubs and part–time jobs, every night to commit to hours of required study in order to actually master English. I guess they feel that the payoff is way too small because only around 10% of the population will get to know a foreigner anyway!
6.   Translation is king. Textbooks are translated word for word. Fluency is not a realistic goal. Reading and writing form the basics of English instruction. In fact, English majors at top universities muddle through great literary works such as *The Grapes of Wrath, Keynsian Economics* and *War and Peace*, translating word for word (in some cases over 500 pages!).

7. Translation takes no real learned ability to teach. Get a dictionary and let's get to it.
8. Junior and Senior high school classes have roughly forty to fifty students with only two and a half hours a week of instruction. There is no time or desire for individual participation. The teacher proceeds at his or her own pace regardless of the student's comprehension. He expects brighter students to carry the slower ones.

Most definitely, this is a superficial discussion of the English education problems facing the Japanese nation today. However, I feel having experienced many of these dilemmas that the above information is true.

Doctor Reishauer, the once famous American Ambassador to Japan, further hypothesized that the Japanese might never master foreign languages due to their "xenophobic" personality. A xenophobic is a person who fears foreign people and hates all things foreign. He felt that the Japanese feared the West and were concerned they would lose their Japanese–ness and their identity if they studied and mastered English properly.

In conclusion, I guess what I'm trying to say is that your role will be as a live example of an English speaking foreigner. The market for jobs will never be in danger and continues to expand outside of Tokyo to more and more remote areas. At last count there were over 12,250 conversion schools in the Tokyo metropolitan area alone!

Recently, some schools such as Bilingual, Plady House, and Nova have closed a few locations. These closures caused quite a stir. However, these failures were not due to declining enrollment but were caused by bad management. The schools invested heavily in real estate and the stock market during the boom and now are paying the price during the 'Bubble Economy' of 1992/1993. The Bubble means that the economy grew too fast and then burst as all bubbles eventually do. They expanded too rapidly and are being forced to downsize to survive. All of these schools are in the heart of Tokyo so they garner a disproportionate amount of attention. In the suburbs and especially in other prefectures (province or state), it is business as usual.   Recent unemployment figures are at 2.5% for Japan compared with 11.6% for Canada. You've got to go where the jobs are to prosper or be one of the herd.

JAPANESE SAYINGS – A TEACHER'S NIGHTMARE!

Just to show you what you're up against if you don't believe what I've written so far, I've compiled a few, short sayings off the shirts, billboards, and vending machines. Even those of you here on corporate postings will run across some of these beauties during your stay. Some are minor, others are outright ridiculous. Take them for what they are – a bit of Japanese culture.

The sad part about this broken English is that the Japanese actually think their slogans represent true–life English! Obviously, whoever writes or corrects these attempts cannot be a native speaker. My biggest wonder is how a company, a respectable company, could print such ridiculous Japanese/English for all foreigners to discover and mock mercilessly. It's beyond reasonable comprehension. By the way, I have written these word for word. No attempt was made on my part to add a sensible period or comma or anything. This is their raw form as discovered by me. Company names have been omitted to avoid any major lawsuits! I've added a few of my own comments and put them in brackets. Read 'em and weep!

1. I want there beautiful forever–Always Romantic Elegance Walk in my Rose Garden It's beautiful.
2. Whoopee let's meet a curious sight.
3. International Baseball–The Baseball player I am very good at fighting He is a man of ability. Fighting Monkey! Don't Give Up! Nice Batting.
4. We have found the significance of our life in following tradition and looking for genuine articles. Now, we have realized a new form of life and the importance of health through clothes making.
5. We are on playing terms for your affection–Sweet studio extend your happy life viva casual. Be nothing loath
6. Set off on a journey Why don't we go together Have an enjoyable day
7. GT club Motorsport. Freedom at full ride
8. Don't be mine. It's time to spreading our wings and fly. Don't let another day
9. Your ticket to drink paradice Every satisfying sip a flavour experience
10. Sports casual fine wear
11. Relaxed wearing fits you best: We only work to produce comfortable clothes.
12. Cut and Parm
13. Green Shower. His never failed him Have the courage one's corrections Student Club The active for the easy life over flowing in the passion. Ice Hockey
14. We believe children should not be gentle and well behavExecuted Finest Originality East boy's Kids wear
15. Casual collections World of youthful play the World Only for the Grown Ups fashion for best your life
16. Women are making bread on Sunday with the high quality milk and powder lie on their face and turn up their sleeves sweat is falling down on the trough Women's finger, hand, and body hot just like burning their blouse seems to be burst swing their rich breast. (on a bread wrapper)
17. American we need that once look back the past and get excited since 1921
18. A Maris Club Garden Maris Country friend work in vegetable flower and nature It is never at the end. This little garden is maked by our hand. It is hard and joyful time for us. The work need great care. If you never do it, plants will be blasted. Work in Nature.
19. We lent a boat that have double cockpit. Enjoy twilight tour on Sun Francisco Bay. Good feel from the U.S.A. TO THE WILD. (My favorite: a

somewhat lively description with choice adjectives and some suspect word combinations.)

20. Designed for fashion minded people. This will refresh your senses.
21. This effects you! Oops nearly overdid it. Despite the fact that the mind enjoyed sensational towering ability this shot somehow epitomizes the car in competition and was taken at Gurston Down Hillclimb in the early 1960's.
22. (Sample menu fare at a restaurant in Shinjuku)

    Wiener Coffee ¥600
    Shrimos Pilaf ¥1380
    Cheese An Assortment ¥650
    Crab meet Rise Gratin ¥1680
    Mix Pizza... ¥850
    Potato and Bacon Burn of Cheese (melted cheese) ¥800

23. Unique, natural, innovative, modern, attractive, trendy. Creates Break Time and Off–Time comfortable. For Human–Front (on a paper cup)
24. BOY–Hard Bitten. Traditional (sweatshirt)
25. Challenge Mate Club. Challenge kids. We have challenge spirits (on a book bag)
26. With con(yes "n")fortable–used good quality of material and it is made research on an excellent fit. We believe the basis of good fashion is neat appearance.
27. Our new technology and distinctive yeast process have made it possible to taste the same enjoyment of beer from fine beer halls
28. Super League of Royce Learn, Play, Compete! Boys Bostonian, Sports in the true Bostonian Spirit Playing Hard, Playing Fair, Playing for Keeps. Boston Mass (on a jacket)
29. It had passed for 5 years since the awful and terrible battle of Tenkaichi–Budouki...
    The world had acquired the extreme peace, obviously Gokou and Chichi of his dearest wife had given a birth to the son Goman before 5 years and it had received a call from the calm and peaceful daily life. Such peace was fragilely gone to pieces due to the sudden appearance of the mystery man who had a strong tail. (on a kid's writing pad)
30. Forcible. Beetle. I am pleased at your honesty Bebe. (T–shirt)
31. The Wind is blowing in the crystal beach competition in Wave. (school bag)
32. California Free Thinking. Think Pink. Great way of climbing. Think Pink was born in Yosemite Nat'l Park to relax your mind and understand nature. (T–shirt)
33. A lamb must be dreaming happy dreams. (sweatshirt)
34. Beetle Freak. The Beetle can go forward and backward. It can go fast or slow. It can go uphill, downhill, and turn around. Isn't that wonderful. (on an eraser)
35. CAMPUS MELLOLY. Catch the new city wave. Sweet campus idol your mind. Milk Garamond City Girl Navy. City Club in Garamond. (sweatshirt)

36. South and North Touch a Person's Heartstrings. (on a jean's pocket)
37. A Pleasant sensation, Radiation of Happiness Poljac Collection 1965. You found new fashion. In this life your new mind Flexible kid Club–Out into the field. Pleasure makes the hours fly with a light foot. Have a ripping good time. (sweatshirt)
38. Marathon: It's so simple; cover your body with pleasant sweat and feel the repletion of the mind. (on an eraser)
39 Belle–Club. Head Gear's 1953–H–Club. Universals at Rubbish. CRABBEDNESS. Star Exposition. Unmitigated Humbug. Propriety–Sham
40. JOINT CAP... The children draw their pictures with bright smiling faces, playfully, thoughtfully, and even proudly. That's how playful kids do it. If you take a peek, you'll see what dreams are made of and dreams are the most important thing we can give. (on a pencil case)
41. All of us have a free spirit somewhere. Harvest of America. Free Spirit. East Boy. (sweatshirt)
42. Big very Basic Style. Big very club, British Taste since 1982. Trustworthy Comfortable Feeling. (sweatshirt)

HOME

BASIC PREPARATIONS

1. Book your ticket NOW!!! Reservations on Asian routes are very busy with some airlines having only one or two flights a week. Space is reserved some times up to one year in advance for the busier holiday seasons like Christmas or the Japanese holidays in May, August or January.

2. Grant power of attorney to your parents, brothers or sisters or someone you can trust. It's very easy to do. Ask for and fill out the forms at your bank. That way they can pay off loans, deposit money and so on.

3. Have nice light cotton stuff for August and September. It's really, really hot here in the summer. Very humid.

4. Make sure you've got about $1,000 in traveler's cheques cashed into Japanese yen before you come. It goes quickly in the beginning and saves you the trouble of going to the bank all the time (which might be closed if it's a holiday season). No need to worry about theft if you're careful. Bring a total of $4,000 to $5,000.

5. Be flexible at your job. Speak slowly! If you don't, you'll lose'em for sure in a big way. Some students you'll love, others you wouldn't care if they gave up immediately. Be prepared for one student or eight students, or no students at all. You'll experience this and everything in between. I taught 2 year olds up to 60 year olds in my classes.

6. Don't bring film from home as it's the same price here in Japan. It just adds weight to your luggage.

7. Some articles to bring: a good raincoat, a daily planner for addresses, directions, notes, schedules, and plans; a Walkman for long train rides or some good books to read.

8. Bring or ship a good winter coat. It gets cold enough to wear it during January and February.

9. Buy a good umbrella upon your arrival–the rainy seasons are just beyond belief in their intensity and duration. (Sept/Oct and June/July).

10. Bring the *original* copy of your university degree. You will need the original to get a Work Visa. Many people have been coming to Japan illegally using fake degrees. Most schools insist upon seeing the original.

11. Bring all medications and prescriptions with you. Don't count on Japan having the exact drug you're looking for. The American Pharmacy in Tokyo will take excellent care of you for reorders.

12. Set up a box of your preferred shampoo, toothpaste, gel and general toiletries and especially make–up at home and have someone mail it to you by seamail once you have a permanent address. On average, such things cost about three times as much in Japan. It will cost about $30 or $40 for a fair sized (10kg) box to be sent.

13. Read about Japan–anything you can find out will help your move here to
be as smooth as possible. Once you arrive, there are some excellent
English language bookstores in Tokyo.
14. All Western kinds of food can be bought here in special supermarkets
(listed in the Shopping section); for example National Azabu in Hiroo.
Prices are higher naturally, but not outrageous.

MORE PREPARATIONS – GET STARTED NOW!!!

The bottom line here in Japan is that it can be very easy to get a job as an
English teacher. VERY EASY!!!

First of all, decide if you really want to come to Japan and if the answer is
yes, simply follow these simple steps and remember, the very end of August is
probably the prime time to come. Here are some suggestions my wife gave to a
friend in Canada.

1. Apply for a one–year Working Holiday Visa at the Japanese Embassy in
your nearest city if you are from Canada, Australia, or New Zealand.
Americans and Brits must come here on a tourist visa good for three
months, find sponsorship from a Japanese company, and then leave the
country to apply for a working visa. Most people go to Seoul or Hong
Kong. This trip takes two or three days. Then you must go back to pick it
up. That's right, two trips: one to apply, one to actually get it. The tourist
visa for three months, by the way, is issued upon arrival at Narita Airport
in Tokyo.

Some people got their tourist visas in the States or England at the Japanese
Embassy and reported that they didn't have to leave the country when it
came time to change their tourist status to a work visa.

At the embassy when applying for the Working Holiday Visa, stress the
fact that you want to have the opportunity to travel and work at the same
time. In fact, you are not supposed to settle down in one location with a
Working Holiday Visa. Also, stress that, culturally, Japan has a lot to offer
and you can't wait to study a little Japanese. You are in effect applying for
a job, so dress and act accordingly. This visa is available to those who are
from 18 to 27 years of age and have a university degree.

Again, regardless of your actual intentions, you'll have to fill out a monthly
itinerary of your plans in Japan. Remember, you can't stay in one place so
plan a hypothetical tour. This is only a technicality, and it is very easy to
get the visa, but the embassy simply wants you to realize that it is a
privilege to enter their country.

The visa enables you to work 20 hours a week and is valid for six months
upon which time you may extend it for another six months at the
immigration office. The reality is you can work as much as you like when
you're here. Also, companies like hiring people who already have Working
Holiday Visas because they can start right away and don't have to leave

the country to be sponsored. You can always change to a work visa without leaving the country if your employer will agree to sponsor you. However, this binds you slightly to a company, and I preferred the independence my Working Holiday Visa gave me.

2. SAVE!!! To get the Working Holiday Visa you need a return ticket and Cdn$1,500, or a one–way ticket and Cdn$3,000. I recommend a return and about Cdn$3,500 or more because you won't get your first monthly salary for about five, six or more weeks depending on your success in finding a job. Korean Airlines has the cheapest deals going out of Canada and the States. They offer a one–year open return ticket with a free stopover in Seoul coming or going for about Cdn$1,250. from Toronto. If you can fly out of New York or L.A. that drops to about US$800! Other possible stopovers through Korean Airlines are Bangkok, Hong Kong, Taipei, Honolulu, L.A., Seoul and Vancouver.

3. Go to a bookstore and buy all the books you can find on Japan and read them before you go. Order the best books from us like our "*1001 Jobs in Japan*" listed at the back.

4. Buy all the clothes you'll need at home, especially shoes and shirts–prices are incredibly expensive in Japan, and it's difficult to find large sizes for men and women. If you're a woman, stock up on make–up and underwear. Keep in mind that Japanese women are not known for being buxom. Men should buy all suits, ties, and shoes, unless they are stopping off in Hong Kong or Thailand first where they can get some great quality custom made suits for about the same price as one off the rack back home.

5. Make up a simple, one–page résumé. Have about ten pictures taken from the $2 mall photo booths. You'll need two for your Alien Registration Card and others to attach to résumés.

6. Make a reservation for the first night or two in a good hotel. It's expensive but it's worth it, especially after the long trip. When you get here you can call Gaijin Houses for a place to stay. These are virtually impossible to reserve from home as they're pretty busy and it's first come first served, so don't waste long–distance phone charges like we did. You'll be amazed at how easy it is to get settled once you're here. We arrived late Friday night, stayed one night in a hotel we found through the airport info desk, moved into a Gaijin house Saturday night, bought the Monday issue of the Japan Times (where all the jobs are listed), called for interviews, went to our appointments on Tuesday, and started working on Wednesday!
    It seems like a big endeavor, but was all so smooth. Our first night could have been cheaper had we reserved one of the excellent Ryokan (Japanese inns) located throughout Tokyo and Japan. For more info, refer to the travel section.

7. From the airport you can catch a bus or train to your hotel. We stayed at the Sunroute Hotel in Shinjuku (Tokyo). It is a major center and our room only cost about Cdn$110 a night: a good price for Tokyo. If you come during July–September, you'll appreciate the air–conditioning.

8. Once you are here buy the Monday edition of the Japan Times as there are plenty of jobs listed for Tokyo and elsewhere. I would at least start working in Tokyo. Also, go to the Kimi Information Center in Ikebukuro. They've got several listings for jobs and apartments for foreigners.

9. Money–wise, expect to make about ¥220,000 for 20 hours work a week. At my two jobs, I work about 25 hours a week and I get around ¥400,000. My wife teaches 30 hours a week and she gets ¥400,000. That's a lot of money! Also, you might get lucky and find some private students willing to pay ¥5,000 to ¥10,000 an hour. Japanese love to spend money.

10. Lonely Planet's *Japan: A Survival Kit* has a great description of all types of short term accommodation available in Japan. My book is not a travel guidebook, but rather a book telling you how to set up on a permanent base. Other writers have thoroughly covered traveling around Japan. If I do have one recommendation, however, it's this: avoid Youth Hostels. They have strict rules, do not allow more than three consecutive nights' stay, have an 11 pm curfew and some even expect you to help with the chores: NOT what you need the first few days. If afterwards you want to try them because they are cheap for traveling, at about ¥2,000 by all means go ahead. Another option for short trips is staying in a Temple or Minshuku (a Japanese family's home that takes guests). Any Tourist Office abroad or in Japan has this information as does *Survival Kit,* so please refer to them. I have included a separate section in this book on Temple Lodgings as this info is difficult to find.

Generally, I prepared about six months in advance, with the last three weeks being the most intense. You are much better off preparing a little beforehand than the fool that hears there's money to be made and hops on the first flight over here not knowing about anything at all or what to expect. Even if you don't remember everything, as long as you set up some kind of support at home that can get you what you need and can't find in Japan, you're home free.

The Japanese experience is probably the best money making cultural opportunity you'll ever have, so take advantage of it before everyone else hears about all the excitement and fun.

NOTE: PLEASE READ ON TO SEE ALL OF THE ABOVE POINTS DESCRIBED IN MORE DETAIL IN LATER SECTIONS.

75 THINGS YOU SHOULD NEVER DO IN JAPAN

Here are some serious and not so serious advance warnings that could prove enlightening if not helpful in the future.

1. Never argue with an Immigration Official no matter how rude he is or how right you are.

2. Never start partying it up in a bar 60 km from home without knowing, FOR SURE, when the last train is.
3. Never stop off to ask directions at a police box without a passport or your Alien Registration Card.
4. Never leave home during the rainy seasons, figuring it'll be a nice day, all day, without an umbrella.
5. Never mix large quantities of beer, sake, shochu, and whisky all in one night. The wickedest hangover you could ever imagine is yours the next day.
6. Never sneeze or blow your nose on the train. You just don't do it here in Japan.
7. Never eat on the train except for long trips on the Bullet Train.
8. Never wear short sleeve dress shirts if you're a man until the specified short–sleeve–for–salarymen–commencement–day August 1st.
9. Never leave home without nylons on if you're a woman. I've actually seen Japanese women in Hawaii on Waikiki Beach wearing them.
10. Never tell Japanese friends or students when asked the question, "So, how do you like Japan?", anything less than–it's great, awesome and unbelievable. Less flattery will surely deflate the person or group hanging on your every word.
11. Never say–"I've never gone to Karaoke, what's it like?"
12. Never walk into any house, apartment, or Inn without removing your shoes.
13. Never use slang.
14. Never brag. Modestly rules.
15. Never flash your train pass quickly figuring the JR guy doesn't realize you're ten stops past your allotted fare. Just try it and see how fast those boys can move. I swear they're given speed and agility tests before being allowed to work the front lines.
16. Never tell an employer you plan to piece together several part–time jobs to make a living. Freelancing is seen as being disloyal.
17. Never leave home without cash figuring credit cards or traveler's cheques will get you by for the day.
18. Never tell a guy with curly, permed hair and part of his baby finger missing to stop hogging two seats on the train and move over so you can sit down. Chances are he's YAKUZA, Japanese Mafia.
19. Never be more than five minutes late for anything. You'll get a bad rep.
20. Never get angry when different Japanese people ask you the same questions over and over again. (See Top Ten Questions Lists page 111)
21. Never whine about the way things are done better back home. If "back home" is so great, then why don't you just go back and stay there.
22. Never speak Japanese while teaching.
23. Never buy a plane ticket originating from Tokyo. (See Ticket section)
24. Never get angry when groups of school children point and yell "GAIJIN" while you're on vacation outside of Tokyo. It's just one of those things

you'll have to put up with. That ain't gonna change for awhile yet, believe me.

25. Never take a teaching job for less than ¥3,000 per hour.

26. Never kiss your sweetheart in public unless you like to attract attention, stares and/or a crowd.

27. Never tip.

28. Never think you're special after having moved to Japan. Tens of thousands of people do it every year, some of them lasting for 30 or 40 years.

29. Never think your Japanese is good. No matter how much you know, you'll always meet someone whose Japanese is better.

30. Never think people who fall asleep on the train are weird. I guarantee that after at least a year, it'll happen to you and you might even fly right by your stop.

31. Never stay in Japan longer than a year at a time without a holiday. Do the words "stir crazy" mean anything to you?

32. Never go looking for an apartment alone. Take a Japanese person along with you.

33. Never leave Japan without first having completed the following:
    1) attending a Baseball Game
    2) seeing a Live Sumo tournament
    3) shopping in the Ginza
    4) slurping your noodles
    5) eating eel, octopus, and natto
    6) climbing Mt. Fuji

34. Never climb Mt. Fuji out of the climbing season from July 1st to August 31st. Everything on the mountain shuts down and if it's late in the year, freak snowstorms could kill you.

35. Never stick your chopsticks straight up in your bowl of rice–it resembles two incense sticks that are placed in front of a tombstone. You are wishing death on those around you.

36. Never pour soya sauce or any sauce for that matter on white rice. It's like asking for ketchup in a fancy French Restaurant. Rice is white, therefore pure. Don't spoil the beauty of it. Try using sauce once and see what kind of looks you get.

37. Never pour your own beer. Etiquette rules that you pour your neighbor's first and vice versa.

38. Never slug down your beer before the traditional "KAMPAI!" (Cheers). It's bad manners.

39. Never visit a Japanese Company without tons of business cards. Basically, no "meishi" (name cards) means no existence for you on this earth.

40. Never lose anything on the train or subway. You'll get it back, but the experience will test your patience.

41. Never overstay your visa. It's a sure way to get deported.

42. Never teach more than 30 hours a week. Your sanity depends on it.

43. Never call home before 11:00pm or after 8:00am. Phone charges are astronomical here.

44. Never wear anything but neat, pressed, dress clothes. You'll be treated with more respect. I guarantee it.

45. Never assume just because one person says something happened to them that it'll happen to you. All of Japan's systems, bureaucracy immigration etc… seem to be decided on a case–by–case basis.

46. Never ask one Japanese friend to do all kinds of favors for you (i.e. telephone calls, translation, apartment guarantor) or you'll soon not have that friend. Spread them out so that you've got a complete, reliable, problem solving network. You'll get better results.

47. Never tell the staff at work that you're going out with a student or students after class. It'll only get you in trouble.

48. Never take a job that doesn't pay for your transportation.

49. Never 'tell it like it is' at company meetings. Speaking your mind and gushing out frank statements displays immaturity and is bad for group harmony. Save your complaints and suggestions for after work drinking sessions.

50. Never embark on long train rides or commutes without adequate reading material and/or a Walkman. If you have mega time to kill on the trains each day, you'll be amazed at how many letters you can write and novels you can read, not to mention how much Japanese language study can be accomplished.

51. Never work at the same school as your wife, boyfriend or girlfriend. That, combined with sharing an apartment the size of your living room back home, will take its toll. It'll put too much pressure on even the best of relationships.

52. Never think that you can breeze into Japan on a whim, unprepared and land a plum business, modeling or editing job.

53. Never lick your fingers after a meal. It just ain't done.

54. Never pass food from chopstick to chopstick. This conjures up images of the Japanese tradition of passing a deceased body's bones at a funeral ceremony.

55. Never mix combustible with non–combustible garbage (see "Gomi" section).

56. Never blow bubbles with your gum.

57. Never, if you're contemplating suicide, jump in front of an oncoming train. Your family will have to pay the clean–up charges.

58. Never assume Yes means Yes coming from a Japanese person. It could mean No, Maybe, Possibly, I understand what you're saying but don't agree, I don't understand and don't care, I hear what you say but think you're crazy, or just plain Yes.

59. Never expect common chivalry or respect from Japanese men. Old ladies, pregnant ladies, guys on crutches, mothers with three kids all have to fend for themselves. Expect to stand on the train, open your own doors, and get knocked around the station during rush hour.

60. Never say you're only here for a year. First of all the money's addictive and second of all, you'll make more friends.

61. Never brave the summer weather or train station washrooms without a handkerchief or Kleenex.

62. Never leave the country without a proper re–entry stamp or your present visa becomes automatically invalid.

63. Never lick a stamp with your tongue at the Post Office. You'll send shock waves of earthquake proportion through those observing you. Use the little watered sponge pad off to the left or right.

64. Never lick an envelope either. Not because it's gauche as in #63, but because Japanese envelopes don't have the sticky part like ours do. They use scotch tape or a bottle of glue found on the counter of all post offices.

65. Never assume that just because you've turned left four times in a row you'll end up where you started. Tokyo's city streets would confuse even the most battle–hardened maze nut.

66. Never help yourself to one of the thousands of bikes littered at every train station in Japan. They could be lost, stolen, or abandoned. Naturally, you'll be blamed for all three if caught by the bike police.

67. Never pick up the little steel balls off the floor at the Pachinko Parlor. It's just not International Pachinko Etiquette.

68. Never put a ¥100 coin into a green telephone because it doesn't give change. Thus, you'd have to talk 30 minutes to get your money's worth as ¥10 equals three minutes.

69. Never forget that all Tokyo telephone numbers are eight numbers long. Before they used to be 345–6789. Now they are 3345–6789. Also if outside the 23 Wards of Tokyo, you must add the area code 03–3345–6789. Not so complicated once you get the hang of it. All numbers in this book drop the "03" code for convenience sake.

70. Never leave home without these two numbers:
    1) Japan Railway English Information Line 3423–0111
    2) NTT's English Help Line 5295–1010
    Number one gets you where you want to go; number two is your personal translator, city guide, and friendly voice during a major crisis.

71. Never try to scam JR by trying to buy a friend a ticket at the Fare Adjustment Window twice in a row. They'll nail you. Machines are equipped with sophisticated software to detect any pass used consecutively within a specified time period. Sorry, I couldn't find out the exact time before there's no problem. (Don't worry if this doesn't make sense now, it will in Japan.)

72. Never put on perfume or cologne before trekking into work on the morning train. The ten Japanese within kissing distance of you won't appreciate it.

73. Never hold yourself back while in Japan, the sky's the limit. It's up to you, however, to make the first move.

74. Never take no for an answer 100% of the time. Just because a Japanese person hasn't done it before doesn't necessarily mean it can't be done. Be a pioneer.

75. Never say never in Japan.

GETTING HIRED AT HOME

In a nutshell, it's risky and not worth it. Companies hiring in Canada or the U.S. need live bodies for far away places. Rarely will they give you a fixed territory before you leave. Most people then are sent two or three hours away from Tokyo, or worse Hokkaido or Kyushu. Usually, your pay is less than you could easily make finding a job upon your arrival. Also, if they pay for your ticket you have to complete your contract in order to receive the return portion home and any bonus they are offering. Not necessarily a nice situation to be in if you are having any difficulties with the school such as class overloading, bad scheduling, excessive pay deductions, or in some cases not enough hours as promised. You may begin to feel trapped and dread Japan. If you are confident in your abilities—wait; it will make all the difference between an okay trip and a great, awesome experience.

By waiting, you will be able to choose the type of organization you want to work for. For example, a large school like Bilingual has over ten locations and roughly 250 teachers. They follow their own rigid curriculum, but if you're single, it's a good place to meet other people. A smaller school, however, uses one of the ready made English texts available on the market (*Streamline Departures American English*, for example) and allows leeway in class for free conversation and the teacher's own curriculum ideas.

Also, if you choose your school at home before coming to Japan, how do you know its atmosphere? You can only tell the type of school by actually visiting it yourself. Is it clean? Are there separate classrooms, or are there small partitions in one big room which makes it almost impossible to hear your students over all the noise? Is there a separate teacher's room, so essential for that rest time between classes and time to finally grab a bite to eat? Is it close to the station? Is it brightly lit, or dull and dreary? You'll know what you like best just by visiting the lobby and talking to the secretaries. Some schools are definitely head and shoulders above the rest, so it's worth making the rounds before deciding on any one in particular. When you go for interviews in your first week (perhaps as many as three or four a day), you will start to become a good judge of what is available and what you want just by the way you are treated and by the location of the school. Incidentally, as soon as you arrive is the best time to phone around because you are fresh and enthusiastic—two great qualities all schools are constantly looking for. Another great asset is a full one—year Working Holiday visa (if you are from Canada, New Zealand or Australia).

Personally, I love the freedom and relaxed atmosphere of a smaller school. I have gotten to know my students quite well and often go out bowling, shopping, drinking, and sightseeing with them, something the bigger schools tend to frown upon. Whatever you decide, remember that once the door is closed you are your own boss, and as long as your students are happy, the school is happy.

SWAP

My partner in Canada first went on this program to London in 1984, and then went back again in 1991 to work as an assistant counselor. So it comes highly recommended.

A lot of Canadians considering the Working holiday experience in Japan participate in the Student Work Abroad Programme (SWAP) of the Canadian Federation of Students.

SWAP has many offices located at Travel CUTS and Voyages Campus in Quebec. The best part is you do **not** have to be a student to participate in SWAP Japan. Applications for SWAP are available at any CUTS office as well as Career and Placement Centers on most university and college campuses.

SWAP arranges to get a visa from the Japanese Embassy without you having to go to a personal interview. Participants must arrange their flights, through Travel CUTS/Voyages Campus. You will get two nights of booked and pre–paid accommodation upon arrival in central Tokyo.

You also receive a Lonely Planet Japan travel guide. You are also allowed to use Council Travel Services, the travel arm of the Council on International Educational Exchange. This organization is probably the world's largest exchange organization. The Council office is located in Tokyo across from Akasaka Mitsuke subway station. Council staff are bilingual (English–Japanese) and will advise you about jobs, housing and adjusting to daily life in Japan. They also have a mail drop exclusively for SWAP participants. In the spring of 1993, the registration fee for SWAP Japan was $225.

JET PROGRAM

You may have seen advertisements for this program at your university. Here's the scoop. The brochure says JET (Japan Exchange and Teaching Program) "seeks to foster an international perspective in Japan at the local level by inviting young adults to take part in international exchange activities and by intensifying foreign language education in Japan". The package for you is pretty good, round–trip ticket plus a monthly salary of about ¥325,000.

I knew of several JET teachers in the Chiba area who were also given accommodation at a reduced rent. They paid only ¥50,000/month, didn't have to pay any key money or agent's fee and got a free bilingual color television. One girl even renewed her contract for another year. Most definitely, JET will help you find an apartment if they don't have any housing in the area you'll be placed.

The teaching consists of assisting Japanese high school teachers in class. Usually, pronunciation is your main function along with providing a real live situation for students to experience. Some participants have lots of problems though. Rotation is common where the JET teacher goes every month, week or even day, to different schools performing a 'one–shot' rock star like appearance. Some teachers thrive on the experience while most complain of burnout and being asked the same simple questions day in and day out.

Another problem is location. The salary and benefits are high because you are usually out in the sticks where no one else will go. Consequently, a feeling of isolation, loneliness, even depression, may set in. If you don't speak any Japanese, in some cases, it's fatal; people give up and go home.

Boredom, of all things, compounds the situation. JET teachers find themselves making great money doing little work and being idle on evenings and weekends. Input is not expected or wanted at most schools. Just towing the line can become very frustrating.

On the other hand, many teachers enjoy the solitude, forced learning of Japanese, and travel. A rural location guarantees close interaction with the locals and their culture. Indeed, 3785 people came in 1993 and the Ministry of Education has plans to bring that number up to 10,000 by the year 2000.

If you do decide to take the plunge, there's one more catch. Japan has several idyllic spots like Kyushu, Kyoto, and Nikko, but **you cannot choose your city!** Jet policy is that they do not inform you until a week before your departure of where your destination will be. Requests for any area or placement with friends, or even with your spouse "cannot be guaranteed", a Japanese way of saying don't hold your breath.

I guess it is about a 50/50 call. Personally, I wouldn't take the chance of ending up somewhere I didn't like or want to go. Remember though, you can apply and back out later if you want. With competition becoming tougher in the Tokyo area, the Jet Program doesn't look too bad for the first year. You could use this time to get yourself organized and a small town might be just what you need to gain the necessary experience to land a good job back in the big city. If you do want an application form and deadlines, check your University Outplacement/Job Center for information or call the Japanese Consulate or Embassy. They'll be able to get you the necessary information.

BUDGET IN JAPAN

You'll need about ¥150,000/month to live on if you're single, slightly less if you're living with someone else and are sharing the expenses, such as rent. Without any effort you should earn around ¥280,000 to ¥300,000 a month. As of September 1993, starting salaries have come down by about ¥20,000 to ¥30,000. Nevertheless, in one year you could still save between ¥1.5 to ¥1.8 million (at ¥105 to the U.S. dollar that's about $14,285 to $17,140 dollars, or at ¥82 to the Canadian dollar that's about $18,290 to $21,950 dollars).

I have already detailed a possible budget pretty close to what I experienced during my stay in addition to some of the major outlays I made upon arrival.

What to Expect Cash–Wise

The cost of living is high, but I never met any teacher who was making under ¥300,000 unless they had other interests like studying Japanese, or just plain loafing around. I mean even some guy teaching only three hours a night from 6 to 9pm (plenty jobs available like this) at ¥3,000/hour, makes

¥180,000/month at around only a 5% tax deduction. Most people teach around 25 hours a week, mainly in the evening. If you are ever offered a day or morning job, snap it up right away because they are so tough to find.

And if anyone ever offers to set up some private classes for you, go for it. They are the best–anywhere from ¥2,500 to ¥10,000/hour depending upon the number of students. Most definitely, if I could make ¥5,000/hour on the side I'd go for it every time. You just sort of luck into these, but as you get to know your students or anyone else, you can start dropping hints. Flyers or pamphlets generally do not work because the Japanese are afraid to meet a foreigner for the first time, especially one who has not been introduced previously by a friend. Japanese are nervous for the first lesson at a licensed conversation school, let alone calling a foreigner 'cold' at his home to arrange a meeting somewhere.

Major Money Setbacks Upon Your Arrival

1. Ticket ¥150,000
2. Delivery of luggage from the airport ¥20,000
3. Guest house (gaijin house) per month ¥50,000–80,000
4. Apartment at ¥70,000/month ¥420,000
   deposit and key money and agent's fee
   (2 months, 2 months, 1 month's rent)
5. Japanese lessons 3 hours a week for six months ¥60,000
6. Futons, pillows, bedding ....¥15,000–¥30,000
7. Heater ¥10,000
8. Travel books and maps ¥15,000
9. Travel to Tokyo from airport, first night's accommodation........... ¥15,000
10. Phone installation (rent a bond from NTT) ¥75,000
    and phone ....¥10,000–¥20,000
11. Electric fan.. ¥10,000
12. Mini gas stove.. ¥10,000–¥15,000
13. Refrigerator (used) .... ¥5,000–¥15,000
    (new) .... ¥25,000–¥100,000
14. Washer (used) ¥5,000
    (new) ....¥25,000–¥50,000
15. Dryer (very expensive and small) .... ¥50,000-¥80,000
    Balcony will dry your clothes just as well.

Monthly Budget

1. Breakfast, lunch, dinner at
   about ¥400, ¥700 and ¥800 a day/per month ¥57,000
2. Video arcade (for us addicts!) ¥4,000
3. Telephone calls home (¥1,000 for 7 min. to N.A. after 11pm.) ¥4,000
4. Newspapers ¥3,000

5.   Apartment ¥70,000
      Average price 2 room apartment over 1 hour from Tokyo.
6.   Video rentals (¥300 each, free membership) 10X a month ¥3,000
7.   Japanese lessons twice/week 3 hours total/week...........................¥10,000
8.   Laundry once/week (expensive at ¥300/wash)............................... ¥4,000
9.   Dry cleaning (a must for white shirts and skirts) ¥2,000
10.   Entertainment (depends on alcohol)..................................¥5,000–¥20,000
11.   Snacks ¥5,000
12.   Haircuts ¥3,000
13.   Toiletries, etc. ¥3,000

Naturally, I may have omitted some articles and I also might have included some that seem foolish. Beer is expensive but cigarettes are cheap, roughly ¥220 for a can of beer and same for a 20 pack of smokes. If you do a lot of cooking at home you probably could cut item #1 in half. The apartment is hard to judge depending on if you live in a gaijin house, single apartment or share with a roommate or mates. Laundry all depends how much clothes you have and how dirty you'll get them.

Entertainment is up to the individual, and if you are lucky the crowd you go out with should pick up your tab for the free English lesson you have just given them. If not, expect to pay at least ¥1,000 for a beer and one or two snacks. Most times that I went out to a Japanese pub cost me closer to ¥3,000. Prices are quoted in Japanese yen rather than in dollars due to the relatively low inflation rate of 3.5%, so it is more of a constant than the ever fluctuating dollar.

Phone calls home depend on how much you miss your loved ones and how much of a dose of some hometown news you need from time to time. Overseas calls aren't cheap and run about ¥1,000/7 minutes to North America. To combat this high cost, we bought two faxes, one for Japan and one for my parents in Canada. I find it the best method of inexpensive up–to–the–minute communication. Most cities in North America have photocopy/fax centers which offer a fax service where you can fax to, where people pay a $3–$5 pick up charge. You can also send to Japan for that rate. Keep this in mind in case of an emergency.

A fax is also becoming a good job search tool in Japan and the better schools simply can not answer the phone all day so instead they choose potential candidates for interviews based on a picture/résumé fax.

NOTE: SEE THE SECTION ON WHERE TO BUY A CHEAP FAX IN JAPAN (ROUGHLY ¥60,000).

THE FOREIGN EXCHANGE MARKET
The Japanese Yen

Every weekday The Japan Times or the Daily Yomiuri gives the best account of how your country's currency is fairing against the powerful Japanese Yen. It's good for you while earning yen to see the U.S., Canadian, Australian dollar and Pound Sterling slide. It's like getting a raise every time it does.

As of September 1993, here are the rough values for the world's major currencies against the Yen:

Australian ($) = ¥72
Canadian ($) = ¥82
U.S. ($) = ¥105
U.K. (£) = ¥160

Recently, the U.S. dollar has slid as low as ¥102, and it looks like it hasn't bottomed out yet. Economists are predicting a drop to around ¥100!

There's never been a better opportunity to be earning Yen. Remember to send money home regularly to avoid any sudden fluctuations in the exchange rate. However, it's a safe bet the Yen will continue to be strong for at least the next few years.

TAX

As far as tax goes, the less you know the better. Most schools deduct between 4% to 7% and sometimes you even get a small rebate the following March. It's best to just pay it and that's that because if you start filing income tax returns, they'll have a record of where you work and live and you could create some difficult times for yourself and your school. Some schools don't report all the hours you're teaching to save tax. Plus if you stay two years, in theory, your rate should go up because it'll be based on last year's income. Your first year, you have no last year's income so your rate is the lowest possible. The second year you should end up paying more tax because it'll be based upon your high income of around ¥300,000/month or more.

I was counseled to just pay the tax and that was it, no problems. Big schools will protect you so you've got nothing to worry about. My wife was told always to have a re-entry permit in her passport whenever we left Japan, even the last time we will leave permanently, or the immigration authorities could theoretically detain us to pay for our back Prefectural and Ward taxes. Rare cases indeed, but why take the chance?

Part-time workers usually don't worry about tax especially the smaller schools who do not put you on their books, saving both of you money. They pay straight cash for straight time. For example: 3 hours at ¥3,000 = ¥9,000 x 4 times a month = ¥36,000.

Call your embassy and they'll have a guide on taxes useful for Japan and your home country. Americans are lucky as they can earn up to $70,000 in one year outside the U.S. and pay no taxes. However, they still must file a return regardless of their income. Canadians have two choices: (1) fill out the tax exemption form which requires you to sever all ties back home, i.e. car, bank account, credit cards, home, furniture, everything for two years; or (2) do not report your salary or report only some of it. Check before you go in any case to know where you stand. We are talking big money for one year if the tax man gets his hands on your stash.

NOTE: SEE NEXT PAGE FOR EXACT INFO ON THE TAX SITUATION FOR CANADIANS.

Paying Taxes in Japan – Survival Tips

There are three kinds of tax returns that wage–earners are required to file every year by the March 15 filing deadline:

1. Japanese Income Tax (Shotokuzei)
2. Citizen's Tax (Shiminzei)
3. Prefectural Resident's Tax (Kenminzei)

Generally, employers automatically withdraw taxes from employee earnings. The employer should provide forms stating earnings and how much tax was withheld. If you have no information about tax matters it is important to communicate with your employer about them.

Whether or not the national tax must be paid and what income is taxed depends on a person's residency and status. Generally, all income from sources in Japan is taxed whether one is a permanent resident, a non–permanent resident, or a non–resident.

For information on the national tax call the Foreign Division of the 1st Taxation Department of the Tokyo Regional Tax Bureau at 3216–6811 ext. 2695 or 3216.

If you must pay the Citizen's and Prefectural taxes, the percentage depends on your visa classification, amount of earnings and when your residency in Japan began.

Canada Duty Free System

To qualify for the one year custom's exemption for Canadians living abroad, you must be away more than one year from the date you left to the date you return. If you qualify for this exemption, you are entitled to mega duty–free items purchased six months before your departure date from Japan. Each item can be worth up to $10,000 and you can bring back as much as you can afford; there's no limit on the number of items. Therefore, if you are out of Canada for over 365 days, you have got the system beat. Remember though, customs requires use, ownership and possession (all personal of course) for 6 months before returning to Canada. So buy your camera, phone, radio, rice cooker, anything like that early on in your stay. It is a great deal! If your stay is under one year, you only receive the $300 tax free allowance per calendar year. Anything over $300, and you are charged a 20% import duty fee.

How to Escape Paying Provincial and Federal Sales Taxes

In Canada, we have the P.S.T. and the G.S.T. which comes to 15% sales tax in my province of Ontario. What the governments don't tell you is that if you are not a resident of Canada, **you do not have to pay these taxes.** If you save all of your receipts you can apply for a rebate for the full value of taxes paid. Personally, my wife and I have applied twice based on three separate trips home and have received four cheques totaling almost $1,000! Not bad for a little paperwork. At the airport you'll find the federal rebate forms, but you'll have to call the provincial office to have theirs sent to you. They don't like to advertise this program too much.

NOTE: YOU MUST HAVE NON RESIDENT'S STATUS TO APPLY FOR THE ABOVE. AS I MENTIONED, YOU MUST CUT ALL TIES IN CANADA. YOU ARE STILL A CANADIAN CITIZEN, BUT JUST NOT UNDER THE TAX SYSTEM WHILE YOU ARE OVERSEAS. YOU MUST BE PLANNING TO BE AWAY FOR TWO YEARS OR MORE TO GET THIS STATUS.

CONTACT THE INTERNATIONAL TAXATION OFFICE, 875 HERON ROAD, OTTAWA K1A 1A8 AND ASK FOR A COPY OF THE DETERMINATION OF RESIDENCY STATUS (LEAVING CANADA) FORM

ARRIVAL

Narita Airport
Recommended First Steps

1.   store luggage.
2.   cash traveler's cheques.
3.   visit the Tourist Information Center.
4.   reserve a hotel or ryokan (Japanese inn) if not yet done.
5.   buy a limousine bus ticket into Tokyo or take a train if someone has given
     you directions.
     It seems like a lot to do but it'll take only 1 1/2 to 2 hours.
     Welcome to Japan!

To and From Narita

Narita Airport is not that big compared to other international airports but
it's handy to know where you are going and to have some sort of plan.

You have several choices for your first night's stay depending upon when
you arrive and where you want to go. If you were smart and booked a Ryokan
before leaving, you're all set. If you didn't, go to the information counter and
ask them to help you find a hotel room or ask them if they'll phone a Ryokan
for you.

You should also cash about $1000 of your traveler's cheques, store your
baggage and go to the Tourist Information Center for maps and pamphlets
(open from 9am–8pm Mon–Fri, 9am–12pm Sat). Storage is best if you've got
tons of baggage like we did. Just take an overnight bag with you and get to
your hotel for the night. The last thing you need after 15 or 20 hours of travel is
to lug around your entire life's possessions. (Well, all the important stuff
anyway.) The company will deliver it to you within 3 days at your Gaijin House
(or apartment, if you're really fast). Up to 30kg. per piece costs ¥1,500/day to
store. Have the hotel or gaijin house manager call in the address for delivery to
make sure there'll be no mistakes.

Depending upon where your Ryokan, Gaijin House or hotel is, there are
several ways into town. For example:

1.   Taxis: over ¥20,000, no trunk space and only 3 people allowed. Most
     convenient only for those with expense accounts.
2.   Narita Express: non–stop from the airport to Tokyo, Shinjuku, and
     Ikebukuro stations. All seats reserved ¥2,890 to ¥6,490 (3381–0131).
3.   Keisei Skyliner: Narita to Ueno station. ¥1750 about 1 hour travel time. Call
     3831–0131.

However, by far, your best bet is to hop on one of the Airport Limousine Buses which go directly to Ikebukuro, Shinjuku, Akasaka, Ginza, etc. for about ¥2,700. Call 3665–7283 for details or 3370–1156 for reservations.

Check the limousine schedule at the ticketing counter in the arrival lobby or ask at the Tourist Information Center. They can take big luggage and go directly to some hotels if you want to splurge ¥20,000–¥30,000 the first night for a little comfort after the long flight.

Baggage Storage at Narita for Delivery

Air Baggage Service Company Ltd. (ABC).................................. 0476–32–8866
Price ¥310 x # of bags x # of days.
Each bag costs ¥310/day.
Maximum 1 month storage.
Weight up to 70kg per item.
Each item is insured for up to ¥300,000.

TCAT

Once established in Tokyo and off for a trip somewhere just reverse the process back to Narita or take a connection of subways and trains once you know the ropes. Call Japan Railways information line to see if you'll save any money or time. (3423–0111 in English)

Another painless way is to find your way to TCAT–Tokyo City Air Terminal (Hakozaki in Japanese). There's an Airport Limousine bus from Tokyo station which takes 15 minutes and costs ¥200. Once there, you can check in your luggage and have your passport stamped and hop on another direct airport limousine bus to Narita for ¥2,500 which will take roughly 70 minutes. Buses leave every 10 minutes and you avoid long line–ups at Narita. Call 3665–7156 for any specific questions.

Delivering Bags to Narita

Any time you leave the country, a reverse delivery service is available. Call the following companies listed below 3 or 4 days prior to your departure and give them the following information:

1. departure date
2. airline
3. flight number
4. departure wing–north or south
5. name
6. address
7. telephone number: work and home

The day before your flight, they'll come pick up your luggage and give you a receipt. On the day of your flight, just go to the delivery counter to pick it up. Anyone who uses this service knows that Narita is small and there's no chance of getting lost. Just ask at any information desk where to find the companies listed below. Expect to pay around ¥3,000 for a couple of bags. Call to find out their exact pricing list.

Here's the list of delivery companies:

Air Baggage Service Company Ltd. (ABC)...3545–1131
N.T.S. Sky Porter...3590–1919
QL Liner 5994–3332
Yamato Transport Ltd. 3541–3411

Be sure to reconfirm your reservation with the company if you make it several days ahead of time. One little trick I always do is to get the name of the baggage handler at the time. For some reason, if you've got a name, the guy's a lot less likely to take liberties and make mistakes. Always make sure you speak slowly so as not to confuse anyone too much.

International Airlines

Narita (New Tokyo International Airport)
    Flight Guide 0476–32–2800
Haneda (Tokyo International Airport)
    Flight Guide 3747–8010
Aeroflot..3434–9671
Air China..3505–2021
Air France (Cargo Service number) 0476–32–7741
Air India...3214–7631
Airlanka 3573–4261
Alitalia 3580–2181
All Nippon Airways..3272–1212
American Airlines (Toll free) 0120–000–860
British Airways...3593–8811
Canadian Airlines International.....................................3281–7426
Cathay Pacific..3504–1531
China Airlines..3436–1661
Continental 3592–1631
Delta...5275–7000
Egypt Air..3211–4521
Finnair..3222–6801
Garuda 3593–1181
Iberia..3582–3631
Iran Air...3586–2101
Iraqi Airways 3264–5503
Japan Airlines (Japanese 5489–1111) ....(English) 5259–3777
Japan Asia Airways 3455–7511

K.L.M. 3216–0771
Korean Airlines 3211–3311
Lufthansa...3580–2111
Malaysia Airlines...3503–5961
New Zealand Airlines 3287–1641
Northwest 3533–6000
Pakistan International..3216–6511
Philippine Airlines 3593–2421
Qantas 3593–7000
Sabena 3585–6151
Scandanavia Airlines...3503–8101
Singapore Airlines...3213–3431
Swissair 3212–1016
Thai Airways International 3503–3311
United Airlines 3817–4411
Varig 3211–6751
Virgin Atlantic Airways 5269–2680

NOTE: AIRPORT DEPARTURE TAX: ¥2,000/ADULT; ¥1,000/CHILD

IMMIGRATION
Visas

As I mentioned earlier, unless you can get the Working Holiday Visa (for Canadians, Australians, or New Zealanders age 18–27), you will need a company to sponsor you for a one year Work Visa. In reality, many people arrive at Narita, get the 3 month visitor stamp, then leave the country a month or two later to apply for their work visa once they've found full time work and sponsorship.

Everyone does this and other teachers and your school staff will be able to give you advice. Do not work full time for a school unless they'll sponsor you, because no other part time job you'll find will be able to sponsor you for a working visa.

Getting sponsored allows you to stay for one year in Japan and work legally. You can then renew that every year with the same school or switch to another that agrees to assume responsibility for your sponsorship. You can also switch in midstream if your employer allows you to do so. Check the numbers at the Labor and Immigration people for accurate case–by–case advice tailored to your needs (listed at the end of this section).

You can also study Japanese and get a Japanese language school to sponsor you for a Cultural Student Visa. This limits you to a maximum of 20 hours of teaching per week, but like the Working Holiday Visa limit of 20 hours per week, most people exceed this by as many as 15 hours with no consequences at all. Keep in mind however, that schools are required to keep attendance records and if you are not a regular student your visa will be revoked. You must pay for and attend 20 hours of lessons a week and then you are all set to start working. Check to see if you have to leave the country to apply for your visa or if you can stay in Japan. Ask the Japanese Embassy if it's possible to be sponsored from home before you go if the school sends you all the information and you pay tuition and have a return ticket and sufficient funds.

Below, you'll find a listing of all the current visas available.

Status of Residence

Status	Applies to:	Period of Stay
4–1–1	Diplomats and consular officials and their families	During mission
4–1–2	Officials of foreign governments or international organizations recognized by the Japanese government, and their families.	During mission
4–1–4	Temporary visitors with the following purposes: sightseeing, rest and recuperation, taking part in sports activities, visiting relatives, going on inspection tours, participating in meetings or short courses, attending business meetings, and other similar purposes.	Usually three months
4–1–5	Persons engaging in management	Up to 3 years
4–1–6	Students engaging in study or research of the junior college level or above.	Up to 1 year
4–1–6–2	Persons accepted by a public or private organization in Japan to acquire new techniques or skills.	Up to 1 year.
4–1–7	Lecturers and professors engaging in full–time teaching at educational or research institutions.	Up to 3 years
4–1–8	Persons engaging in activities of a high level in the arts and sciences, (music, fine arts, literature, science,)	Up to 1 year
4–1–9	Paid entertainers such as singers, actors, professional athletes, their managers and entourage.	Up to 2 months
4–1–10	Persons dispatched to Japan by foreign religious organizations to conduct religious activities (including non–paid educational or medical activities).	Up to 3 years
4–1–11	Persons dispatched to Japan for news gathering purposes by foreign newspapers, radio and TV broadcasters and other journalistic organizations (excluding free–lance writers, etc.)	Up to 3 years

4–1–12	Persons invited by public or private organizations in Japan for the purpose of furnishing high–level or specialized skills and know–how........ Up to 3 years
4–1–13	Persons engaging in skilled labor (eg., cooks in Chinese or French restaurants, Western–style confectionery, etc.).............................. Up to 1 year
4–1–14	Persons seeking to reside permanently in Japan. ....Permanent
4–1–15	Spouses and unmarried minor children of any person coming under status 4–1–5 through 4–1–13 above (excluding minor children who are college students, employed, or otherwise engaged in any activity which falls under another status of residence category). ....Same as supporting spouse or parent
4–1–16–1	Spouses or children of Japanese nationals (in the case of residing in Japan as family members of Japanese nationals). .... Up to 3 years
4–1–16–3	Persons who do not fall under any other status but are permitted to reside by the discretion of the Minister of Justice (under this status medical doctors, teachers at foreign language schools, students at Japanese language schools, dependents of Japanese nationals, etc. are permitted to enter and stay). .... Up to 3 years

Visa Problems/Legal Consultation Offices

Asia Student Culture Association, Student Counseling Section
....3946–7565
Mon–Fri 9am–5pm, Sat 9am–12pm.
Foreign Residents Advisory Center 5320–7744
Mon–Fri 9:30–12pm, 1–4pm. English, French, Chinese, and Korean. *The best service as far as I'm concerned.*
Human Rights Counseling Center of Tokyo Legal Affairs Bureau
....3214–0424
Open Tue (lawyers on duty) and Thur 1:30–4pm.
Labor Counseling for Foreigners 045–201–1350
Open 1st and 3rd Sat 1–5pm.
Relief Center for Foreigners' Human Rights 3581–2302
Open Thur only1–3pm.
Tokyo Bar Association, Gaikokujin Jinken Kyusai Center
....3581–2201
Thursdays only 1–4pm. Inquiries in person, telephone calls not accepted.

Tokyo Legal Affairs Bureau Civil Liberties Department Jinken Sodan Shitsu 3214–6231
Tues and Thur 1:30–4pm.
Tokyo Metropolitan Government Counseling Service for Foreigners
....5320–7744
Mon–Fri 9:30am–4pm.
**Tokyo Metropolitan Government,
Labor Counseling Center** 5320–6110
Open 2–4pm Mon to Fri.
Tokyo Union 3770–3471
Mon–Fri 10am–8pm. They speak English, Japanese, and Chinese.
Tokyo YWCA, Foreign Student Counseling Section 3293–5421
Mon–Sat 2–5:30pm. Closed Wed.

Private Groups

Asian People Friendship Society..3964–8739
Open daily 9am–8pm.

Also the Labor Relations Office gives free advice to foreigners on Tuesday and Thursday from 9am to 3pm, 3814–5311. They have contracts with employers and if you follow their orientation, you can apply for one job a day. Not outstanding, but their expertise lies in interpreting the law regarding your stay in Japan.

Working Holiday Visa Center

The Working Holiday agreement was signed between the governments of Japan and Australia on December 1st 1980, in New Zealand on July 1st, 1985, and in Canada on March 1st 1986. This visa is "intended to promote a greater mutual understanding and to broaden the international awareness of youths."

To register you simply have to bring your passport, two photos (they have a booth there where you get 4 photos for ¥520) and fill out the application form. They will give you an I.D. card for the validity of your stay in Japan.

The Working Holiday Center is of great use, not only for jobs, but for the free legal advice they offer on holidays, contracts, visa renewal, hours, and pay. I used it many times for clarification on what my employers told me was the law, just to make sure they were telling me the truth. For example, my company had me sign a legally invalid contract. They demanded one month's notice of termination or else I'd have to pay a one month salary penalty. The contract also said that they could fire me anytime for wrongful conduct like fraternizing with my students after class. Both of these stipulations are illegal.

Labor regulations state that:
1.   The employer is prohibited from making a contract which fixes in advance the sum payable to the employer for breach of contract, or the amount of indemnity for damage.

2. The employer must give at least 30 days advance notice in the case of dismissal or pay one month's salary for immediate dismissal.
3. The worker or employee can resign anytime as long as he gives 14 days advance notice.
4. The employer must pay all outstanding wages within 7 days of the employee having ceased work.
5. As for going out with students, of course it's completely illegal to tell a person who they can or cannot see after work. It's against all common sense. However, do not flaunt it or make plans openly in front of the office staff. What you do on your personal time is your own business. Just don't start taking business away from the school by offering cheaper private lessons. Then you've gone too far and they just might fire you. They may not admit it's for stealing private students from them, but probably for other stuff – lateness, appearance, style, whatever. Be discreet.

Working Holiday Center 3389–0181
fax 3389–1563
JR lines or Tozai line to Nakano. North exit 1 min. Nakano Sun Plaza Bldg. 7F. Open 9:30–12pm, 1–5:30pm. Closed Sat, Sun and holidays.

> Japan Working Holiday Center
> Sun Plaza
> 4–1–1 Nakano, Nakano–ku
> Tokyo 164.

Working Holiday Visa Renewal

After six months has expired on your Working Holiday Visa, you'll be required to submit an application for extension of your stay for another six months. Do this at the immigration bureau nearest your home or school. Check this book's list or ask your school. The school will provide you with all the info you need. They have an interest in keeping you, and its ten times faster if they put all information together with a map on how to get there. Renewal costs ¥4,000. Bring at least ¥10,000 just in case for any surprises such as having to take new photos, having to wait a long time and buying lunch there, or getting a re–entry permit which costs ¥6,000.

Try to time when you go to the last possible day, because the immigration officials stamp that day's date in your passport which will only be good for 6 months forward. Only necessary if you have a specific departure date in mind, but not usually important because most travelers arrive with a one–year open ticket which can be changed without any hassle.

Visa Extension and Re–Entry Permits

Also, at the same immigration office you can obtain a re–entry permit. If you go anywhere outside of Japan during your one year stay, you must apply for a re–entry permit. If you don't, you automatically forfeit your current visa as soon as you leave Japan and will only be granted the usual Tourist Visa upon re–entry.

Re–entry permits cost ¥4,000 for one trip or ¥6,000 for multiple trips during an entire year. Documents to be submitted are:

1.   Application for Re–entry permit;
2.   Document identifying yourself, i.e. Certificate of Employment;
3.   Document explaining the nature of your travel;
4.   Passport; and
5.   Alien Registration Card.

Also note that even if you spend months outside Japan, your original expiration date will not be extended to allow for the time that you spent outside of the country. Larger schools will prepare the guarantee for you while smaller schools may need some guidance.

Re–Entry Permit Offices

Tokyo has three visa main offices, the main one being Otemachi. Nihonbashi appears to be your best bet because it's less crowded and more friendly. See the list of offices in detail under the Regional Immigration Bureau's section.

IMMIGRATION PROCEDURES AND WORKING VISA ONCE IN JAPAN

For Americans, Brits and other nationalities, changing your status from a Tourist Visa to a Working Visa, the situation is fairly complicated. Call the number in this book to determine which immigration branch you can go to (i.e. Chiba, Tokyo, etc.) and ask your school to give you all the necessary papers and a map.

Here's what you'll need from your school:
1.   **Annaisho** – a company brochure outlining their activities.
2.   **Koyomeibo** – a list of all the teachers and staff and those who are currently sponsored by the owner.
3.   **Tohon** – business registration of when the company was established.
4.   **Keiyakusho** – signed contract from your company stating your job description.
5.   **Hoshosho** – letter guaranteeing that your company will pay your way home if necessary.
6.   **Kyuyohosho** – contract of your salary and working hours.
7.   **Nozei Shomeisho** – company's national tax certificate.
8.   **Tomin–zei** – company's business tax certificate.

You have to bring:

1. Your passport.
2. Alien Registration Card (Note: you have 3 months to register for that, so it is better to wait until after you have changed your working visa status or you will have to get it twice as your status has changed. Each change of status requires a new Alien Registration Card).
3. **Original** copy of university Degree. *No original, no visa – period.*
4. Résumé.
5. Short letter describing why you want to change your status.

As you can see, schools prefer those who already have a Student, Cultural, or Working Holiday Visa. Americans and Brits must leave the country to receive their working visa. I also believe Australians, Canadians and New Zealanders must do the same if they didn't get a Working Holiday visa beforehand. Check with your Japanese Embassy before you go as the visa situation changes frequently, and it's decided purely on a case–by–case basis at Immigration.

I sincerely mean this last statement. Immigration officials have a tough job in Japan and most could not care less about all of your troubles. Always be courteous, answer all questions no matter how ridiculous, 3 times if you have to. Never raise your voice and generally kiss a little ass. I changed from a 90 day tourist visa to a 1 year spouse visa in this manner. The official, a woman, kept me writing a letter of explanation 3 times before she stamped my passport.

Most people in that situation have to leave to country within two weeks and apply elsewhere. She wanted me to complain, but I kept my temper, so she was nice and gave me special treatment. That is why I say check with your Embassy on the latest policy. The application process is scary to say the least, but remember your manners and patience and all should go well.

Arrive early (8am) to stand in line for an hour and get out in 3 to 4 hours, although it's sometimes less. Bring some sandwiches and a drink.

Call a few of the immigration numbers listed in this book to get accurate up to date information on your particular case. In the end however, the Work Visa situation is pretty inflexible, so be prepared for a little work to get it. It's worth its weight in gold.

The Japanese consider you an outsider and consider it a privilege for you to experience their beautiful country and refined culture. "We are doing you a favor" is generally their attitude. Personally, I think that's why they're surprised when foreigners go back home after 1 or 2 years. "Why go back – don't you like Japan?" They can't understand that your family, friends, and loved ones are waiting for you back home and that all things considered, Japan is nice, but not your first choice.

Once at a school where I was teaching, three teachers left all within one month of each other. They each had one to two years experience in Japan. It caused a big uproar among the students because two of the teachers moved on to other schools and cities for a change of pace. The students felt abandoned and that their school was bad. In general, the Japanese are very insecure at times about their English speaking ability, their food, and their country. In fact, some have become so worried about Japan bashing abroad, they lose all reason when a foreigner quits to go home.

Otemachi Immigration Advice

Whatever you do, don't be a schmuck like me and wait for hours in Otemachi's Immigration lobby. That's for amateurs. Upon handing in your documents, you are given a number like in a supermarket. Watch for 15 minutes or so to count how many numbers go by. Multiply that according to your ticket and you're all set. Give yourself 15 minutes leeway though. I arrived back 3 minutes before my number was called! After one and a half hours, I finally got smart and asked where a restaurant was and went for a beer and peanuts, wrote some letters and generally turned an unpleasant afternoon into a very productive one. Bring a book, study Japanese, do anything but waste away your valuable time. Otherwise you'll sit there complaining and whining with all the other aliens! The place I went to is called the Lavender Tea Room (telephone 3215–9749). Also, check out the 24 hour phone service listed below for immigration information before you chug all the way down there and find out you do not have all the proper papers.

Code List for Telephone Service for Information on Procedures of Foreigners' Entry and Residence Phone 3213–8141 (push–button phone only)

How to use the telephone service system:

1. Find the code number of the information you want from the code list attached. eg.: "001" Main Amendments in the Immigration Act
2. Call 3213–8141
3. After hearing the instructions, choose the language you want by pressing 1 for Japanese or 2 for English. Then press the code number of the information you want.

Hints for Users:

The 'code system' information service is available through push button phones only. You will not be able to use push button phones that do not beep as you push the button. You can hear more than one code at a time. The information of certain code numbers may be removed due to the amendment in the Immigration Act. As a rule, the code list is revised annually. This service is available 24 hours a day seven days a week.

If you want to hear the information again, press the asterisk button. If you press the # button, this instruction will start again and you will be ready to choose another number from your code list.

NOTE: IF YOU CANNOT FIND THE INFORMATION YOU NEED FROM THE CODE LIST, CALL 3213–8523/7 THE GENERAL INFORMATION CENTER FOR FOREIGN RESIDENTS.

Code List

001	Main Amendments in the Immigration Act
002	Immigration Basic Plan
003	'Certificate of Eligibility' system
004	Application Procedures for 'Certificate of Authorized Employment'
005	Illegal employment of foreigners
006	Procedures for foreigners who stayed over their period of stay
007	The opening of the Tokyo Regional Immigration Bureau Nishigaoka Office and the transfer of divisions

Information on address and office hours

101	The address of the Tokyo Regional Immigration Bureau and how to get there from Otemachi station
102	How to get to the Tokyo Regional Immigration Bureau from Tokyo station
103	How to get to the Tokyo Regional Immigration Bureau from Shinjuku station
104	How to get to the Tokyo Regional Immigration Bureau from Ikebukuro station
105	How to get to the Tokyo Regional Immigration Bureau from Shibuya station
106	Office hours of the Tokyo Regional Immigration Bureau
107	The address of the Tokyo Regional Immigration Bureau Nishigaoka Office and how to get there
108	General Information Center for Foreign Residents
111	The address of the Narita District Immigration Office and how to get there (Departure procedures)
112	The address of the Narita District Immigration Office and how to get there (Procedures for entry)
113	The address of the Narita District Immigration Office and how to get there (Extending your stay and getting your re-entry procedures)
114	The address of the Narita District Immigration Office and how to get there (Overstaying residents and their departure permit)
115	The address of the Narita District Immigration Office and how to get there (Conveniences and General Affairs)
116	Telephone number of the Inspection and Record Control Division of the Narita District Immigration Office (Record of entry and departure, notice of departure)
117	Group departure registration at the Narita District Immigration Office (Procedures for group departures)
118	Telephone numbers of each facility at the Narita Airport

Information on passports

Information on Alien Registration Certificate

Entry Procedures

Foreigners who are permitted to earn an income in Japan through business management or by working for others:

301	Immigration Procedures for foreigners coming to Japan to teach at universities, colleges or other equivalent educational institutions
302	Immigration Procedures for foreigners coming to Japan as an instructor
303	Immigration Procedures for foreigners coming to Japan for religious activities
304	Immigration Procedures for foreigners coming to Japan for medical services
312	Immigration Procedures for foreigners coming to Japan as a researcher
313	Immigration Procedures for foreigners coming to Japan as an engineer
314	Immigration Procedures for foreigners coming to Japan as a specialist in humanities or international services
321	Immigration Procedures for foreigners coming to Japan as a journalist
322	Immigration Procedures for foreigners coming to Japan for investment or management
323	Immigration Procedures for foreigners coming to Japan for legal or accounting services
324	Immigration Procedures for foreigners coming to Japan as an intra–company transferee
325	Immigration Procedures for foreigners coming to Japan to use their skills
403	Immigration Procedures for foreigners coming to Japan under the status of residence "Temporary Visitor" (Visa–exempt country: U.S.A.)
404	Immigration Procedures for foreigners coming to Japan under the status of residence "Temporary Visitor" (Visa–exempt countries: Peru, Mexico)
405	Immigration Procedures for foreigners coming to Japan under the status of residence "Temporary Visitor" (Visa–exempt country: Brunei)
406	Immigration Procedures for foreigners coming to Japan under the status of residence "Temporary Visitor" (For countries without visa–exemption)
411	Immigration procedures for foreigners coming to Japan to study as a college student
412	Immigration procedures for foreigners coming to Japan to study at Japanese language schools or vocational schools

621   Procedures for students to stay in Japan for higher education
           after graduating from a Japanese language or vocational
           school
622   Changing status of residence for students who wish to work
           in Japan after graduating from school
623   Procedures for students who have married a Japanese
624   Changing status of residence of 'College student' or 'Pre–
           college student' to that of 'Trainee' (without practical
           training)
625   Changing status of residence of 'College student' or 'Pre–
           college student' to that of 'Trainee'(with practical training)

Foreigners holding a certain personal relationship or status:
701   Extension procedures for a spouse or child of a Japanese
           national
702   Changing status of residence to that of 'Spouse or child of
           Japanese national'
703   Extension procedures for a spouse or child of a permanent
           resident
704   Changing status of residence to that of 'Spouse of Permanent
           Resident'
705   Extension or change procedures for 2nd and 3rd generations
           of Japanese
711   Application for permanent residence
712   Application for naturalization to Japan
713   Procedures when a permanent resident's baby is born
714   Procedures for new babies of an Agreement permanent
           resident (not recorded in English)

Re–entry application procedures
801   Application procedures to obtain your re–entry permit
802   When you lost your re–entry permit overseas

Regional Immigration Bureau Locations

Tokyo Immigration Bureau 3213–8111
    Dai–ichigo–kan, Otemachi Godo–chosha, 1–3–1 Otemachi, 2F and 3F
    Chiyoda–ku, Tokyo 100.
    Exit C2 Otemachi Subway Station.
    Area covered: Tokyo, Kanagawa, Niigata, Saitama, Gunma, Chiba, Ibaraki,
    Tochigi, Yamanashi, Nagano.
    Hours: Mon–Fri 9–12pm and 1–5pm; 1st and 3rd Saturday 9–12pm.
Hakozaki Immigration Branch Office 3664–3046
    English line.. 3665–7157
    Tokyo City Air Terminal Building
    42–1 Nihobashi Hakozakicho, Chuo–ku.

Hours: Mon–Fri 9–2pm and 1–4pm; 1st and 3rd Sat 9–11am.
Hanzomon line to Suitengumae. Exit 1.

Meguro Immigration Branch Office 5704–1081
3–6–3 Higashiyama Meguro–ku.
Hours: Mon–Fri 9–12pm and 1–4pm; 1st and 3rd Sat 9–11am.

Yokohama Branch ....(045) 681–6801
Yokohama Chiho Godo–chosha, 37–9, Yamashita–cho, Naka–ku,
Yokohama–shi, Kanagawa 231. Area covered: Kanagawa.
Keihin Tohoku line or Tokyo Toyoko line to Sakuragicho. Bus #8 or #58 to
Yamashita–futo Iriguchi, Yokohama Chiho Godo–choshamae stop.

Narita Branch ....(0476) 32–6771
P.O. Box 175, New Tokyo Kokusai.
Kuko Passengers Terminal Biru, 1–1, Sanrizuka, Narita–shi, Chiba 286–11.
Area covered: New Tokyo International Airport area in Chiba.

Osaka Immigration Bureau ....(06) 941–0771
Osaka Daini–homu Godo–chosha,
2–31, Tani–machi, Higashi–ku, Osaka–shi, Osaka 540.
Area covered: Osaka, Kyoto, Hyogo, Nara, Shiga, Wakayama.

Kobe Branch ....(078) 391–6377
Kobe Chihou Godo–chosha, Kaigan–dori, Chuo–ku,
Kobe–shi, Hyogo 650.
Area covered: Hyogo excluding Osaka Int'l Airport area.

Nagoya Immigration Bureau ....(052) 951–2391
Nagoya Homu Godo–chosha, 4–3–1, San–no–maru, Naka–ku,
Nagoya–shi, Aichi 460.
Area covered: Aichi, Mie, Shizuoka, Gifu, Fukui, Toyama, Ishikawa.

Hiroshima Immigration Bureau ....(082) 221–4411
Hiroshima Daini Godo–chosha, 6–30, Kami–Hatchobori, Naka–ku
Hiroshima–shi, Hiroshima 730.
Area covered: Hiroshima, Okayama, Yamaguchi, Tottori, Shimane.

Fukuoka Immigration Bureau ....(092) 281–7431
Fukuoka Kowan Godo–chosha, 1–22, Okihama–cho, Hakata–ku,
Fukuoka–shi, Fukuoka 812.
Area covered:Fukuoka, Saga, Nagasaki, Oita, Kumamoto, Kagoshima,
Miyazaki, Okinawa.

Naha Branch ....(092) 281–7431
1–15–15, Toikawa, Naha–shi
Okinawa 900.
Area covered: Okinawa.

Sendai Immigration Bureau ....(022) 256–6076
Sendai Daini Chiho–homu
Godo–chosha, 1–3–20, Gorin, Sendai–shi, Miyagi 983.
Area covered: Miyagi, Fukushima, Yamagata, Iwate, Akita, Aomori.

Sapporo Immigration Bureau ....(011) 261–9211
Sapporo Homu Godo–chosha
12 chome, Odori Nishi, Chuo–ku Sapporo–shi, Hokkaido 060.

Area covered: Hokkaido.

Takamatsu Immigration Bureau .... (0878) 22–5851

Takamatsu Homu Godo–chosha, 1–1, Marunouchi, Takamatsu–shi Kagawa 760.

Area covered: Kagawa, Ehime, Tokushima, Kochi.

Takasaki Branch Office 0273–28–1154

2–1, Tsurumi–cho, Takasaki–shi. Near JR Takasaki Station, West Exit.

NOTE: ALL THE ABOVE OFFICES OFFER BASICALLY THE SAME SERVICES: EXTENSION OF PERIOD OF STAY; PERMISSION TO ACQUIRE OR CHANGE STATUS OF RESIDENCE; RE–ENTRY PERMISSION; AND CONSULTATION FOR RESIDENCE PROCEDURES.

Alien Registration Card (ARC)

No matter what kind of visa you have, you've got to go and get an Alien Registration Card at your city (town) hall before the end of 90 days, starting the day you entered Japan. The nearest City Hall (Shiyakusho) can be found by calling the NTT information line and asking for the closest one in your area. Also, you could ask your school to find out for you.

When you go, you will have to give them your passport, two passport size photos and a completed application form. They might fingerprint you as well, a policy that continues despite heavy protest from foreigners. Supposedly, starting January 1993 they were to discontinue this process. After you hand in your application, they'll give you a slip of paper stating a date with a few days of leeway to come back and pick it up a week or two later.

Before getting the ARC, it's a good idea to carry your passport around because you'll need it to do just about everything: open a bank account, get a room at a gaijin house, cash travelers cheques, or get a job. Afterwards, just slip the ARC plastic card (like a credit card) in with your monthly JR commuter pass. (See Japan Rail and Passes section) If for some reason in the future you have to show your ARC to the police and you don't have it, you may be required to write a formal letter of apology. Again, this is strictly a case–by–case basis. It all depends how the morning is going for them and how apologetic you can be on cue.

They sell neat little wallets that carry both of these cards in shops everywhere for ¥1,000 to ¥2,000. Buy one. That way you'll never forget the stupid thing one day when you stop to ask for directions at the police box and the policeman asks to see your ARC card. If that happens, it's a bitch unless you've got someone at home who can come to the police box with your card. You'll be released only after having written a profuse letter of apology. If nobody's home, then your day might be lost if they won't accompany you to your home: a distinct possibility if you're anywhere else but your home station. They definitely won't travel on the train with you for an hour to get it. In that case, someone where you work or a friend will have to do it. Either way just carry it at all times to be safe.

JOB HUNTING

Please see the end of this book under the Book Order Section on how to buy *1001 Teaching, Modeling, Editing and Hostessing Jobs in Japan* complete with addresses, phone numbers, salary, and in many cases an actual contact person.

Résumé/C.V. Translation

If you can't manage to get your resume translated before you leave home, you can get it done after you arrive. It might even be cheaper– so compare.

Several companies are specialists in certain fields so call and ask about specific work. Of course, everyone speaks English! You don't even have to visit them if you don't want to as you could do everything by fax. The going rate is different at each place, so call around. Usually though, the companies adhere to the size to be translated:

1. English to Japanese for 400 characters (verify work) per page. Anywhere from ¥3,500 to ¥5,000.
2. Japanese to English. A4 letter size paper, double spaced. Roughly 22 or 23 lines. Anywhere from ¥5,000 to ¥7,500.

AAA Communication 3295-0611
Alpha Corporation Business Center 3230-0090
Central Translation Service 3361-2839
DHC Corporation 3478–2061
ILC Limited 5395–5561
ISS Service Inc. 3265-7891
Japan Translation Center 3291-0655
Nexus International Corporation 3584–5034
TSS (toll free) 0120–25–8461

Typing Services

Prices start at around ¥1,500 and shoot up to about ¥2,500. Usually they will do the work the same day if it's only a few pages, however some might levy a surcharge for rush orders. Call to find out exact prices and directions. You could also do by this fax if you are in a hurry and can't make it there in person.

ISS Service Center Inc. 3265-7891
AMO 5485–9381
JSC 5276–4085
Profit Systems 3200–5407
Tokyo International Business Center 3343–2575

Typing Documents By Yourself

Kimi Information Center 3986–1604

You can type for ¥500 per hour or have your resume typed for ¥4,000 per page.

Temporary Center (Tokyo)..3508-1431

105 offices in Japan.

Tempstaff Company (Ginza) 3573-2931

Over 20 locations.

Business Cards

At some point, once you've settled down in your apartment and have a telephone, you should order yourself some business cards to present to friends, business associates and prospective private clients. They're an indispensable part of doing business in Japan. Lots of teachers don't have them but if you want to give off a professional attitude, here's where to get them.

Express Corporation...3760–4081

fax 3760–4464

5–8–2 Himonya Meguro–ku.

Mon–Fri 9am–3pm, English okay.

Owner: Tatsuo Yoshigaki .

Secretary: Urabesan.

Double sided, words in English and Japanese.

Cost: ¥5,000 for the first 100 and ¥1,000 for each additional 100.

A regular order is ready the next day delivered to your door.

Nadia's Lines 3400-7137

Graphic design, illustration, corporate stationary, business cards etc. Great prices on business cards. Fax is preferred and is the same number as the telephone.

Press Man 3211-7916

fax 3211-7937

Ready in 48 hours. ¥3,500 Jap/Eng. 100 cards, doubled sided. Near Yurakucho station.

Japan Times Insight

I always buy the Japan Times on Mondays. I like to know what jobs are out there and at what rate. Some companies advertise every week, while others are smaller schools looking for one or two positions for departing teachers or are creating a new job due to increased demand. Be warned that you will be chasing the same job as lots of other newly arrived foreigners, however, if you have a Working Holiday visa and you're Canadian (Canadian accents are 'softer' than British, Australian or American accents), your chances of landing the job you want are considerably better. You're just less hassle than the Americans and Brits who have to leave Japan to apply for their Work visa and therefore need time off from work.

NOTE: GO TO YOUR JAPANESE EMBASSY TO READ BACK ISSUES AND TO MAKE
PHOTOCOPIES OF RECENT ISSUES OF THE JAPAN TIMES.

International Networking In Tokyo

Previously, I mentioned finding work in other areas besides teaching. I
wrote that it's possible to use headhunters or employment agencies. Quite
often though, like back home the best jobs are never advertised, but come
from other sources such as friends, family or business contacts.

There are several organizations in Japan to help you make these contacts.
These groups also provide support for those experiencing difficulties at work
or in Japan in general. After all, Japan is still very cliquish and insular, so it's
nice to go somewhere, speak natural English and make a few friends at the
same time.

Three prominent business clubs are:

Sætar Japan

Sætar Japan (*Ibunkakan Komyunikeishon Kenkyukai*) is for university
researchers, professors, students, English teachers, and those who work in the
International Department of their company. Founded in 1985, it now has over
100 members, 60% Japanese and 40% English. Its goals are to: (1) "train
Japanese going overseas and foreigners coming to Japan" and (2) "to educate
Japanese about the different values, behaviors, and assumptions that exist in
other cultures."

Annual membership costs ¥3,000 for students and ¥10,000 for individuals.
Monthly meetings are held at Omotesando or Ginza subway stations and cost
¥200 for students, ¥1,000 for members and ¥2,500 for non–members. Former
guest speakers have discussed multicultural marriages, and values in Japanese
and American corporations.

Contact Membership Director Lisa Grant at 3380–1696.

FCC (Forum for Corporate Communications)

FCC was established in 1979 and now has 150 members of whom 65% are
Japanese and 35% non–Japanese. The application fee is ¥3,000 plus ¥12,000 per
year. Dinner meetings are held on every third Tuesday of each month: ¥4,000
for members, ¥6,000 for non members.

Tel: 3221–9764
Fax: 3230–2817

Kaisha Society

Kaisha means company in Japanese. The society was started in 1987 to
help foreign employees of Japanese companies swap grievances and make

contacts. Over 250 members have joined and only non–Japanese may participate in meetings and events.

Excellent opportunity for newcomers to seek guidance and support and to get the scoop on Japan. Quite possible for you to find a good full–time teaching job here or just to pick up some private lessons from departing members.

Annual membership fee costs ¥15,000. Meetings are held at the Foreign Correspondent's Club on the third Wednesday of every month. The cost is ¥3,000 for non–members and ¥1,500 for members. Authors of books about the Japanese (Robert Collins' Max Danger series) are popular speakers. Probably the best choice for those of you just looking for a place to talk and meet some new people.

Contact the Membership Director by fax at 3668–3095.

Headhunters, Employment Agencies

Much has been written on the subject of modeling, translating, rewriting and television work. To be honest, I didn't meet many people doing that who didn't have some sort of experience back home, especially modeling. Let's face it, not everyone has the perfect look, so don't feel bad. My advice is not to pursue something you wouldn't feel comfortable doing at home, or you just might end up wasting valuable teaching time on lost causes. By all means though, ask around for other types of work if you're interested. It's hard to believe, but so much is based on how you look and especially who you know in Japan; it borders on being tremendously shallow. When in Rome... Play the game. Mention your interests, like a new business, a franchise opportunity, import/export, whatever. You'll know soon enough if whoever you're talking to will be able to help you or not by the amount of interest they show in your proposal, or if they mention it to you again.

There are lots of success stories. I mean, big dollars earned by people you'd never even think of, but that's life I guess. Unless you work extremely hard, ask around and get a lucky break from time to time, be happy with your teaching dollars which is more than enough to allow you to live well and save cash for the future.

Some Employment Agencies to Contact

JT Consultants, Inc. 3408–7196
    Hokushin Building, 1–22–11
    Kanda–Jimbocho, Chiyoda–ku, Tokyo 101.
Able Corporation 3242–6506
    Time Life Building
    3–6 Otemachi 2–chome, Chiyoda–ku, Tokyo 100.
Borgnan Human Development Institute, Ltd................................. 3989–8151
    fax 3983–4897

Daisan Taihei Bldg.
1–25–3 Higashi–Ikebukuro, Toshima–ku, Tokyo 170.

Cambridge Corporation 3582–8931
Kowa Building, No. 3
11–45 Akasaka 1–chome, Minato–ku, Tokyo 107.

Casters Japan, Inc. 3238–0341
Ematanaka Bldg 3F,
2–5–2 Iidabashi, Chiyoda–ku, Tokyo 102.

JAC Japan Comany Ltd. 3262–8171
4th Floor, Hirakawacho Koizumi Building
9–5 Hirakawacho 1–chome, Chiyoda–ku, Tokyo 102.

OA Consultants 3496–9443
1405–2–1, Udagawa–cho,
Shibuya, Tokyo 150.

Selnate Co. Ltd. 3234–5071
Recruitment Promotions Department
Fujibo Bldg 2F, 22-10-28 Fujimi, Chiyoda–ku, Tokyo 102.
They publish *Adapt* magazine which lists Japanese companies looking for
foreigners to work in Japan.

Some Modeling Agencies to Contact

Get a portfolio made before you come, and send it out when you arrive.
Or call them when you arrive and make an appointment. Some experience
would be helpful as the competition is stiff.

Barbizon Academy 3746–0088
4-24-13 Jingu Mae, Shibuya–ku, Tokyo.

Central Fashion 3405–9111
2–24–15 Minami Aoyama, Minato–ku, Tokyo.

Japan Fashion Model Center 3400–4004
5–10–14 Minami Aoyama, Minato–ku, Tokyo.

K and M Promotion 3404–9429
Vira Aoyama, 2–10–25 Kita Aoyama, Minato–ku, Tokyo.

Pueblo Models Tokyo 3468–1051
55–7–303 Moto Yoyogicho, Shibuya–ku, Tokyo.

World Fashion Agency 3280–3488
5–2–6 Shirokane, Minato–ku, Tokyo.

Remember this: you must have a goal and be persistent. Go out and get
the job you want. Don't wait for it to appear in The Japan Times. Only about
10% of all jobs are advertised that way, the rest come from friends and
contacts. The Japanese hate to meet someone 'cold' without an introduction.
The more people you meet, the more contacts you'll have. Teaching English

gives you the opportunity to expose yourself to all types of people and maybe get your foot in the door somewhere else if you want a change.

The Interview

"During the interview, usually with a Japanese, but now sometimes with a native speaker, I always speak slow."

That was the best piece of advice that I got upon landing in Tokyo from a friend at a gaijin house. The interviewer usually speaks fairly good English, but will be checking your pronunciation and enthusiasm. Sometimes they'll ask you to describe a newspaper article or a small dialogue to a Japanese secretary as a test of your abilities.

Just relax and be yourself, and don't speak fast or try to explain too much of the article or of yourself if asked. Even if a native speaker interviews you, again speak slow to show him or her you can adjust your speed for your students. Most likely, this person will bring in the Japanese boss for the final approval.

I repeat, go slow, enunciate, and of course, no slang, whatever you do!

Second interviews are, in my experience, non–existent. They either hire you or don't hire you. However, some bigger companies (100 teachers plus such as ALA, Bilingual, Plady House, Britannica Pacific, GEOS, ELS, NOVA, Sony, Berlitz) might ask you to call them back the next day or at the end of the week and come in a second time. It's nothing to worry about as they're so flooded with calls, they're busy choosing the best candidates. Just set up another interview somewhere else to keep your options open. If one school doesn't take you, another will. That's a personal guarantee! Recently, the big schools in Tokyo have over 100 candidates to choose from for each position. You've got to impress them right off with a great business look, clean–cut image, Japanese résumé, and good pronunciation.

Appearance

I cannot stress enough about appearance on the job: dress smart! You'll be treated so much better if you're dressed for success. Guys, get a couple of *nice* suits made in Hong Kong or buy them before you come to Japan. Dark blue business suits, white shirts, black shoes, and some nice ties. Short hair is in. Long hair and facial hair is not good for job prospects.

I don't mean here that you won't get the job. I was offered every job in The Japan Times I applied for because I called early and set up an interview as soon as possible. I just feel you'll make friends easier and people will respect you more; respect being *very* important here in Japan. Dressing well helps your confidence, too, so why not? Make the effort and it'll pay off in maybe a higher salary, better hours, more friends and ultimately more fun.

Personality

Along with appearance comes a friendly personality. A good "can–do" attitude is what employers look for the world over, so why would Japan be any different? Smile a lot, don't be forceful or brag, just present a full–of–energy character that's willing to try and to experience new things in Japan. Don't worry that you've never taught English before. I'd say at least 90% of us didn't before we came either!

Presenting an enthusiastic attitude in the interview will land you the job every time. I should mention that quiet, shy, reserved people may not like teaching too much. Japanese students need to be prodded and a lively class taught by a complete novice will win every time over a guy with a Ph.D. in English who puts his students to sleep with grammar, spelling or other useless stuff. The Japanese on a whole spend over 10 years studying verbs, vocabulary, and spelling. They need practice speaking and communicating, pure and simple.

Your school will know it too if people are canceling and not renewing their tuition contracts. They won't fire you, but you'll feel indifference towards you. English is a big business and they've got to make money. Help them out by doing your part in a lively, energetic way and you'll get your way with them every time you ask a favor. Once they know you're good, they'll do quite a lot to keep you: holidays, home leave, bonuses, a raise, or more hours if you want them.

I personally have been working for over 3 years for the same school and have secured numerous benefits:
1. 3 week Christmas Vacations (every year).
2. 1 week Golden Week Holiday in May (every year).
3. 1 week Obon Holiday in August (every year).
4. 5 week Vacation (First year) to Canada in Aug/Sept.
5. 6 week Vacation (Second year) to Hawaii/Canada in May/June.
6. Month vacation (third year) to visit friends and family in Canada in May.
7. Salary increase from ¥3,000/hour to ¥4,000/hour starting after the second year.
8. ¥200,000 completion bonus at the end of my second year teaching.

NOTE: I ALWAYS MAKE SURE MY STUDENTS COME FIRST AND THE REST JUST FALLS INTO PLACE.

What to Bring to the Interview

Naturally when applying to all English Schools, bring your passport and a clear one–page résumé with a color picture in the top corner. Also bring an original copy of your degree. The original–not a photocopy. You can get them from your university Registrar. Japanese schools are worried about fakes, so why give them any reason not to hire you?

I also got my résumé translated into Japanese for Cdn$20 by a lady who advertised in my local newspaper. It was a big hit and helped me get several jobs over the years. It showed a kind of interest and understanding most other foreigners didn't bother with. It'll give you that extra edge and help you stand out for the better jobs. It only makes sense that the Japanese who is interviewing you would feel more relaxed with a résumé in his native tongue than one which might be at too difficult a level for him to understand. If you're really keen, there's a standard résumé form you can buy at bookstores that all university graduates use. Ask a student to get some for you.

Interview Questions to Ask Potential Employer:

1. What textbook do you use?
2. How many levels of classes do you have? (i.e. beginner, intermediate, advanced)
3. Will I have a mix or predominantly one of the above levels?
4. Can I use outside materials (i.e. photocopies of other exercises, newspaper clippings)
5. What is the hourly pay, or how much salary per month?
6. Are there any paid vacations or national holidays?
7. Can I ask for time off (without pay) if I need to do so? (i.e. can you find a replacement teacher for a couple of days, or longer for a refresher trip back home?)
8. When will my first pay come? And after that?
9. How much tax will be deducted?
10. Do you pay all transportation costs?
11. What if no one shows up for class? Do I still get paid? Do I have to do other work like proofreading a student's composition or school texts?
12. Will you sponsor me now (or later if you have a Working Holiday Visa)?
13. Do you have any housing available for teachers? If not, can you recommend a real estate agent (Fudosanya)?
14. Will you be my apartment guarantor?
15. Is there a contract completion bonus, or monthly bonus system? (Bilingual school used to have a 10% bonus every month for teachers ranked "A" by their students one week out of every month. Other schools such as Plady give you a ¥100,000 bonus upon completion of a one–year contract.)
16. Will I get a raise after a certain period of time?
17. Is there paid company training? How long and how much?
18. How many teachers are there?
19. How big are the classes? (maximum student limit – 5 being ideal)

Make sure you ask about your actual working hours. I mean how long classes are, when are your breaks and what happens if your class is canceled. Can you go home? Do you have to stay? Do you get paid or not? Will you have to do other work like proof reading or can you just read the newspaper and relax?

Also, if you're full time, find out about staying time. For example, you may only teach 25 hours, but you have to remain at the school for 40. (i.e. 1–9pm Monday to Friday with 25 or 30 teaching hours)

Work Hours

A good work set–up is easy to get going, but I recommend that any job you come across advertising morning or day hours, you should grab it as soon as you can. Some schools have early morning company classes from 7:30am to 9:30am, but unless you're near the company I don't recommend them. You'd have to get up at least at 6am to eat, shower, get dressed and fight the rush hour crowd into Tokyo for your 30 to 60 minute ride.

What's better are morning hours starting at say 9 to 10 or 11am and going for about 3 hours. Then you can relax, go home, have lunch, or possibly go study some Japanese during an afternoon class. The fitness center, aerobics, kendo, or judo are other options.

After that, you then proceed to your evening job of anywhere from 2, 3, 4 or even 5 hours of teaching. Most evening company classes start from 5 to 7pm and last two hours. The rate of pay should be higher at ¥4,000 to ¥5,000. I wouldn't take anything less than that because you've basically shut off your night for any other teaching at schools, unless you have some private students. Otherwise you can work at a conversation school for the going rate of ¥3,000 an hour working usually from 5 to 9pm or 6 to 9pm.

Therefore, a good set up, I think, would be as follows:

1. 2–hour company class or 3 morning hours at a school Monday to Friday at ¥4,000 and ¥3,000 per hour respectively. Depending on if classes could be found for all five days, you could make some serious money, say around ¥150,000 a month.
2. Get company classes lined up for Monday to Thursday at ¥8,000 to ¥10,000 per night meaning around ¥128,000 to ¥160,000 per month.

NOTE: FRIDAY COMPANY CLASSES ARE ALMOST NONEXISTENT SO CONSIDER YOURSELF LUCKY IF YOU NAIL ONE. FRIDAY CLASSES EXIST AT EVERY LANGUAGE SCHOOL IN JAPAN, IT'S JUST THE SALARYMEN WHO DON'T LIKE THE IDEA OF CLASSES ON FRIDAY NIGHT.

So now you're making roughly anywhere from ¥120,000 to ¥420,000 per month with the average being around ¥300,000. Anybody not earning the basic minimum of 3 hours per night at ¥3,000 an hour for ¥180,000 a month should definitely go home. You could find a job like that calling from Narita Airport in Tokyo upon your arrival in Japan. If mornings are difficult to find in the beginning, although it really is just a matter of calling enough schools to find them, you have another option. Most schools operate on Saturdays and some even on Sundays. I worked for Plady House in Chiba for one year every Saturday and Sunday 6 hours a day at ¥3,000 for ¥144,000 a month. I started at 10:30am and finished at 6pm including breaks and lunch. I still had plenty of time to go out if I wanted to. Most likely though that sounds a bit extreme, since I was also working full time Monday to Friday for another school. I was a bit tired sometimes, but a couple of hours at ¥3,000 per hour can add up to some significant play money at the end of the month. For example:

2 hours on Saturday @ ¥3,000 per hour = ¥24,000 per month
3 hours on Saturday @ ¥3,000 per hour = ¥36,000 per month
4 hours on Saturday @ ¥3,000 per hour = ¥48,000 per month.

I found the most preferable position is to work part–time at two or three schools due to the flexible schedule, variety, more materials from all the schools to draw upon and choice of teaching methods, not to mention more money than full timers. That way you can always jump ship if for some reason you have a better offer or are simply bored and want a new location. The part–time route will give you a better chance to be exposed to many more students and their different lives.

My advice is to have a serious goal in mind before you set out on your interviews. The temptation is to say yes to everything that comes your way in the beginning, and the next thing you know you don't have any time left to explore around town, go out with friends or just plain relax. It's something you and only you know about yourself; how much is enough. Set a goal of how much money you want to save, and that'll help your decision. Also try to calculate just how much money you'll need every month based upon suggestions and prices in this book about housing, food, travel, entertainment, and clothes. The more prepared you are in setting a fixed amount of hours, the more control you'll have, thus leading to a higher income and more enjoyment out of your experience.

National Holidays

Something to consider if you go the part–time route for jobs is that you won't be paid for National Holidays, so take this into consideration. Full–time work at most, if not all English schools, will pay you for these holidays as you are paid a fixed salary for so many hours a week. These holidays add up to two weeks without pay for part–timers. Add to the holidays the inevitable cancellations by Japanese students, and a good paying part–time job, (i.e. at ¥4,000/hour) becomes less and less money by the end of the month. Also, most schools close down from around December 22nd or 23rd until after the New Year and open again around January 4th or 5th. More time lost for part–timers, but a bonus for the salaried English teacher. Don't forget Golden Week in May and Obon Week in August, a potential two weeks of holidays with or without pay depending upon the company. Listed below are the 14 National Holidays in Japan:

January 1	**New Year's Day**. Visits to family, shrines and/or temples to pay respects to ancestors and to pray for good luck and fortune in the coming year. Several stores and most businesses are closed until January 3. Ganjitsu in Japanese.
January 15	**Adult's Day**. Festival for young adults who have reached 20 years of age and thus adulthood and the right to vote. Seijin no Hi in Japanese.

February 11	**National Foundation Day**. To celebrate the accession to the throne of the first Emperor, Jimmu. Kenkoku Kinen no Hi in Japanese.
March 21	**Vernal Equinox Day**. First Day of Spring. Shunbun no Hi.
April 29	**Green Day.** Tree Planting Ceremony. Midori no Hi.
May 3	**Constitution Memorial Day**. Commemorates Japan's new postwar constitution. Kenpo Kinenbi.
May 4	**People's Holiday**. Kokumin no Shukujitsu.
May 5	**Children's Day**. Used to be called Boy's Day. To celebrate the growth and health of children. Kodomo no Hi.
September 15	**Respect for the Aged Day**. Keiro no Hi.
September 23	**Autumnal Equinox Day**. First day of Autumn and a chance to visit ancestors' graves. Shubun no Hi.
October 10	**Health Sports Day**. Taiiku no Hi.
November 3	**Culture Day**. To encourage love, peace, freedom and culture. Bunka no Hi.
November 23	**Labor Thanksgiving Day**. Thanksgiving for a good rice harvest and work. Kinro Kansha no Hi.
December 23	**Emperor's Birthday**. The Imperial Palace is open to the public. Tenno Tanjobi.

NOTE: APRIL 29 TO MAY 5 IS COMMONLY REFERRED TO AS GOLDEN WEEK. MASS EXODUS OF THE JAPANESE TO FOREIGN COUNTRIES. AVOID TRAVEL AT ALL COSTS DURING THIS WEEK. REALLY GOOD TIME TO SEE TOKYO AS IT IS PRETTY DESERTED. PRICES FOR AIR TRAVEL ARE ASTRONOMICAL—UP TO THREE TIMES THEIR NORMAL VALUE! SAME SITUATION APPLIES DURING OBON WEEK IN AUGUST. CHANGES EVERY YEAR, SO VERIFY WITH FRIENDS OR COMPANY. ONLY IF YOU ARE SMART AND ARRANGED AN EXTRA STOPOVER WILL YOU BE ABLE TO AVOID TOKYO'S ASTRONOMICAL AIRFARES DURING GOLDEN WEEK. FOR EXAMPLE, WE ALWAYS BUY A TICKET FROM NORTH AMERICA TO A FURTHER DESTINATION LIKE HONG KONG, THAILAND, OR SEOUL WITH A STOPOVER EN ROUTE TO TOKYO. IN THIS WAY, WE CAN CONTINUE OUR JOURNEY FROM TOKYO TO ANY OF THE ABOVE MENTIONED CITIES DURING GOLDEN WEEK ANY TIME WE WISH FOR FREE. IT IS LIKE HAVING TOKYO PLUS ANOTHER ROUND—TRIP TICKET VALID FOR A WHOLE YEAR. SEE THE SECTION ON BUYING TICKETS FOR MORE INFO.

KAROSHI – DEATH FROM OVERWORK

A sober note on working in Japan must be told. People are dying in Japan due to overwork. The Ministry of Labor says 'karoshi' is "exaggerated". Japanese workers claim the actual situation is 20 times worse. By definition, karoshi means "sudden death by cerebral hemorrhage" and/or "cardiac arrest due to overwork and stress". Over 60% of Japanese salarymen feel they work too much overtime and fully 30% are afraid of dying from overwork! I recently read an article that stated over 7,000 karoshi deaths per year occur in Japan. In fact, in the past eight years in Japan over 55,000 people have perished, to the 56,000 lives lost between 1965 and 1973 during the war in Vietnam!

People rarely drop dead at work but die from such maladies as strokes, heart attacks, cancer, and liver or kidney diseases. Unfortunately, Japanese families who are in danger of losing their breadwinner receive compensation only five out of a hundred times. Six–hundred cases were reported in 1992 alone. Imagine being asked to work 18 hour shifts seven days a week four times a year. Tell me you wouldn't get sick or depressed or maybe even die.

During all my time in Japan I was always astonished by tales of woe from businessmen and their wives.

Some of my student's comments were:
1. "I'm tired today. I worked 80 hours this week."
2. "My husband plays with the children on Sunday if he's not golfing. During the week and some Saturday nights he usually gets home at midnight."
3. "I commute four hours everyday by bicycle, train, bus and on foot."
4. When asked what they did on the weekend, several of my students (male and female) replied "I slept".
5. A 12 year old told me he couldn't do his homework because his day started at 6:45am and didn't finish until 9pm Monday to Sunday! He was literally out of the house during this time at school, juku (cram school), piano lessons, English lessons, swimming lessons and *golf* lessons.

What this means for you is that a little bit of the work fever will get you too. Your life will become fairly organized with teaching English (or other work), studying Japanese, working out and other activities. You'll constantly be on a train, subway or bus somewhere, off to make your next appointment. You'll practically never have guests at home or even be invited to anyone's home unless you make a point of inviting yourself. You won't be able to watch your favorite T.V. programs anymore either, unless you like: *Night Rider, Fame, Little House on the Prairie , Hillstreet Blues,* or *Remington Steele.* Most of your entertaining will be done in an "Izakaya" (a Japanese–style pub) after work with colleagues.

Of course everyone's different, but try to keep a healthy balance and don't go overboard on the teaching hours. It's so easy to say to yourself, "Wow, they're paying me $30 bucks an hour to shoot the breeze on any subject I want!" Save some time to go out with students and explore the many sights and sounds. The last thing you want is to become one of the stressed–out, vitamin–drinking, chain–smoking, beer guzzling, dying salarymen shuffling around Tokyo like zombies. It's up to you to judge for yourself whether or not the above is true or exaggerated. Seeing is believing!

HOUSING

You'll probably have to stay in a gaijin house or a very cheap ryokan (inn) while looking for a place to stay. Personally, I had no idea what a good area for an apartment was when I came. Get your job first and then ask the staff to assist you. You'll need the school as a guarantor anyway, so you might as well involve them in the search. Try to live near a rapid train stop station rather than a local one as this will save you time when traveling about town. Call JR info at 3423–0111 to get this information and ask them the times and how long the trip takes to your job. Count on a 30–60 minute commute, the latter usually closer to reality.

If you're single, I recommend a Foreigner (Gaijin) House (see list) because it will be furnished with a phone (about US$700 to install in Japan) and other foreigners will be around to talk with after a long day of broken Jap–lish (Japanese/English). If you're married, an apartment is better because it offers more privacy. You'll need lots of cash, five months rent in order to move in, plus a sponsor–no mean feat. Your school should sponsor you, but there are no guarantees. No sponsor, no apartment. Period.

To this day, a ridiculous practice persists regarding renting and apartment in the Kanto area. You will have to pay 5 to 6 months rent up front in order to move in: 2 months deposit (refundable after any damage and a small fee is deducted), 2 months 'key' money (a non–refundable gift to the landlord) and 1 to 2 months real estate agent's fee (non–refundable). Add to these fees your first months rent and you now have a grand total of 6 to 7 months @ ¥70,000 to ¥100,000/month. There's no way around this rip–off and all Japanese are accustomed to this rule.

For the short term visitor under one year, guest houses are best. If you plan to stay more than a year, an apartment is worth the initial set up fee. Guest houses require one month deposit and are around ¥50,000–¥70,000 per month for a single room.

Apartment Hunting Suggestions

1. Look for restaurants around the area
2. Is there a 24 hour 7–Eleven or Family Mart nearby?
3. Laundromat – make sure it's nearby and not at the next station or you'll get sick of this set–up in a hurry.
4. Is there a post office nearby?
5. Can you park a bike at the apartment?

After this, go to the rental agency with a Japanese secretary or student (offer them free English conversation for the morning or day in exchange for their help) and ask for prices and availability in that area. You might run into some discrimination but don't worry, it's all part of the game.

Don't expect anything big – probably 108 sq. ft. with a kitchen and bathroom area of 72 sq. ft. Rent should be around ¥60,000–¥90,000/month. Definitely check the place out before you sign – *caveat emptor* – let the buyer (gaijin) beware!

NOTE DO NOT ATTEMPT TO FIND AN APARTMENT ON YOUR OWN. I REPEAT, GO WITH A JAPANESE SPEAKING PERSON, PREFERABLY SOMEONE FROM THE AREA IN WHICH YOU'RE LOOKING. EVEN BETTER, IF ONE OF YOUR STUDENTS KNOWS A FUDOSAN (REAL ESTATE AGENT) BY ALL MEANS TAKE HIM UP ON HIS OFFER. DO NOT FEEL YOU'VE GOT TO GO IT ALONE. COLD CALLING A FUDOSAN IS LIKE TRYING TO SELL ELECTROLUX VACUUM CLEANERS OR DICTIONARIES DOOR–TO–DOOR BACK HOME. THINK FOR A MOMENT ABOUT WHAT I MEAN. WHAT DO YOU USUALLY DO WHEN ONE OF THOSE SALESMEN COMES TO YOUR DOOR? EXPECT THE SAME RESPONSE IN JAPAN IF YOU'RE NOT PROPERLY INTRODUCED.

Check below for a list of associations that will help you out if you feel you're getting a raw deal.

Apartment Related Problems, Landlord/Tenant Disputes and Rental Agencies

Arai Housing Company Ltd. 0473–98–3370
Apartments located in Gyotoku. One room up to 2DKs. Deposit but no key money or agent' s fee. Big foreign population lives here.
ARS Vivendi Company Ltd. 3440-8710
Apartments inside Tokyo for foreigners. English contracts. One month's finder's fee.
Center for Domestic and Foreign Students 3359–5997
Rooms in Tokyo, Chiba, Saitama and Kanagawa. Anywhere from ¥20,000 without a bath to ¥180,000 for deluxe accommodations. The great news is this service is free for students with a proper visa.
Foreign Residents' Advisory Center 5320–7744
Open 9:30–12pm, 1–4pm Mon to Fri. As I said before, simply the best counseling available.
House Information Center 3352–4108
Guest houses and monthly mansions in and around Tokyo. From about ¥45,000.
Manshon Consultation Center 3344-6936
Shinagawa Tenant Leases Association 3786-6047
You have to pay for a lawyer. You must become a member (¥5,000 membership fee and monthly dues of ¥1,000). Open Wed, Thur and Fri 10am–12pm, 1–5pm. English only.

Tokyo House Bureau 3501–2496
They charge a one month finder's fee. Mainly deals with embassy staff and corporate clients on big expense accounts.

NOTE: AN APARTMENT IS GENERALLY MADE OUT OF WOOD AND A MANSHON IS CONSTRUCTED OUT OF CONCRETE. A MANSHON BEING MORE PREFERABLE DUE TO INCREASED SOUND AND HEAT INSULATION. MIGHT EVEN STAND A BETTER CHANCE DURING THE NEXT BIG EARTHQUAKE!

Useful Phrases

1.   Itsu hairemasu ka?
     When can I move in?
2.   Yachin wa, ¥50,000 (goman), gurai made ni shitai n desu.
     I want a rent of up to 50,000 yen.
3.   Misete itadakemasen ka?
     I'd like to see it.
4.   (Reikin, Yachin, Shikikin, Zappi) wa ikura desu ka?
     How much is the (key money, rent, security deposit, administrative costs)?
5   Keiyaku kikan wa dono kurai desu ka?
     How long is the lease?

Insurance for Valuables

Protect your apartment against theft, fire, or earthquakes.

If you're like me, getting robbed was the last thing on your mind when you were thinking of coming to Japan. Well, it happened to me when someone stole my bag with a new pocket computer in it. I was sorry I hadn't known about insurance possibilities in Japan.

Afterwards, I discovered the British Insurance Group while I was waiting for a train to arrive. Staffed by expatriates, they'll insure all your stuff against everything, even an earthquake, which the major insurance companies in Japan won't do because they'd go bankrupt if they did.

It'll cost about ¥6,000/year to cover ¥1,000,000 worth of goods, plus another ¥6,000 to cover fire, theft and earthquake. There's a ¥25,000 deductible. They'll cover your possessions worldwide and up to ¥150,000 cash if it's lost or stolen. For US$100 a year, you can't go wrong.

This insurance is especially practical if you're planning some trips to such places as Thailand, the Philippines, Hong Kong, or Korea. Anything can happen while traveling so it's best to be protected. Their phone number is 3214–6921. There is also an American Insurance Group in Japan. Their number is 3238–0111. Check the English Yellow Pages or call NTT at 5298–1010 for other companies.

Garbage – *Gomi* – Apartment Dwelling Etiquette

To facilitate your entry into your new surroundings, I strongly recommend you at least attempt to separate your garbage. To be honest, I never knew of many foreigners who did do this, but here's the scoop if you're the least bit an environmentalist. If you're in a rural area and the only gaijin about, don't give your neighbors anything negative to say about you. They'll all be aware of the new foreigner in town so why not impress them with your deep understanding of Japan by blending in as much as possible. Besides, everyone will know it's you who is screwing around with the system if you don't divide your combustibles from your non–combustibles! Just exactly what are combustibles and non–combustibles?

1. Paper bags are combustibles or in other words stuff you can burn totally–ordinary garbage (Futsu gomi).
2. Plastic bags are supposed to contain non combustibles (stuff you can't burn) like rubber, plastic, glass, bottles, metal, etc. (Bunbetsu gomi)
3. Dry Batteries. Put them in a see–through plastic bag and put it out on the day for unburnable garbage.
4. Spray Cans. Make a few holes in the can and set them out with unburnable garbage.

NOTE: SOME AREAS USE DIFFERENT COLORED MILK CARTONS FOR BEER CANS, BOTTLES AND TIN CANS. JUST THROW THEM INTO THE CORRECT BOX.

Number 1 is collected three times a week, number 2 once a week.

Sodai Gomi, or big garbage, is collected once a month. Not that you'll have lots of big stuff to throw out but this is where you can find your chairs, tables, shelves, and T.V.'s for free. Ask the T.I.C. or NTT. in English for the telephone number of the ward office in your area, or see my list under Local Government Offices, page 87. Then have the secretary at your school or anyone you know who speaks Japanese call to get all the times and places.

I finally did figure out their system. As I mentioned above there are three days a week for burnable garbage (*Futsu gomi*), one day a week for non burnable garbage (*bunbetsu gomi*) and once a month for large items (*sodai gomi*). There's a specific place and time for everything in my neighborhood. If you can, get all this information from the Fudosan (rental agency man) when you sign the apartment contract. There's even a garbage truck that collects paper (newspapers, magazines, and books) then gives you toilet paper in exchange (*Chirigami kokan*), usually on Sunday mornings. Ask the Fudosan or *koban* (Police Box).

Furnishings

All apartments are unfurnished, so you've got to run around here and there and pick stuff up when you can. The local *gomi* (garbage dump) can be a great source for all kinds of really useful articles. I found a cassette radio,

T.V., bookshelf, desk and chairs. To find out where and when the nearest big item gomi is ask a Japanese friend to help you. I recently read an article in the Tokyo Journal about several foreigners who had nailed down all the choice gomi drop off points and times in Tokyo, and had started a neat little business selling the goods for cash. Only in Japan!

Japanese people throw a lot of things away because there's virtually no used market like back home. Once something is old, out it goes and in comes the new. Apparently, the Japanese have a fear of anything dirty or touched by other people. Their homes are so crowded and cluttered with tons of stuff. They just don't have the attic, garage or basement space like we do in North America to store old possessions.

Another good source of furnishings is the Salvation Army. They must have the cheapest stuff around beside the gomi, and they deliver! It's basically a free–for–all on Saturday mornings from 9am–1pm. You could furnish your entire apartment here as its cheap and usually of good quality. Of course, you can buy everything new and shiny at the huge, well–stocked department stores, but if you only plan to be here a year or so, its not worth the extra cash. Refer to the general telephone number section for the coordinates, page 84.

Supermarkets have lots of gadgets that you'll need to clean up your place: clothespins, hangers, cleaning fluids, etc. Two supermarkets in Tokyo that cater to the foreign clientele also have bulletin boards where people advertise moving sales, English lessons and the like. They are National Azubu Supermarket near Hiroo subway station on the Hibiya line and Meidiya Supermarket (2nd floor) near Roppongi Staion on the same line. They're both within walking distance of each other.

As I mentioned previously, the Japanese do not like to buy used articles, however the foreign community here doesn't worry about this aspect of the culture and on every Sunday *The Daily Yomiuri* newspaper has a free classified section for its readers. Just like back home there's an Articles for Sale column. It's a great idea, and there are always sayonara sales. Many people sell their phone bond here for about ¥65,000 which you can then sell to someone else for the same amount when you decide to leave.

Finally, depending upon where you live there might be some second–hand furniture shops in your area. Ask at the Police Box where the *chuko* (a second–hand store), the *shichiya* (a pawnshop), or the *disukaunto shoppu* (the discount shop) are located.

Necessary Appliances and Furniture

Gas or electric heater. Go for electric although it costs more to run. There's no smell of gas or danger of killing yourself during the night. Japanese apartments have no central heating and are usually made of wood. For November, December, January, and February you'll pay maybe ¥4,000 a month. A new heater costs around ¥10,000.

Refrigerator. A necessity if you're going to cook at home. Something I rarely did the first year, but nice to have anyway. We bought ours used from a friend for ¥3,000.

Gas stove. Around ¥10,000. You'll need it to boil water or cook.

Futon, pillows, sheets, comforter. About ¥5,000 to ¥10,000 for the futon; ¥2,000 each for the pillows; ¥1,000 each for the sheets; and around ¥5,000 to ¥10,000 depending upon the size for the comforter.

Lights and lamps. Buy new at your nearest appliance store for around ¥3,000 to ¥5,000. They plug on into the ceiling socket.

Plates, forks, eating utensils. Salvation Army, moving sales or new from the supermarket.

Rice Cooker. New for ¥10,000 or get it from a moving sale in Sunday's *Daily Yomiuri* for around ¥2,000. You'll get into making rice a lot while you're here. It's healthy and relatively cheap.

NOTE: FOR A COMPLETE LISTING OF WHAT YOU'LL NEED SEE THE PREVIOUS SECTION ENTITLED BUDGET IN JAPAN AND MAJOR SETBACKS UPON ARRIVAL.

Gaijin Houses

A Gaijin house is like a dormitory or rooming house. They're really the only cheap sleep you'll find in Tokyo for around ¥1,500/night. They're furnished with a bed or futon, dresser, closet, sometimes a fan, heater or air conditioner (very rare) and they've got a kitchen with utensils, refrigerator, and stove. Sometimes they have a lounge area with a T.V. and coffee table. They will be equipped with a shower, bath, and maybe even a washer and dryer.

Some are clean and a great place to stay, others are *Animal House* revisited. Check around before you choose. You've usually got three choices:
1. dormitory: youth hostel type idea
2. shared: 2 or 3 people to one room
3. private: 1 person 1 room, 1 very small room
    I think private is the best way and it's not much more expensive. For example:

	Per Night	Per Week	Per Month
Dormitory	¥1,300	¥10,000	¥35,000
Shared	¥1,400	¥12,000	¥40,000
Private Room	¥1,800	¥17,000	¥50,000
(single)			
double	¥2,000	¥26,000	¥80,000

The best thing about Gaijin Houses is that you're only required to pay for one month's deposit. So, for a private room in Tokyo for the first month it would cost about ¥60,000 rent and ¥60,000 deposit. Sort of like the first and last month's rent system back home. What's wrong with that? When you leave, you'll get your ¥60,000 deposit back. And they say this is the world's most expensive city to live in?

The Gaijin house, especially if you're single, is the best place to cope while getting your bearings straight in Tokyo, especially if you're from a small town. Every city in Canada, even Toronto and Montreal, is small compared to Japan. At 2.3 and 1.8 million people respectively, it rates low. Consider these facts: Shinjuku train station alone has roughly 1,000,000 daily users alone! If you include metropolitan Tokyo, Chiba, Saitama, and the Kanagawa surrounding areas you'd have about 30,000,000 people, more than the entire population of Canada, squeezed into a 100km radius.

There's usually someone at a Gaijin house who can help you get started or tell you where to go and how to get there; not in broken Japanese English either. This is something you'll come to appreciate in the future as the months whiz by. A friend who speaks flawless native English and who understands you without the use of sign and body language and a dictionary is like a Godsend.

Questions for the Gaijin House

1. Who's the manager – a foreigner or a Japanese (Japanese is better: more conscientious and clean and can help with the language).
2. Does the manager live in the House or nearby? (Better in, to keep down parties or stupid behavior to a minimum)
3. Is there a curfew or anything like it? (probably never)
4. Is there a fridge, stove, T.V., phone? Who cleans this area?
5. Can you get a refund if you leave before your stated time?
6. How many people in total live in the house?
7. Mainly what nationality is it?
8. How many showers are there? Are they free? (Some have a ¥10 coin system for three minutes of hot water – kind of annoying after awhile.)
9. Is there a refundable (100%) deposit?
10. Is it a private room, or are you sharing with others?

Suggestions on Choosing a Gaijin House

1. Find a place on the map near the center of Tokyo because for the first week or two you'll go for interviews in this area.
2. Always ask for the manager when you call these places and remember you must speak slowly and clearly and not use any slang.
3. Get directions from the station or ask if there is someone who can meet you. Personally, I'd never take anything for more than a week because, in the meantime, you never know what might happen – your new job is too far away, bad roommates, you found an apartment, or even were offered a job in a different city. Once you're in there's no problem renewing at the end of the week as it's first come first served. If you decide to stay then you can ask for the cheaper monthly rate.

4. Everyone should stay at a Gaijin House first while they get the feel for Tokyo, get a job(s), and look around. Ask your school or other teachers where to live. Waiting two months before you move into an apartment is not so long considering your first salary will come about 6 to 8 weeks after you start. You are paid monthly in Japan. Each company has a different system, but most pay 2 weeks after the end of the month. So, depending upon when you arrive during the month, add the rest of that month plus 2 weeks before your first pay comes in!

5. Make the rounds and visit at least 10 before you find a good one. You can't reserve from abroad because it's first come first served as I mentioned previously.

Some people spend their entire stay (1 year or more) in Gaijin houses totally avoiding the whole apartment key money–agent's fee–deposit scene (around $3,000 to $4,000). If you do choose to stay at a Gaijin House, you'll be able to ask others staying there all kinds of things it would take you months to find out on your own.

NOTE: THAT FIRST NIGHT IS ALWAYS THE HARDEST, SO IF YOU WANT A LITTLE COMFORT BEFORE CHOOSING A GAIJIN HOUSE AND CAN'T AFFORD A $150 TO $200 HOTEL, TRY BOOKING A ROOM AT A RYOKAN OR MINSHUKU. THESE LODGINGS CAN BE BOOKED AHEAD OF TIME AND COST ROUGHLY ONE–THIRD OF THE ABOVE MENTIONED HOTELS. JAPANESE STYLE ROOMS WITH OPTIONAL BREAKFAST AND DINNER PLANS. A RYOKAN IS A JAPANESE INN, WHILE A MINSHUKU IS LIKE A BED AND BREAKFAST SETUP BACK HOME.

Japanese Inn Group (Ryokan) 3822–2251
Minshuku Center (Family–run lodging) 3216–6556

Gaijin Houses Tokyo Area

Ajuna House 3331–4607
Nakano and Musashisakai.
Bilingual House 3200–7082
Four locations.
Cosmopolitan House 3926–4746
15 minutes from Seibu–Shinjuku.
Egerton House 3381–7025
15 minutes from Shinjuku.
Friendship House 3327–3179
Many locations.
Fuji House 3967–4046
25 minutes Hibiya St.
Greenpeace 3915–2572
8 minutes Ueno, 15 min Shinjuku.
International House 3326–4839
20 minutes Shinjuku.

International Guest House 3623–8445
    15 minutes Ginza.
Lily House 0482–23–8205
    29 minutes Ueno.
Lucky House 048–881–8707
    15 minutes Shinjuku.
Maharajah Palace 3748–0569
    12 minutes Gotanda.
Marui House 3962–4979
    5 minutes Ikebukuro.
Sun Academy 0449–434–4450
    20 minutes Shibuya.
Tokyo English Center 3360–4781
    10 minutes Shinjuku.
Tokyo House #1 3391–5577
    10 minutes Shinjuku.
Tokyo House #2 3995–5306
    15 minutes Shinjuku.
Tokyo House #3 3610–8808
    15 minutes Otsuka.

Call JR Info at 3423–0111. Tell them what station you're at and where you want to go. They'll direct you perfectly, in English. Of course, make sure you have your *Tourist Map of Tokyo's Trains and Subways* handy to visualize what the operator is talking about. Believe me, Tokyo's transportation system is quite difficult until you get the hang of it.

NOTE: BUY A COPY OF THE TOKYO JOURNAL FOR A COMPLETE, UP–TO–DATE LISTING OF ALL GAIJIN HOUSES ON TOKYO. AS FOR THE MAP, GET THAT FREE AT ANY TOURIST INFORMATION CENTER LISTED UNDER THE TRAVEL SECTION, PAGE 194.

SENTO

In all neighborhoods, there are public baths. Years ago, it was the usual place for people to bathe, talk and relax. They are declining in popularity quite a bit, but if you must try one just check around your neighbourhood or ask a student to show you one. The sentos are usually open to around 11pm. After having tried the worst, why don't you try one of the best below.

Saunas

Nowadays, the best saunas have added special services to entice more customers away from the traditional public baths.

Reminiscent of a European Spa, these new saunas offer karaoke, dining, massage, T.V., video games, lounge chairs, and a variety of other features. Almost all offer 24–hour bathing! I went to Utopia and really thought it was a great place. Most places cost around ¥2,000 to ¥3,000 to enter.

Green Plaza Sports Sauna..3207-4922
Shinjuku.
Kojimachi Rebirth... 3262–7561
Yotsuya station. Open Mon–Fri 9:30am–9pm. Sat until 8pm.
Relaxation Sauna Bath..3344-0305
Shinjuku.
Sauna Beach Shinjuku Finland 3209–9196
Shinjuku station, E exit. Open 24 hours a day.
Sauna Komazawa 3412–8951
Komazawa–daigaku station. Open Mon–Fri 1pm–12am. Sat and Sun 12pm–
12am.
Sauna Sanpia 3987–0201
Men only. Ikebukuro station, W exit. Open 24 hrs daily.
Shibuya Supersonic Spa 3409-4882
Shibuya.
Sunflower.. 3208-5217
Shinjuku.
Utopia.. 3398–4126
Ogikubo station, W exit. Open 24 hrs daily.

MOVING OPTIONS

The day will arrive no matter how long you stay in Japan, that you move. Maybe you'll move from one apartment to the other or move to another city within Japan or move back home altogether. In any of the above cases, you'll need numbers to call. Some people will be lucky and their company will pay for everything. If you're not transferring to another school branch location, here's the info you'll need to know.

Prices vary depending upon who does the packing. Make an appointment with two or three companies and they will visit your spread to give you an estimate.

Procedures to Follow When Moving

Face the fact that everything will be twice as hard as it is back home. Then, after it's all said and done, you won't feel so bad. It's going to be a lot of work. For example, you'll have to change: your mailing address, telephone number, electricity, gas, water, National Health Insurance (only if you change wards), Alien Registration Card, Ward Tax and other particulars. Make a list and make sure everything gets done on time.

Before Moving

1. **Mail**: Get a card called the *tenkyo–todoke* . This will forward your mail to your new address for a period of up to one year.
2. **Telephone**: Call NTT Information at 5295–1010.

3. **Utilities** (electricity, gas and water) See the numbers listed below for further instructions.
4. **National Health Insurance**: If you leave your present ward, you have to reapply at the new one.

After Moving

1. **Alien Registration**: The authorities will write your new address on the back of the card, but don't worry about taking any more pictures or fingerprints as the old ones still apply.
2. **Electricity**: Turn the power on. A postcard addressed to Tokyo Electric Power Company should be hanging near the electrical box. Fill it in and mail it right away. Have a friend do it in Japanese.
3. **Water**: Normally the water is already connected.
4. **Gas**: Fill in and send the card. Some guy will come by later to check to make sure everything is O.K.

For the above services, call these numbers to find out where your nearest office is:

Tokyo Gas Co. Ltd 3433–2111
Tokyo Electric Power Company..3501–8111
Tokyo Waterworks Bureau, Public Relations Section 5320–6327

NOTE: HAVE A JAPANESE FRIEND CALL FIRST.

Domestic Services/Choices
Moving companies

Within Japan it costs about ¥15,000 per room charge (1DK–One room, dining/kitchen all together) for a two ton truck, one workman carrying the boxes in and out (packing charges separate) within the same city. The same room charge can jump up to ¥30,000 if your new place requires a lot of travel.
Contact:

ABC Moving Service 3368–5995
Alba Moving Service 5399–1625
Art Corporation 3502-0123
FourWinds 3593–3191
Japan Express (toll free) 0120–228–322
Nippon Express (Heartliner).. 3572-4301
Orient Moving System..3254–1230
Phoenix Transport 045–212–3251
T.S. Brothers..045–785–0633
Yamato Transport (toll free) 0120–008–008
Japan Moving Bureau (toll free) 0120–333–125

NOTE: ENGLISH SHOULD BE NO PROBLEM AT MOST OF THE ABOVE COMPANIES.

Parcel–Home Delivery

If you're just moving a few boxes or bulky items, try a convenience store. Many have a service called *Takkyubin* (Home–Delivery) and it's very cheap, about ¥1,000 per suitcase or box in the Tokyo area. Try 7–11 or Lawson or any of the other big franchises.

Station–Wagon Taxis

You load up the taxi, pay for the time it takes, then pay for the fare. Carries both you and your stuff. Probably not the best solution because you can rent a truck for about the same price (see below). But if you don't have a driver's license, this is a good option.

Contact in Japanese only:

Checker Radio Taxi Co–op 3573–3751
Hinomaru Transportation 3808–1191

Truck Rental

Up to a one–ton truck with an ordinary International Driver's License or a normal Japanese license is possible. (See the Transportation and License section on how to get either one, page 77) It will cost about ¥10,000 for up to 6 hours and ¥13,000 for 12 hours.

Call in English:

Avis 3583–0911
Budget 3779–0543
Hertz 3796-8002
Isuzu Rent–A–Car 3334–2411
Nippon Rent–A–Car 3485–7196
Nissan Rent–A–Car 3587–4123
Opal Rent–A–Car 3995–2014
Toyota (Tokyo) 3364–0100
Toyota Rent–A–Lease (Narita) 0476–32–1020

NOTE: FOR A SMALL CAR, HERTZ HAS THE BEST RATES AT ¥8,800 FOR 24 HOURS, PLUS
FOREIGNERS CAN APPLY FOR A DISCOUNT CARD WHICH GIVES 15% OFF.

Overseas Moving Services

Much more complicated and expensive.
Points to consider:
1.   Residence–to–residence, or residence–to–seaport or residence–to–airport.
2.   Charges include: domestic transport, packing, air transport, custom clearance and second country domestic transport.
     Companies:

Alba Moving Service 5399–1625
Ark Moving (toll free) 0120–359–359
Art Corporation 3249–0123
English OK.
Crown Lines Company 045–661–1913
Dean International 045–662–7870
Econoship (toll free) 0120–22–2111
Global International 3589–0830
JTB Moving Service Center 0120–154–007
Nippon Express Company Ltd 3572–4301
No problem with English.
Overseas Moving Service 3760–1180
Will send a free brochure.
Phoenix Transport Japan 045–212–3251
Rakudo Line Company 5607–2925
Yamoto Transport (toll free) 0120–008–008

LIVING IN JAPAN

TRANSPORTATION

Trains and subways really are outstanding in Japan. They run on time and they're never late except when tormented students hurtle themselves onto the tracks of oncoming trains to relieve the burden during examination hell (February in most cases).

Mass transit is also really, really safe with the exception of drunken salarymen (businessmen) who sometimes want to talk to a foreigner, especially women. The worst is if they throw up – a frequent occurrence late at night. Otherwise, transportation is a real pleasure.

Don't expect a seat during rush hour unless you are at the first station of the line. By this I mean Japan has hundreds of separate train tracks or lines like the Sobu line, Chuo line, Keiyo line, and the Yamanote line. Each line runs from A to Z for example. A or Z are great places to get a seat because everyone gets off and the train starts back in the direction it just came from. When getting an apartment this can be a real bonus.

A typical line starts at A, stops at B, C, D, E and so on all the way to Z. It waits a few moments, then starts its way back from Z to Y, X, W, V etc. The best place to get a seat is at A or Z as all passengers have reached their final destination and must exit leaving the train totally empty. However, most teachers work from 1–9pm so 1 o'clock is no problem as the rush hour is long over. 9pm depends where you are in the city, but you should get a seat 50% of the time. A big deal considering most people commute an average of 1–2 hours each way to work (you included!).

Until you establish a routine to and from your work place(s) just buy the cheapest train or subway ticket ¥120 and ¥140 respectively. You do this by locating the ticket machine and put in the coins and press the red LCD button indicating ¥120 or ¥140 when the light comes on. You then hand this to the ticket puncher and you go through the gate.

At the end of your destination just go to the *Fare Adjustment Window* which is written in English and pay the difference – very simple. Some of the bigger stations like Shinjuku or Tokyo have an automatic ticket machine. Instead of handing your ticket to be punched by the gate attendant upon entering, you just slide it into the slot in the direction of the pointed arrow written on the ticket. It comes out on the other side of the turnstile for you to scoop up.

Upon exiting, the same process applies. However, if your ticket purchase price is less than the distance you've just traveled, the turnstile freezes shut and bells go off alerting you as a train thief to all around. You'll then have to go to the *Fare Adjustment Window* and pay the difference. It's best to check at the window until you establish a routine and know the exact fare.

NOTE: ANY TICKET YOU BUY EXPIRES AT THE END OF THE DAY. I MADE A MISTAKE ONE DAY, BOUGHT THE WRONG TICKET FOR ANOTHER SUBWAY LINE AND TRIED TO USE IT THE NEXT DAY FOR AN INTERVIEW I HAD. THE MACHINE JUST SPIT IT BACK IN MY FACE. LIVE AND LEARN IS ONE OF MY MOTTOES IN JAPAN.

After you accept a full time position, buy a commuter's pass (at the tekiken uriba) between your two destinations for one, three or six months. Most schools want it monthly for accounting reasons, and will reimburse you at the end of each month's pay. The pass allows you to get on and off anywhere between any of the stations designated on your pass. For example, Makuhari Hongo station to Chiba station which is a total of 6 stations and a 13 minute train ride is about ¥5,000/month. I could have got off or on at any of the four stations in between at no extra charge. All platform station identification is in English telling you the previous and next stop.

There are times when you can out–smart Japan Railways. However, that's an initiation process I must leave up to you or else I'll get sued in a big way! Suffice it to say, JR loses somewhere in the neighborhood of $300 million dollars every year due to 'kiseru'. It's interesting that the Japanese even invented a separate word to describe train fare cheating.

I recommend that you get a free copy of the Tokyo map from your embassy before you arrive. Once you arrive in Tokyo, go to the Tourist Info Center in Ginza. Maps are free and you should ask for 2 or 3 as you'll wear them out in a hurry in the first month or two. Tell them they're for a friend.
Tourist Information Center...3502–1461

Once you get your routine down, it's helpful to know when you can catch your train. JR supplies free schedules at each station. They print new schedules in April, so depending upon when you arrive they may be out. I made up a little chart for my station going in both directions so I could time my departure from my apartment and my arrival at school. This skill can make a long trip into a shorter one if you save 10 minutes each way. Black is for Monday–Friday, blue is for Saturday, and red is for Sundays and national holidays. These color coded schedules are in plain view on the platforms where you wait for the trains to arrive.

Useful Phrases (Directions)
1. chikaku desu ka?
   is it near?
2. hidari
   left
3. migi
   right
4. mae
   before
5. soba
   beside, nearby

6.　ushiro
　　behind, in back of
7.　tonari
　　next to
8.　muko
　　opposite
9.　kado
　　corner
10.　shingo
　　traffic light
11.　massugu
　　straight
12.　＿＿＿ onegaishimasu.
　　Please take me to ＿＿＿.

Bus

Some buses have a flat rate of ¥120 and you get on at the front of the bus and take a seat. Others are pay–as–you–go types which you enter from the middle and take a ticket from the dispenser to your right. The distance is divided into zones and the zone number will be printed on your ticket. You then pay according to the prices at the front of the bus next to the driver listed on the red display screen. At each bus stop there's a post with the times of arrival on it. I always found out beforehand the name of my stop wherever I was going and asked the driver if he went there. I sat up at the front and he usually gave me a little signal to let me know it was my stop. All buses have a high shrilly female voice telling you each stop's name in Japanese. Until you get used to it, it's difficult to comprehend. Even for a native Japanese speaker it's difficult to understand.

You can buy a set of 11 tickets for the price of 10, 'kaisuken', between two points valid for three months. Also you can get a bus pass, 'teiki', good for one or three months. The booths are located at the bus terminals. Your ward office might have schedules and destinations in English so check it out.

Most buses stop running around 10:30pm, and like trains and subways, they might not do the full route on their last run. Don't worry about having the exact change because all buses have a coin changer that takes a ¥1,000 note plus ¥500, ¥100 and ¥50 coin slots that automatically give you the correct change. The transportation bureau of the Tokyo Metropolitan Government has a free city bus route map in English. It's called *Toei kotsu no Goannai*. You can find it at:

1.　Kinshicho Stn. S Exit. Tokyo Traffic Kinshicho Bldg. 1F.
2.　Shinjuku Stn. W Exit. Bus Terminal, B1. Next to the Police Box.

Cars

If you've heard any stories about the traffic jams in Tokyo they're all true. We're talking massive lengths of metal more than 75km, sometimes close to

100km if it's a peak day during Golden Week in May or New Year's in January. That's not an exaggeration. If you're *still* interested in driving, second hand cars can be had very cheap anywhere from ¥100,000 and up. English Language publications like the *Tokyo Journal*, *Tokyo Weekender*, and the *Daily Yomiuri on Sunday* have classified sections. If you can get a Japanese person to read the Japanese Dailies and call around your choice is unlimited.

The problem with owning a car in Japan is a system of insurance, user registration fee, road tax and a safety check called *Shaken*. Shaken could best be described as road maintenance insurance; making sure your vehicle is suitable to drive. It starts three years after a new car is bought and then every two years later regardless of who owns the car. It costs about ¥100,000 yearly. That's why some cars can be had so cheaply if their Shaken expires within a couple of months. I've seen some cars listed for ¥50,000 due to a fast–approaching Shaken deadline. The Shaken is transferable to the new owner and it's expiry date remains the same regardless of ownership.

If you're looking for a car to do some touring in after a year or so, it might save you and a couple of friends some train fare, not to mention the freedom of going where and when you want. If three or four people each put in ¥35,000 to ¥50,000 you could buy a great car for a couple months of travel then sell it again when you're done.

Train fares add up in a hurry and just to give an example look at these Shinkansen (Bullet Train) prices for a one–way trip from Tokyo to:

Kyoto	¥12,970
Osaka	¥13,480
Nagoya	¥10,380
Hiroshima	¥17,700

Therefore if the situation is right, a car wouldn't be a bad investment for group travel.

What are the other drawbacks of having a car in Tokyo? In addition to paying Shaken, you'll need a parking spot certificate – proof you won't leave it on the street. In the Akasaka financial district in Tokyo, the going rate for a prime parking spot sells for around $800,000. Naturally, the farther out you are the cheaper a spot is, but then your commute is longer. Monthly parking rent at your apartment's lot might be had for around ¥10,000 if they're not full. Otherwise a private company will cost about ¥30,000 per month. When you get into town, parking by the hour, if you are lucky enough to even find a meter or car park, could be anywhere from ¥300 to ¥1,000 an hour. All in all it just ain't worth it.

There is one last option for those people who want to take a car around just for a day and that is to rent a car. It's a great way to see some sights. You'll need your passport and a valid driver's license. Driving is on the left so be careful. I recommend everyone rent a car at least once. Our neighbor did it so he could move one Sunday because it was easier and cheaper to load the car once than take the train several times.

NOTE: FOR A LIST OF CAR RENTAL AGENCIES, CHECK UNDER TRUCK RENTAL IN THE MOVING SECTION, PAGE 71.

Licenses

If you don't get an International Driver's License before you come to Japan you can change your ordinary one here. You'll need:
1.   driver's license (with date of issue stamp) from home
2.   passport
3.   alien registration card
4.   passport size color photo

Test centers are open from 8:30–11am Monday to Friday. The cost is ¥3,000, valid for three years (until your third birthday), renewable for three more years each time after that. It's a long process taking about two to three hours. Call the Tourist Information Center (3502–1461) for the nearest test center near you or try:

1.   **Koto Driving Test Center**..3699–1151
   1–7–24 Shinsuna, Koto Ku.
2.   **Samezu Driving Test Center**..3474–1374
   1–12–5 Higashi–Oi, Shinagawa–ku.
3.   **Fuchu Test Center** 0423–62–3591
   3–1–1 Tama, Fuchu–Shi.

Lonely Planet's guide to Japan has an excellent section on driving in Japan. It mentions driver's attitudes, safety, road conditions, and much more. *Lonely Planet* also has a section on hitch–hiking (something I never saw, but might be possible). Also, *Your Life in Tokyo* delves further than *Lonely Planet* describing all road signs, violations, insurance, and taxes. These two publications will be able to answer any further questions you'll have if you decide to take the plunge and buy a car. Both of these books are available through our mail order service at the back of the book.

Motorcycles and Scooters

I think this is smarter than a car, a lot more fun, quicker and cheaper. I got a 90cc scooter for free, fixed it up for ¥20,000, and have been using it ever since! A gaijin had bought a new scooter and it was easier for him to give it away than to dispose of it legally. To do so he would have had to have paid a special garbage charge. Big items in Central Tokyo cost extra money to throw out. It's an honor system so I don't know how many people actually use it, but it exists. Most people just dump stuff near the garbage center and wait for it to be picked up by someone else who could use it themselves. A scooter might have cost my friend about ¥2,500 so he put up a note at the Tourist Information Center in Ginza instead, advertising a free scooter to anyone who would come and pick it up at his apartment. Tokyo's full of stories just like mine.

Anyway, you can buy a scooter or motorcycle cheap. If it's under 250cc no *shaken* (insurance fee of around ¥50,000 for bikes) applies. With 250cc or more you can drive on the highways from 11pm–6am, anything smaller is forbidden at all times. Ueno station has tons of motorcycles for sale but take a Japanese person to negotiate for you. New 50cc scooters start at around ¥90,000. Naturally, a helmet is required.

Japan Rail and Passes
Everyday Travel

Bargains at Japan Rail exist. A regular one month commuter pass is 30 times the one way fare plus 3% tax added. Three month and six month passes are also available at a slightly cheaper rate.

A Japan Rail pass between A and E for example allows you to stop at B, C, and D for free just by flashing your pass to the ticket puncher. Also, always ask how far you can go before you buy your pass because sometimes you can often include the next stop (i.e. F) for the same price as A to E.

Buy your pass from the green window near the ticket vending machines. No Japanese required. Just point on the map where you want to go and write your name down. If in doubt or you want to check several prices, call the Japan Rail info line which gives excellent English service for everything related to Japan Rail (3423–0111).

A special one day ticket which would be useful for your first few days of travel looking for a gaijin house or a job, costs only ¥720 which includes all JR lines in Tokyo. For the subway system a one day fare costs ¥620.

Also, you can buy blocks of 11 JR tickets for the price of 10. These are for travel between 2 set stations like our example of A to E. No stops are allowed in the middle. Pre–paid tickets are good if you've taken a short term part–time job, or if you regularly visit another station to go shopping, to see a movie, or to go a fitness center that is not on your pass which your school supplies free of charge. The tickets are valid for 3 months. A good buy all around as transportation is expensive in Japan. Anytime you can save yen buying specials or whatnot, go for it.

Long Distance Travel

Japan Rail also has a one, two or three week all–inclusive anywhere in Japan (Bullet Train included) pass which must be bought outside the country and used within three months of entry. It starts the day you validate it at any one of the major stations. Call JR to find out the closest to your home or hotel.

One of my friends who had lived in Japan for eight months skirted the official policy of having to buy the pass outside of Japan by having his parents buy it for him and send it to Japan. He then went to Ueno Station, (over 800,000 people use this station a day) and validated his pass for Golden Week in May with no problem whatsoever. The official only checked his picture, passport number and issued his pass. He didn't bother to check his date of entry into Japan and the purchase date of the pass which were obviously way off. Since then I've heard of several people doing the same thing. The passes are meant for foreign nationals on a Tourist Visa only. If there is any reason why your pass cannot be validated, you can refund it at a 10% loss.

When you travel always carry a map and check the platform signs to make sure you're going in the right direction. If in doubt ask the guys wearing the blue suits: just point to the train and say the destination – nothing more – they say yes or no (in which case they'll tell you the proper track number). Bigger stations have lots of exits marked 1A, 1B, 1C, South, West, East, North, so it's easy to get lost. Make sure you notice which one you come out of and always ask for the exit number if going for a job or meeting someone.

You just can't imagine the crush of people at a JR station like Shinjuku. It has over one million users a day making it the world's busiest station. It's literally like being in a can of sardines. Forget about running or even walking fast. People seem to crisscross all over and it's easy to get lost, but hey, that's half the fun, not every day, but once in awhile it's really neat. If that happens to be where you live or work, well, just learn to grin and bear it or it'll drive you crazy.

JR East Info Line 3423–0111
Shinkansen Reservation 3540–9200

Train Savvy

Always always always know when your last train is at night. This is my best advice to any newcomer. Trains shut down around 1am and start around 5am depending upon where your station is situated. Call the above JR info line to get exact times.

If you're out drinking or dancing or just drinking a coffee, jot down in your schedule planner the station's last few train times or better yet go to the Ticket Window and ask. Tell the man where you are now and where you want to go. For example: Shinjuku –> Funabashi last train when? Or the Japanese equivalent: Shinjuku kara Funabashi made wa saigo no densha wa itsu desu ka?

If you blow it some night and miss your train you've got several options:
1. Continue to party until the first train 4:30–5am.
2. Take a taxi home (more expensive at night and depending on where you live they might not go there if it's too far out and the driver's afraid he won't be able to find a fare back). A thirty minute taxi ride could cost you about ¥10,000.
3. Go to a coffee shop (if you're in a large area, like Roppongi, Shinjuku, or Shibuya) and wait it out. You only have to buy one coffee for about ¥400.
4. Sleep on the train station's floor or bench as some businessmen do!
5. Rent a capsule hotel (only metro Tokyo from ¥3,000 to ¥4,000/night. The rooms are the length of your body plus one meter, about 1.5 meters high (you couldn't stand up) and 1.5 meters wide. You could touch both sides

of the walls if you outstretched your arms. Usually filled with salarymen who are on business or who missed the last train like you. Some businessmen even rent them during the weekdays as cheap accommodation, visiting their homes in the suburbs only on weekends. You should try it once just to say you did it. See the Travel Section labeled Capsule Hotels for further info.

6. Go to a Love Hotel. Also described under the Travel Section.
7. Midnight express buses called *Midnight Arrow* are another late–night option. They run daily except Year–End, New Year's Holidays, 'Obon' summer holidays, Sat, Sun and National Holidays. The cost runs about ¥2,000 to ¥3,000 depending upon the distance traveled. The latest departure is 1:15am so might as well make the effort to catch the last train. They depart from Ikebukuro, Shinjuku, Shibuya, Shimbashi and Yurakucho only. Call JR info at 3423-0111 or NTT info at 5295-1010 for further details
8. Tokyo Metropolitan operates *Midnight 25* buses, which run inside the metropolitan area for ¥320 per ride. Ikebukuro, Shinjuku, Shibuya, Shinagawa, Shimbashi, Tokyo, Oji, Kinshicho and so on. For detailed information, call 5600–2020 or 5320–6074.

Useful Phrases

1. Tsugi wa *Shinjuku* desu ka?
    Is *Shinjuku* next?
2. Koko wa doko desu ka?
    Where are we now?
3. Kono densha wa ___ e ikimasu ka?
    Does this train go to ___?
4. Orimasu.
    I'm getting off.
5. Yamanote–sen wa doko desu ka?
    Where's the Yamanote line?
6. Ikebukuro made ikura desu ka?
    How much is it to Ikebukuro?

Reserving a Ride on the Bullet Train

Awesome speed, extremely accurate departure and arrival times, clean seats and speed make a ride on the Shinkansen (Bullet Train) a joy. If you've got a JR Weekly Pass, just validate it and make your reservations as you please. You have unlimited travel anywhere in Japan from one to four weeks.

Here's how the system works.
1. Make a reservation at a Green Ticket Window in any JR station. You don't necessarily have to go to a Shinkansen station. Or call Shinkansen Reservations at 3540–9200 in English.

2. If you don't have a pass, tickets go on sale at 10am one month prior to the departure date (for example, tickets for April 2nd go on sale March 2nd). Don't go earlier like me and waste your time. They just don't bend the rules here.

3. There are two types of Shinkansen trains; the Hikari and the Kodama. The Hikari stops only at major stations, while the Kodama stops at every Shinkansen station. Also, there are more unreserved cars on the Kodama.

4. Travel is not cheap as can be witnessed by some of these one-way fares:

Tokyo–Kyoto	¥12,970
Tokyo–Shin–osaka	¥13,480
Tokyo–Hiroshima	¥17,400
Tokyo–Hakata	¥21,300
(Tohoku)	
Tokyo–Sendai	¥10,190
Tokyo–Morioka	¥11,700
Tokyo–Nigata	¥9,600

5. If you are traveling a long distance (for example, Tokyo–Hiroshima), you can start using your ticket from your local JR station. Most people don't know this and pay extra to get to Tokyo or Ueno Station which are the two major Shinkansen starting points. Sometimes there are discounts so call the JR Infoline at 3423–0111 for more info.

NOTE: ALL SHINKANSEN TRAINS HAVE TELEPHONES WHICH IS PRETTY COOL TO TRY ONCE. ANNOUNCEMENTS ARE MADE IN BOTH JAPANESE AND ENGLISH, SO DON'T WORRY ABOUT MISSING YOUR STOP. FIRST CLASS IS CALLED THE GREEN CAR. FREE DRINKS AND MAGAZINES PLUS BIGGER SEATS.

Police Boxes – On the Spot Directions

A great service when you're out and about are the *Kobans* (police boxes) right beside every station in the country! The boys (police) help everyone out including the Japanese who have just as much trouble as us foreigners do in finding out where they are and how they can get to where they want to go. (P.S. always have your passport or Alien registration card with you – or the day has just been lost to Japanese bureaucracy. See section on Alien Registration Card.)

1. Ichiban chikai eki wa doko desu ka?
    Where's the closest station?
2. Mo ichido itte kudasai.
    Please say that again.
3. Wakarimashita.
    I understand.
4. Wakarimasen.
    I don't understand.

Taxi

Flag down a taxi with your hand anywhere or find them at train stations parked near the entrance. There's a taxi stand where you have to wait and in most cases you have to line up and wait your turn. There's no cheating and if you try to flag down one out of the loop, the driver won't even acknowledge you. No New York style budding in permitted in Japan. A red light means empty, green means full. A basic fare of ¥600 and distance traveled is charged. Have the address of where you're going written down or else the driver won't understand you. If where you're going is not a station or big landmark make use of the directions section – straight, right, left, and so on listed previously.

Don't grab the handle as the door swings open automatically–same when getting out; the driver does this for you. Unlike Thailand, Hong Kong, or Korea, all taxis have meters. There's no bargaining and no tipping either. Fares cost about 30% more between 11pm and 5am. If you reserve one by phone, it'll cost an extra ¥500 to ¥600.

Checker Radio Taxi Co–op 3573–3751
Daiwa Motor Transportation 3563–5151
Eastern Motors...3742–1461
Green Cabs 3202-5381
Hinomaru Transportation 3811-1151
Keio Motors..3378–3211
Odakyu Kotsu 3541–2294
Teito Motor Transportation 3288–1211

All the above are strictly Japanese speaking. If you lose something in any taxi, try calling this lost and found number in Japanese:
Tokyo Taxi Kindaika Center 3648–0300

TELEPHONES

Much has been written about the complexity of Japan's telephone system. The way to avoid this is to buy a telephone card for ¥1,000 which gives you 105 units of local calls each three minutes long.

You then go to the green phones and stick your card in. The red numbers will indicate how fast your units are being used and how many you have left. Green phones also have special free buttons for the Police, the Fire Department and a Free Ambulance service to the nearest hospital. When calling from public phones for job interviews and the like, go into big banks' lobbies or other big office complexes because you'll appreciate the absence of all the noise to be found outside on the sidewalk.

Getting an actual phone line installed depends on your circumstances. If you're in a Gaijin house, you won't need one and people will take messages for you. However, if you rent an apartment you'll have to buy a phone line bond for about ¥75,000, pay for the installation fee of ¥10,000, and shell out dough for the monthly user fee of ¥1,600. You can sell the phone line bond back when you leave Japan for ¥65,000 or so. You might also go to Kimi Information Center and check out their bulletin board for people who are selling their phone lines as they are leaving the country. They'll be slightly cheaper at around ¥60,000–¥65,000. (See page 49 for Kimi's phone number) Also, check the Sunday edition of *The Daily Yomiuri* in the Classifieds. It's a seller's market so if you find it hard to get hold of a used phone line, head to NTT. You'll pay full price, but sometimes it's worth it to have a phone immediately.

You'll also have to buy a phone for around ¥10,000–¥15,000 (with an answering machine, which is essential for busy teachers). At Kimi they'll take messages for you for ¥2,500/month. Not bad, because they'll handle Japanese/English calls from friends or job prospects or employers. Another full time answering service like the ones that exist back home cost around ¥10,000/month (call 3291–3596 Mita line Jimbo Cho Station Exit A5).

Personally, we lived for 10 months without a phone. We both could have received emergency calls at work if needed and when we called home we used the ¥1,000 telephone cards.

Our reasons for using a public telephone were:

1. Limits calls home as you see your money disappearing directly into the slot.
2. Gives a buzzer warning for you to put in another card when the original one is close to expiring.
3. Is definitely cheaper in the long run compared to all the costs involved in the initial set–up price. You can phone home once a week and still come out ahead and save money.

Call NTT's Japan Hotline 3586–0110 or NTT's English Information 5295–1010 for information on where to get a phone from the nearest branch of NTT. NTT is open from 9am–5pm Mon–Fri, 9–12pm Sat.

There is another company that will rent you a phone line for ¥3,000/month, but you can't make international calls. You can receive them but not make them. A good money saver. You'll still pay the ¥1,650/month basic fee, plus you'll need to rent a touch tone phone. My feeling is why bother unless you're an orphan and won't be making any calls home. NTT will be able to help you out greatly with any other conceivable questions you might have on these matters.

General Telephone Numbers

Asahi Evening News 3543–3321

Daily Yomiuri English Subscription Office 3216–8866
This paper has a free classified section on Sundays for articles for sale and a message board. Good place to pick up a used phone line for around ¥65,000 and there are always sayonara sales by departing foreigners. This book was drafted on a free computer that I found in one of the ads.

English Information (run by NTT) 5295–1010
Mon–Fri 9am–5pm, Sat 9–12pm.

Foreign Residents Advisory Center 5320–7744
Government run program to assist foreigners with the usual questions
about housing, insurance, or hospitals. Very good resource base. Mon–Fri
9:30am–4pm.

Imperial Palace Visit (extension #485) 3213–1111

International Direct dialing ....001, 0041, or 0061
(I find 0061 to be the cheapest to Canada. It has the same discounts from
11pm to 8am as in North America.)

Japan Hotline 3586–0110
Mon–Fri 10am–4pm. Will assist in phone number checks, language
difficulties and more.

Japan National Tourist Organization 3502–1461
(reservations and general info)

Japan Railways Hotline 3423–0111
Will answer questions about JR prices, schedules, itineraries, and discount
tickets.

Japan Times 3453–5311
The best source for foreigners who are looking for teaching jobs. Monday's
issue is when all the schools advertise for one day only as rates are quite
expensive.

Japanese Homestay 3261–3451
One, two or three week stays with a Japanese family. Cost for example for
a couple for one week is ¥42,000.

Mainichi Daily News 3212–0321

Narita Friendship Club 0476–24–1734
English club that organizes trips, Bar–B–Q's, and Karaoke sing–a–longs.

Overseas Operator 0051
Will place collect calls, check numbers etc.

Post Office Information 5472-5851

Salvation Army (Nakano)...3384–3769
Kanda 3237–0881
Great bargains on just about everything you could think of that you might
need for your stay in Japan. Best time is Saturday mornings 9am–12noon.
Call to confirm schedule.

Servas...3721–1507
A non–profit homestay with a Japanese family for a maximum of two days.
Nine thousand hosts in over 100 countries. Apply for membership in your
home country before departure. Over 350 hosts in Japan. For more
information write: U.S. Servas Committee Inc., 11 John Street, Box 406,
New York, New York 10038. (212) 267-0252. Also check the page 222,
Homestay Programs Servas Japan for info on how to join.

Student Travel (ISIC) 3379–6311
For students who are valid members and have the International Student
Identity Card. Information on cheap accommodation, tickets and more.

Teletourist Service 3503–2911
Calendar events, entertainment.

  Great for maps and travel information. Also they can arrange the popular Home Visit for one night with a Japanese family. Allow at least one day's notice, preferably two or three. Free evening in a Japanese home. A small gift from your home country would be appropriate. They will also book ryokans (Japanese Inns) for you anywhere in Japan free of charge. A great service and you could save all of the long distance charges.

Ward Office–Check the Ward you're living for any English information. Many wards offer a wide range of services including pamphlets, culture courses, cooking classes, and sometimes free Japanese lessons. They are like the YWCA back home. See page 87.

  A non–profit welcome organization for newly arrived foreigners in Japan. Free info kit containing maps and pamphlets of Tokyo. Five free Coke coupons!

Counseling

  Mon–Fri 9am–4pm.
  A Government–approved social welfare agency. Problems such as adoptions, citizenship, marriages, divorces, social security, benefits.
Emmaus Japan–picks up clothes, appliances and donates them to the needy.
  Toll free number 24 hours a day from anywhere in Japan which will handle any personal or family problems.

Lawyers for Foreign Laborer's Rights 3357–5506
Le Leche League (baby breast feeding) 0422–20–2888
Metropolitan Police 3581–4321
Overeaters Anonymous 3630–3118
Quit Smoking 3583–6126
Rape Crisis Center of Tokyo 3207–3692
Substance Abuse 5481–4347
Tell (Tokyo English lifeline) 5721–4347
    9–1pm and 7–11pm. Trained volunteers to listen to your problems.
Tokyo Center for Human Rights for Foreigners 3581–2303
UNICEF 3475–1617

Credit Card Companies
American Express 3220–6000
    Lost Card (toll free) 0120–376-199
Diner's Club Japan 3499–1311
    Night 3499–1181
Master Card 3464–6611
    Lost Card 052–201–2121
Visa 3233–1141
    Lost Card 3459–4700

Emergency Telephone Numbers
Ambulance Tokyo Shindai 3357–1421
Emergency Hospitals (see complete list under Hospitals).................3212–2323
Fire and Ambulance Service 119
Police (throughout Japan) 110

Hospitals (English Speaking)
American Pharmacy 3271–4034
    The best place to have any prescription filled by English speaking
    pharmacists. Mon–Sat 9am–7pm. Holidays 11am–6pm. Near Yurakucho
    Station JR.
Sanno Clinic 3402–3151
Seibo Hospital (International Catholic Hospital) 3951–1111
St. Luke's International Hospital 3541–5151
Tokyo Sanitarium Hospital 3392–6151

Immigration and Work Related Problems
Central Immigration Office 3580–4111
Immigration Information Office 3213–8523/7
    Mon–Fri 9am–4pm. First and Third Sat 9–12pm.
Narita District Immigration Office, Narita Airport...................... 0472–32–6812

Ministry of Justice 3214–0424
   Visa, health, and work related problems. Otemachi Subway Station Exit C2.
   In Japanese ask for Godo Chosha Sangokan, 4th floor.
Labor Union Organization 0425–76–9030
   Gives info for foreign workers on Japanese labor rights and benefits.
Tokyo Center for Human Rights for Foreigners 3581–2302
   Thur 1–4pm. Free legal advice. No appointments, in person only. Tokyo
   Bar Association 1–1–4 Kasumigaseki.
Tokyo City Air Terminal (TCAT) Immigration Office 3664–3046
   Info about re–entry permits. Mon–Fri 9–12pm and 1–5pm.
Work Relations Labor Board 3814–5311
   Tue and Thur 9am–3pm.
Working Holiday Visa Center 3389–0181
   You can register for ¥500 and they provide you with a booklet outlining
   your rights in Japan. They have a job board and bulletin board there as
   well. Definitely worth the visit.

Local Government Offices

   If I've failed to list any of the Ward office telephone numbers, please call
the Foreign Residents' Advisory Center at 3211–4433 Mon–Fri 9:30–12pm and
1–4pm to get a complete list.

Adachi 3882–1111
Arakawa 3802–3111
Bunkyo 3812–7111
Chiyoda 3264–0151
Edogawa 3652–1151
Itabashi 3964–1111
Katsushika 3695–1111
Kita 3908–1111
Koto 3647–9111
Meguro 3715–1111
Minato 3578–2111
Nakano 3389–1111
Nerima 3993–1111
Ota 3773–5111
Setagaya 3412–1111
Shibuya 3463–1211
Shinagawa 3777–1111
Shinjuku 3209–1111
Suginami 3312–2111
Sumida 3626–3151
Taito 3842–5311
Toshima 3981–1111

   Most of the above Wards have English books and guides available but I
wouldn't try calling them in English for anything. Ask a Japanese friend to do it

for you or just go and pick up what they've got in the lobby. However, some wards and cities are staffed to handle us gaijin. Here are the phone numbers of the wards and cities where English personnel will handle your inquiries:

Fuchu City 0423–66–1711
Kita Ward...3908–1111
Kunitachi City 0425–76–2111
Minato Ward..3578–2053
Nakano Ward 3389–1611
Suginami Ward 3312–2111
Toshima Ward (largest foreign population of all Wards)....................3981–1111

Lost and Found

If you ever lose anything, for example your passport (like me!), train pass, books, bag, or purse, you'll have several spots to check out before you can officially swear that your article is hopelessly lost. The Japanese seem to delight in going out of their way to return lost parcels, and every foreigner has a "You–won't–believe–what–I–lost–and–got–back" story. Chances are that even money will be returned to the nearest authority, surprising as that may seem.

Police Box: Go and fill out a lost and found form. Bring your Alien Registration Card to show your name and address. There's a chance someone already found it and it's there waiting for you.

Japan Railways: Go to the nearest station to where you think you lost your item and explain what it was. They have a little storage compartment and all you have to do is sign for it if they found it. If it's not there, they will phone ahead to the end of the line and see if the man who walks through the train found anything. People have lost entire sets of luggage and retrieved them within two hours. I've been able to get a lost shopping bag back twice both within ten minutes. After I realized I had left my bag in the train and watched it pull out, I immediately went to the small office located on every train platform in Japan. I told them that the previous train had my bag. They asked me approximately what car it was, which side of the train, then called ahead a few stations. There, a JR guy dashed in when the train arrived, retrieved my bag and kept it waiting for me until I caught the next train and arrived there. All pretty fast and like a James Bond movie.

Police Station: Not the little police boxes beside each station, but the main office. For serious articles such as passport or alien registration you'll need to fill out their form. Phone the NTT info line to find out where the nearest one is and get there as soon as you can.

Items such as umbrellas and bikes are a different matter as they disappear on a more frequent basis and are almost impossible to trace.

Hopefully, you won't need this section, but if you do, you may experience a very positive side of the Japanese personality. I lost rough copies of this book twice and retrieved them both times through the help of all three of the above. Believe me, I was pretty worried but greatly impressed with their efficiency.

NOTE: TRANSPORTATION COMPANIES WILL HOLD YOUR STUFF FOR A FEW DAYS, THEN SEND IT TO THE LOCAL POLICE STATION FOR ONE MONTH. THEN IT IS MOVED TO THE METROPOLITAN POLICE DEPARTMENT LOST AND FOUND. AFTER SIX MONTHS, YOU NO LONGER HAVE THE RIGHT TO CLAIM IT. IF YOU'VE LOST YOUR PASSPORT, SOMETIMES THEY'LL CALL YOUR EMBASSY AND ALERT THEM. IF YOU LOSE YOUR COMMUTER PASS, TRY THE STARTING AND ENDING STATION'S LOST AND FOUND. CALL THE JR INFO LINE AT 3423–0111 FOR ASSISTANCE.

Lost and Found Telephone Numbers

JR–Tokyo Station	3231–1880
JR–Ueno Station	3841–8069
Subway Metro	3818–5760
Subway Teito	3834–5577
Taxi (open 24 hours)	3648–0300
TOEI, Bus, Subway	3818–5760
JR Info Line if you're not sure what Stn to call they will direct you. 10am–6pm Mon–Fri only.	3423–0111
NTT Info Line (in English) Mon–Fri 10am–4pm.	5925–1010
Metro Police Department Tsuyaku Center	3581–4321

Money/Taxes

Consultant Office, Tokyo National Tax Bureau 3216–0511

Political/Volunteer

Agape House 0120–461–996
    Toll free hotline for those experiencing cross–cultural difficulties.
Amnesty International...3203–1050
Friends of the Earth 3770–5387
    Global and environmental issues, Sunday hikes.
Japan International Volunteer Center 3834–2388
Japan Tropical Forest Action Network.. 3770–6308
    Global deforestation problems.
People to People Partnerships (Help for Filipinos).................... 0429–72–6946
The Citizens Cycling Recycling 3228–6800
Republicans Abroad tel/fax 3794–4691

Travel

Airport Baggage Service (ABC) 3284–2525
> Located at Narita Airport. Handy pick–up and delivery service. Especially useful when you arrive with ten suitcases and only need one to live from until you settle in. Reasonable prices. Worth paying to avoid dragging your luggage around from hotel to gaijin house to apartment each time you move. They will also store your bags for a fee on a daily basis. For more info see section on Arrival at Narita.

Haneda Flight Information 3747–8010
Narita Flight Information 0476–32–2800

NOTE: UNDER THE ARRIVAL SECTION THERE IS A LIST OF ALL THE INTERNATIONAL AIRLINES SERVICING JAPAN.

Utilities

Tokyo Electric Power Company, Customer Service 3501–8111
Tokyo Gas Customer Service Office 3273–0111
Tokyo Telephone Information line, NTT 5925–1010
Tokyo Water Bureau, General Affairs 3212–6796
> All the above are English Hotlines.

Making An International Call From Japan

Several numbers to call and several companies to choose from can complicate matters for you until you know the ropes. Here's what I've found out over the years. There are three international companies:

1. 001–Government Run. Service around the world.
2. 0041–Private. Cheap. Service to most countries.
3. 0061–Private, Cheapest. Same as above. Will cover every country you will ever call while in Japan, unless your family lives in Tonga or Iceland.

To make a call using one of the above, it goes like this:
A)   001+ country code + area code + number or;
B)   0041+ country code + area code + number or;
C)   0061+ country code + area code + number

A, B, and C are three different telephone companies. As I mentioned previously, I find 0061 to be the best value. There are no sign up charges as in the United States. Just dial and it automatically clicks in. In a month or so, you'll receive your bill. These companies can be used at home or in an International Telephone Booth. Amazing.

NOTE: IF YOU ARE USING A TELEPHONE BOOTH, YOU HAVE TO CHOOSE THE GREEN ONE WITH A GOLD PANEL ON THE FRONT THAT SAYS "INTERNATIONAL TELEPHONE".

If you don't know the number of someone you'd like to call, but know their city, you have two options:

1. Use one of International Telephone Companies mentioned above in A, B, or C. Then dial the country code, the area code, and 555–1212 as your telephone number. 555–1212 is a world wide number for operator assistance. You will be connected with an operator in that city. You will be billed for the long distance charge.

2. Dial "0039" + Country Code. You will be connected to an operator in your country directly. You can call collect with a credit card, from your home phone or from the green phones with a gold plate.

Here are the special country codes for "0039". The normal country codes for the 3 other Long Distance companies are listed on the next page

Areas	Dialing Number
U.S.A. (mainland)	0039–111/0039–121
Hawaii	0039–111/0039–181
Canada	0039–161
Brazil	0039–551
United Kingdom	0039–441
France	0039–331
Italy	0039–391
Spain	0039–341
Netherlands	0039–311
Finland	0039–358
Australia	0039–661
New Zealand	0039–641
Singapore	0039–651
Thailand	0039–662
Taiwan	0039–886
Korea (Rep. of)	0039–821
Hong Kong	0039–852

NOTE: JAPAN FOLLOWS NORTH AMERICA'S LONG DISTANCE DISCOUNT STYLE:
NO DISCOUNT ON WEEKDAYS FROM 8AM TO 7PM;
20% REDUCTION WITH ECONOMY RATES FOR WEEKDAYS FROM 7PM TO 11PM;
20% OFF ON SAT, SUN, AND HOLIDAYS FROM 7PM TO 11PM;
40% REDUCTION FOR LATE–NIGHT CALLS, 11PM TO 8AM.

Country Codes and Time Differences

Here is a list of the country codes that A) 001, B) 0041, and C) 0061 use.

ASIA

Areas	County Code	Time Differences
Bahrain	973	–6
China (People's Rep. of)	86	–1
Hong Kong	852	–1
India	91	–3.5
Indonesia	62	–2 to 0
Korea (Rep. of)	82	0
Kuwait	965	–6
Malaysia	60	–1
Philippines	63	–1
Singapore	65	–1
Taiwan	886	–1
Thailand	66	–2
United Arab Emirates	971	–5

NORTH AND SOUTH AMERICA

Areas	Country Code	Time Differences
Argentina	54	–12
Brazil	55	–12 to –14
Canada	1	–12.5 to –18
Chile	56	–13
Colombia	57	–14
Mexico	52	–15 to –17
U.S.A.	1	–14 to –17

OCEANIA

Areas	Country Code	Time Differences
Australia	61	–1 to +1
Guam	671	+1
Hawaii	1	–19
New Caledonia	687	+2
New Zealand	64	+3
Saipan	670	+1

EUROPE

Areas	Country Code	Time Differences
Denmark	45	–8
France	33	–8
Germany (Fed. Rep. of)	49	–8
Greece	30	–7
Italy	39	–8
Netherlands	31	–8
Spain	34	–8
Switzerland	41	–8
United Kingdom	44	–9

AFRICA

Areas	Country Code	Time Differences
Egypt	20	–7
Kenya	254	–6

POST OFFICES

You can do tons of stuff at the post office besides just buy stamps and mail letters. For example, it's possible to:
1. pay phone, gas and utility bills,
2. pay for National Health Insurance,
3. send money to another person in Japan,
4. buy life insurance,
5. open a savings account which can pay more interest than some banks or,
6. get a post office cash card (yubin chokin kyasshu) to take out money from any Post Office ATM and some banks.

Most people don't need all this, especially us guys just interested in sending a letter back home. However, as I explain in my How to Send Money Overseas section, the post office has cheap rates. If you do want to know exactly how much everything costs, write or fax:

> The Postal Bureau
> Research Section
> International Affairs Division
> Ministry of Posts and Telecommunications
> 3–2 Kasumigaseki 1–chome
> Chiyoda–ku, Tokyo 100–91
> fax: 3593–9124

They have a large 30–page brochure outlining everything in English, free of charge. It's called *How to Use the Post Office*. It outlines the services that you may need over the course of your stay. For further info get your own copy. The book lists info about:

1. How to buy commemorative stamps.
2. How to buy New Year's Lottery Post Cards. Send a New Year's wish to a friend and they have a chance to win money and prizes with the special number written on their card. Very popular.
3. How to get a cash card and use the Automatic Teller Machines.
4. How to transfer money abroad.
5. Mail Forwarding–good for up to one year. Give them your home address when you leave Japan or if you move. Mailed back to point of origin.
6. Mail Order Food and Craft Specialties from all over Japan. Catalogue is available at major post offices. Furusato Kozutsumi in Japanese.
7. Mail Order Specialties (International)–same concept. Warudo Yu Pakku (World Yu–Pack).
8. Special Book Shipping Rate–Must use their bag to wrap around your box. Max. weight is 30kg. About US$100 for seamail.
9. The correct way to address a letter in Japanese.
10. Withholding Mail–good for when you take home leave. Valid for 30 days and then held for another 10 for pick up.

There's more but I think you get the picture. Now, back to the simpler stuff. The ' 〒 ' is the mark for a post office. **The mail box has two slots: Left–Domestic; Right–International–all over Japan.**

One thing I noticed over the years is that it's cheaper and quicker to send mail or parcels from a larger office because it'll take less time to be handled domestically. Most post offices are open from 9am–5pm on weekdays, and until 1pm on Saturdays. Some are even open in the mornings on Sundays and Holidays. When you're settled in, call to find out the exact schedule of the one nearest you.

Azabu Post Office (1–6–19 Azabudai, Minato–ku)
Mail Sending 3582–3806
Mail Delivery...3583–8712
Shiba Post Office (3–22–5 Shimbashi, Minato–ku)
Mail Window 3431–4504
Mail Delivery...3431–9661
Shibuya Post Office (1–12–13 Shibuya, Shibuya–ku)
Mail Sending (Ordinary) 3409–5163
Mail Sending (Special Delivery, Registered Letters) 3409–5164
Mail Delivery...3409–5165
Shinjuku Post Office (1–8–10 Nishi–Shinjuku, Shinjuku–ku)
Mail Sending (Ordinary) 3342–9222
Mail Sending (Special Delivery, Registered Letters) 3342–2070
Tokyo Central Post Office (2–7–2 Marunouchi, Chiyoda–ku)
Domestic Mail Sending 3284–9539

Foreign Mail Sending 3284–9540
Mail delivery 3284–9556

You can even buy stamps and send domestic and international mail 24 hours a day at a special all night wicket.

Tokyo International Post Office (2–3–3 Otemachi, Chiyoda–ku)
Foreign Mail Information 3241–4891
Ordinary Sea Mail 3241–5901
Sea Mail Parcel Post 3241–5908
Airmail Parcel Post 3241–3544

NOTE: FOR TIMES, RATES OR ANYTHING TO DO WITH THE POST OFFICE, CALL THEIR ENGLISH HOTLINE AT 5472-5851.

Lastly, when you're not home, the mailman's going to leave you a non–delivery notice if someone sends you a large parcel or a registered letter. The greatest thing about the Japanese system is that you can call them back and specify a re–delivery. Fantastic service. You can choose to:
1.   send it to your apartment on your day off.
2.   send it to a neighbor.
3.   have it delivered to your office.
The latter has got to be the best because a secretary will always be at your school or office. If you're really in a hurry, you can go pick it up at the post office yourself. Just ask a Japanese person to tell you which post office it is and have him write down the address for you in English.

The Fastest Way to Send Stuff in Japan Post Office

There is a one–hour delivery service called Super Express Mail. A messenger will come and pick up your package then deliver it. This service is only for the 23 wards of Tokyo. Packages can weigh up to 10kg. The size limit is 90cm adding length plus width plus height. Call the Super Express Mail Center at 3546–1123 (Open Mon–Sat 8:30am–7pm). Not available on Sundays and holidays.

Private Delivery Companies

There is a *Baiku–bin* (motorcycle delivery) service. A guy on a motorcycle will come to your office or home and deliver. They will deliver anywhere in Japan on the same day in most cases.

Rates are based on distance traveled. There is a minimum of ¥1,000–¥2,000. Most companies do not speak English. They are usually open Mon–Fri 9am–7pm, and 9am–5pm on Sat. Closed Sun and holidays.

Business Kyubin 3780–1111

Delivery Service Hashiriya (toll free) 0120-013-455
San'ei Kyubin (toll free) 0120-006-995
Super Bike Express BSA (toll free) 0120-285-600
Tokyo Baiku-bin (toll free) 0120-332-666

BANKING

Banking is only difficult if you let it be. Go to a major branch of a big bank like Sumitomo, Dai Ichi Kangyo or Mitsubishi where they have English speaking staff. Better yet call the Tourist Information Center for help in finding the closest branch to your apartment. Often times your school will suggest a bank to you. It will make things easier as your salary is automatically deposited into your account for you.

Naturally, you should bring your passport with you. Apply for a cash card at the same time. It's the same word in Japanese with a slightly different pronunciation and spelling but they'll know exactly what you mean. Put a token deposit of ¥100 in the beginning. You might even get lucky and get some free Kleenex or something equally elegant for joining the fold.

NOTE: CITIBANK HAS AN ENGLISH TOLL-FREE NUMBER AT 0120-322-522. SEE PAGE 97 FOR OTHER MAJOR JAPANESE AND FOREIGN BANK'S HEAD OFFICES.

Useful Phrases

1.   I'd like to open an account.
      Ano, koza o hirakitai no desu ga.
2.   Please show me how to use the cash machine.
      Kyasshu mashin no tsukaikata o oshiete kudasai.
3.   Where's the cash corner?
      Kyasshu kona wa doko desu ka?
4.   Where's the Quick Corner?
      Kuikku kona wa doko desu ka?
5.   Where's the service corner?
      Sabisu kona wa doko desu ka?

Automatic Teller Machines (ATM's)

You need to use them because the banks are hardly ever open here. Plus, it's one less hassle trying to speak Japanese or fill out the right form. In fact, you never have to deal with the bank face-to-face unless you're sending money home.

First of all, your pay is automatically deposited into your account. Secondly, you can deposit, withdraw or just check your balance with your card so why bother with tellers?

They're usually open from 8:45am–7pm on weekdays and until 5pm on Saturdays, Sundays and holidays. Don't ask me why they haven't figured it out yet, but it seems simple to me to just leave them open 24 hours a day, seven days a week. But then that would be too convenient, wouldn't it? No wonder domestic demand is so low now as no one can get any cash to buy anything.

If you open an account with one of the banks listed below, you automatically become enrolled in the BANCS system which allows you to withdraw from any of the other banks. Ask if they have an English pamphlet to explain ATM's.

1. Bank of Tokyo
2. Daiichi Kangyo Bank–the only bank with **bilingual** cash machines
3. Daiwa Bank
4. Fuji Bank
5. Hokkaido Takushoku Bank
6. Kyowa Saitama Bank
7. Mitsubishi Bank
8. Sakura Bank
9. Sanwa Bank
10. Sumitomo Bank
11. Tokai Bank

There are also literally thousands of CS (cash service machines) in shopping centers, train stations and department stores. It will cost you ¥103 to use a bank other than your own and CS machines only dispense ¥10,000 bills.

American Express, MasterCard, Visa

Go to any bank and you should be able to make a cash withdrawal on the above cards. Make sure it's a big branch, not the little one on the corner out in the boonies. If they don't accept your particular card, they will give you the name of the bank that does and point you in the right direction.

If you have a personal identification number (P.I.N.), you can withdraw cash from certain ATM's.

American Express (AMEX) Card Offices

You must register your secret P.I.N. with American Express Japan. For other American Express ATM's outside of the Tokyo area, call their toll free line at 0120–010–120.

Visa Card and MasterCard

Refer to the section on General Telephone Numbers, page 86, and call them to find out the nearest cash machine in your area.

Banks (Main Offices)

The Federation of Banker's Association of Japan 3216–3761
Ginko Kyokai Bldg 1-3-1 Marunouchi, Chiyoda-ku

Bank of Japan 3279–1111
   2–1–1 Nihombashi–hongokucho, Chuo–ku
Bank of Tokyo Ltd....3245–1111
   1–3–2 Nihombashi–hongokucho, Chuo–ku
Daiichi Kangyo Bank, Ltd........................................3596–1111
   1–1–5 Uchisaiwaicho, Chiyoda–ku
Daiwa Bank, Ltd....3231–1231
   2–1–1 Otemachi, Chiyoda–ku
Fuji Bank, Ltd...3216–2211
   1–5–5 Otemachi, Chiyoda–ku
Hokkaido Takushoku Bank, Ltd.............................3272–6611
   1–3–13 Nihombashi, Chuo–ku
Industrial Bank of Japan, Ltd.................................3214–1111
   1–3–3 Marunouchi, Chiyoda–ku
Kyowa Saitama Bank, Ltd...................................... 3287-2111
   1–1–2 Otemachi, Chiyoda-ku
Long–Term Credit Bank of Japan, Ltd..................3211–5111
   1–2–4 Otemachi, Chiyoda–ku
Mitsubishi Bank, Ltd....3240–1111
   2–7–1 Marunouchi, Chiyoda–ku
Nippon Credit Bank, Ltd....3263–1111
   1–13–10 Kudan–kita, Chiyoda–ku
Nippon Trust and Banking Co., Ltd.......................3245–8180
   3–2–9 Nihombashi, Chuo–ku
Sanwa Bank, Ltd... 5252-1111
   1–1–1 Otemachi, Chiyoda–ku
Sumitomo Bank, Ltd....3282–5111
   1–3–2 Marunouchi, Chiyoda–ku
Tokai Bank, Ltd...3242–2111
   2–6–2 Otemachi, Chiyoda–ku

Foreign Banks (Branches, Offices) Europe

Barclays Bank, P.L.C. 3214–3611
   Mitsubishi Bldg., 2–5–2 Marunouchi, Chiyoda–ku
Lloyds Bank International Ltd................................3214–6771
   Ote Center Bldg., 1–1–3 Otemachi, Chiyoda–ku
Midland Bank, P.L.C...3284–1861
   AIU Bldg., 1–1–3 Marunouchi, Chiyoda–ku
National Westminster Bank, P.L.C.........................3216–5301
   Mitsubishi Bldg., 2–5–2 Marunouchi, Chiyoda–ku
Standard Chartered Bank 3213–6541
   Fuji Bldg., 3–2–3 Marunouchi, Chiyoda–ku
Banque Indosuez...3585–2982
   Indosuez Bank Bldg., 1–1–2 Akasaka, Minato–ku

Banque Nationale de Paris 3214–2881
 Yusen Bldg., 2–3–2 Marunouchi, Chiyoda–ku
Banque Paribas.. 3214–5881
 Yurakucho Deiki Bldg., N, 1–7–1 Yurakucho, Chiyoda–ku
Crédit Commercial de France 3595–0770
 Hibiya Kokusai Bldg., 2–2–3 Uchisaiwaicho, Chiyoda–ku
Crédit Lyonnais 3214–4561,284–1291
 Hibiya Park Bldg., 1–8–1 Yurakucho, Chiyoda–ku
Société Générale 3503–9781
 Hibiya Central Bldg., 1–2–9 Nishi–shimbashi. Minato–ku
Union de Banque Arabes de Francaises–U.B.A.F. 3595–0801
 Fukoku–seimei Bldg., 2–2–2 Uchisaiwaicho, Chiyoda–ku
Bayerische Vereinsbank AG 3284–1341
 Togin Bldg., 1–4–2 Marunouchi, Chiyoda–ku
Berliner Handels–und Frankfurter Bank 3213–1983
 Marunouchi Mitsui Bldg., 2–2–2 Marunouchi, Chiyoda–ku
Commerzbank AG 3502–4371
 Nihon Press Center Bldg., 2–2–1 Uchisaiwaicho, Chiyoda–ku
Deutsche Bank AG 3588–1971
 Ark Mori Bldg., 1–12–32 Akasaka, Minato–ku
Dresdner Bank AG.. 3224–6411
 3–2–15 Nihonbashi–muromachi, Chuo–ku
Westdeutsche Landesbank 3216–0581
 Kokusai Bldg., 3–1–1 Marunouchi, Chiyoda–ku
Credit Suisse 3589–3838
 Ark Mori Bldg., 1–12–32 Akasaka, Minato–ku
Swiss Bank Corp. 3214–1731
 Furukawa Sogo Bldg., 2–6–1 Marunouchi, Chiyoda–ku
Union Bank of Switzerland 3214–7471
 Yurakucho Bldg., 1–10–1 Yurakucho, Chiyoda–ku
Algemene Bank Nederland N.V. 3211–1760/9, 1789
 Fuji Bldg., 3–2–3 Marunouchi, Chiyoda–ku
Amsterdam–Rotterdam Bank N.V. 3284–0701
 Yurakucho Denki Bldg., s., 1–7–1 Yurakucho, Chiyoda–ku
Nederlandsche Middenstandsbank N.V. 3212–6481
 Kokusai Bldg., 3–1–1 Marunouchi, Chiyoda–ku
General Bank 3287–0481
 Yurakucho Denki Bldg., N, 1–7–1 Yurakucho, Chiyoda–ku
Banca Commerciale Italiana...................................... 3242–3521
 Nihon Bldg., Annex, 2–7–1 Otemachi, Chiyoda–ku
Credito Italiano Societa per Azioni 3595–1261
 Hibiya Kokusai Bldg., 2–2–3 Uchisaiwaicho, Chiyoda–ku
Banco Hispano Americano 3582–4111
 Landic Akasaka Bldg., 2–3–4 Akasaka, Minato–ku

North America

American Express Bank, Ltd.................................3504–3341
 3–8–1 Kasumigaseki, Chiyoda–ku
Bankers Trust Co...3214–7171
 Kishimoto Bldg., 2–2–1 Marunouchi, Chiyoda–ku
Bank of America NT and SA 3587–3111
 Ark Mori Bldg., 1–12–32 Akasaka, Minato–ku
Bank of California....................................... 3214–2411/5
 Palace Bldg., 1–1–1 Marunouchi, Chiyoda–ku
Bank of Hawaii 3588–1251
 Akasaka Twin Towers, 2–17–22 Akasaka, Minato–ku
Chase Manhattan Bank, N.A..............................3287–4000
 Tokyo–kaijo Bldg., 1–2–1 Marunouchi–Chiyoda–ku
Chemical Bank... 3214–1351/9
 Mitsubishi–shoji Bldg., Annex, 2–3–1 Marunouchi, Chiyoda–ku
Citibank, N.A...3279–5411
 Shin–otemachi Bldg., 2–2–1 Otemachi, Chiyoda–ku
Continental Illinois National Bank and Trust Co. 3216–1661
 Mitsui–seimei Bldg., 1–2–3 Otemachi, Chiyoda–ku
First Interstate Bank of California 3211–0757
 Kokusai Bldg., 3–1–1 Marunouchi, Chiyoda–ku
First National Bank of Boston........................... 3211–2611
 AIU Bldg., 1–1–3 Marunouchi, Chiyoda–ku
First National Bank of Chicago................... 3502–4951, 4955
 Hibiya Central Bldg., 1–2–9 Nishi–shimbashi, Minato–ku
Irving Trust Co. 3595–1131
 2–2–2 Uchisaiwaicho, Chiyoda–ku
Marine Midland Bank, N.A. 3214–6737
 Kishimoto Bldg. 2–1–1 Marunouchi, Chiyoda–ku
Manufacturers Hanover Trust Co. 3242–6511
 Asahi Tokai Bldg., 2–6–1 Otemachi, Chiyoda–ku
Mellon Bank 3216–5861/4
 Shin–yurakucho Bldg., 1–12–1 Yurakucho, Chiyoda–ku.
Morgan Guaranty Trust company of New York............3282–0230
 Shin–yurakucho Bldg., 1–12–1 Yurakucho, Chiyoda–ku
National Bank of Detroit...................................3214–7301
 Togin Bldg., 1–4–2 Marunouchi, Chiyoda–ku
Rainier National Bank 3214–5781
 Fuji Bldg., 3–2–3 Marunouchi, Chiyoda–ku
Seattle–First National Bank 3587–3178
 Ark Mori Bldg., 1–12–32 Akasaka, Minato–ku
Security Pacific National Bank 3587–4800
 Ark Mori Bldg., 1–12–32 Akasaka, Minato–ku
Wells Fargo Bank, N.A. 3214–1771
 Fuji Bldg., 3–2–3 Marunouchi, Chiyoda–ku

Bank of Montreal 3246–0103
    Mitsui Nigokan, 2–1–1 Nihombashi–muromachi, Chuo–ku
Bank of Nova Scotia 3593–0201
    Fukoku–seimei Bldg., 2–2–2 Uchisaiwaicho, Chiyoda–ku
Canadian Imperial Bank of Commerce 3595–1531
    Hibiya Kokusai Bldg., 2–2–3 Uchisaiwaicho, Chiyoda–ku
Royal Bank of Canada 3595–1531
    Hibiya Kokusai Bldg., 2–2–3 Uchisaiwaicho, Chiyoda–ku
Toronto–Dominion Bank 3214–4485
    Fuji Bldg., 3–2–3 Marunouchi, Chiyoda–ku

Oceania

Australia and New Zealand Banking Group Ltd. 3271–1151
    Yanmar Tokyo Bldg., 2–1–1 Yaesu, Chuo–ku
National Australia Bank, Ltd. 3241–8780
    Mitsui Nigokan, 2–1–1 Nihonbashi, Muromachi, Chuo–ku
Westpac Banking Corp. 3501–4101
    Imperial Tower, 1–1–1 Uchisaiwaicho, Chiyoda–ku

SENDING MONEY OVERSEAS
Useful Phrases

1. What is the fastest way to send money to_____?
    _____ ni okane o okuru no ni ichiban hayai hoho wa nan desu ka?
2. What is the cheapest way to transfer money?
    Furikomi tesuryo ga ichiban yasui no wa nan desu ka?
3. How much will this cost?
    Kore wa ikura kakarimasu ka?
4. How long will the transfer take?
    Kono furikomi ni wa nannichi kakarimasu ka?
5. How do I fill out this form?
    Kono fomu wa doo kinyu shitara ii desu ka?
6. I would like to transfer money to my overseas account.
    Kaigai no watashi no koza ni okane o okuritai no desu ga.
7. Please deduct the transferred money and the charges from my account.
    Watashi no koza kara okane to tesuryo o hikiotoshite kudasai.
8. Do I need to have an account at this bank/post office to transfer money?
    Okane o furikomu no ni koza o hiraku hitsuyo ga arimasu ka?
9. I would like to exchange ____ into yen.
    ____ o yen ni kaetai no desu ga.
10. How will I be notified that the beneficiary has received the transfer?
    Uketorinin ga okane o uketotta ka do ka tsuchi saremasu ka?

Credit Card

I heard about this from my partner in Canada who used it when he was traveling in Europe. First you get a second card (from your account) issued to someone back home. Then when you want to make a transfer, you go to a bank in Japan and deposit the funds to your credit card account. Then the card holder back home goes to your local bank branch and gets a 'cash advance'. That's it. Simple. Your credit card company does the currency conversion for you. Make sure to check the exchange rate before you deposit. Works in the other direction also.

Costs will vary according to your credit card company, but it is peanuts compared to some of the other methods.

Demand Draft (Yokyubarai Kawase)

It's cheaper than the telegraphic transfer and as fast as post offices in Japan and your country. For roughly ¥2,500 you buy a check from the bank in the foreign currency you want. Next, you send this check by registered mail to the bank or individual of your choice. However, if it's lost, it'll only be replaced if it hasn't been cashed by someone else.

Post Office

One of the cheapest methods has to be the post office. Go to a major post office in Tokyo and ask for an International Postal Remittance (Kokusai Sokin). It's the longest route (7–10 days U.S.A. and Europe, 20–30 days Canada, New Zealand and Australia) but definitely the cheapest:
1.   ¥1,000 charge for up to ¥100,000 remittance
2.   ¥1,500 charge for up to ¥100,000 to ¥200,000 remittance
3.   ¥2,000 charge for up to ¥200,001 to ¥500,000 remittance
4.   Add ¥500 for further increments of 200,000.

If you're paying off a car loan, student loan or mortgage, this is definitely the way to go. Please refer to the previous section on the Post Office. In that section, I provide a post office guide in English and where to get their English language brochure. The guide takes a full two pages to describe clearly the transfer of money through the post office.

Telegraphic Transfer

It will cost about ¥4,500 to send money home regardless of the amount. This is called *furikomi* (telegraphic transfer). This goes directly into the bank account of your choice in about a week (4 or 5 banking days). This is definitely the safest method.

NOTE: THIS COST VARIES WILDLY. I SENT HOME ¥700,000 FOR ONLY ¥2,500 PLUS ¥684 HANDLING CHARGE AT MITSUBISHI BANK (FUNABASHI BRANCH). CALL AROUND TO GET THE BEST RATE.

Traveler's Cheques

Same as buying them back home. However, you have to sign and endorse them before you send them. If they're lost or stolen in the mail, you're out of luck unless you say they were lost or stolen in Japan.

HEALTH CARE SYSTEMS

If you get sick, you'll need to see a doctor or go to an English speaking hospital, which there are several of in Tokyo. In your neighborhood there will be a clinic–type family doctor who examines your minor aches and pains. Bring a phrase book along and point to which sentence is appropriate or ask someone to come along to translate.

Pills, hospitals and doctors like everything else are expensive, about ¥10,000 each visit plus prescriptions. Hospital beds are about ¥10,000 a day with relatives expected to do a lot for the patient like special food, bathing and so on.

Unless your company has a special program, you can enroll in the National Health Insurance Program. I would hazard to guess that 95% of all English teachers are not covered by their employer, therefore they register by themselves.

The premium costs the following:

107% of resident's tax the previous year (in your case 0);
plus ¥12,000 flat rate ÷ 12 = monthly pay.
Therefore, you pay only ¥1,000 a month for health care that covers 70% of all expenses except cosmetic surgery, childbirth, shots for diseases (immunizations), yearly check ups, and intentional personal injuries (suicide).

If your bill goes over ¥54,000 in any given month at the same hospital or clinic, the program will pay 100% of all expenses above this amount.

If you are enrolled halfway through the year, your premium starts from the month of application. When you leave Japan and withdraw, they will charge you with the premium until the preceding month of your withdrawal. You'll receive your first installment bill by mail and you can pay it like any other bill at the bank or post office. The medical card will be effective on the day you apply. So if you're a procrastinator, and get sick, you can always enroll immediately.

However, if you stay in Japan for longer than one year, you're looking at a hefty increase of probably nine or ten times the ¥12,000 you paid for your first year. This hike is due to your high monthly salary that you will have earned from the previous year which your premiums are now based upon. When you first came to Japan, you had no previous Japanese income, so you paid the minimum ¥12,000 charge. After one year you're in for a shock.

Try and find out beforehand where the nearest clinic or hospital is in your area. It's better to do this in the beginning when you're not so busy, or not so sick. There's nothing worse than being ill and feeling like there's nowhere to go.

Also it's a good idea to carry around a copy of an emergency medical card with you in English and Japanese. List any allergies or special medical conditions on it. Put it in your wallet with your train pass, Alien Registration Card or Passport.

Once you enroll you are not permitted to withdraw from the National Health Insurance program (*Kokuho*) as long as you are in Japan. In other words, you're locked in. Even if you leave Japan, cancel all ties, apply for a new visa, change schools after one year, your new application will still be based on your previous yearly earnings in Japan. You'd have to wait a full year at home to escape the increase in the user fee which will occur your second year in Japan.

Further on I've listed the major English pharmacies, hospitals and clinics in Tokyo. If you live far from these hospitals or anywhere outside of Tokyo, you should phone the T.I.C. at 3502–1462 or T.E.L.L. at 3264-4347 (9am–1pm, 7pm–11pm) for information about the nearest medical care facility.

Another good idea is to sign up for Travel Accident Insurance when you take those all–important R & R trips back home or wherever. By this time, you'll probably have canceled your health insurance in your home country and signed up in Japan. However, you'll need extra coverage while abroad. Enter AIU Insurance company. Telephone 3216–6611. Call for an application form to be sent to you by fax or mail. Currently, Mr. Nagasawa is in charge.

For one month coverage of sickness, accident or death, from AIU you'll pay about $100. Peanuts, if you actually do need medical care anywhere when traveling. I'm not a worry–wart but there's no sense taking unnecessary risks. Think about it.

NOTE: YOU CAN ALSO SIGN UP FOR PREFECTURAL (STATE OR PROVINCIAL) PROGRAMS TO COVER YOU WHILE YOU'RE OUTSIDE OF JAPAN FOR AROUND $50 TO $60/MONTH. CHECK TO SEE WHAT'S AVAILABLE. THEY'LL PAY ALL MEDICAL BILLS IF YOU HAVE TO BE FLOWN BACK IN AN EMERGENCY INCLUDING THE PLANE TICKET AND ANY PAID ASSISTANTS YOU'LL NEED. THE PROBLEM WITH THIS SYSTEM IS THAT YOU'LL HAVE TO PAY OUT OF YOUR OWN POCKET, THEN WAIT FOR A REIMBURSEMENT.

What To Do If You Get Sick

If you do get sick and have to go to a clinic or hospital, here's how it goes. First of all, don't go without at least ¥20,000 to cover the examination and prescription. Second of all, call to make sure the place is open. Ask a Japanese person to call, or just assume that if someone answers they are receiving patients.

Next, after you've found your way there, give your health insurance card to the secretary and point to the phrase list in the *Berlitz Japanese Phrasebook*. If you're good at miming, just point and grimace. It would be wise, however, to know what you want to say to the doctor specifically. Sign language will get you in, but Japanese will get you healed.

If in a clinic, you will be asked to wait to see the doctor. If in a hospital, she will give you a card and direct you to the correct department for your ailment. Now wait. Usually three hours. One exception to this system is the Tokyo Medical and Surgical Clinic which takes appointments.

Inside, the doctor will size up the situation very quickly and give you a prescription written in German. Time is money here, so a couple of minutes is all you'll get. Please have a dictionary to point out any allergies you might have, like Penicillin for example. If he wants to see you again, he'll tell you. Go back to the secretary, get your medical card, prescription and bill. Go to the cashier, pay your 30%, then go to the Hospital Pharmacy or to a pharmacy near your home.

Pharmacies

The best pharmacy in Japan is the **American Pharmacy** located in the Hibiya Park Building, 1–8–1 Yurakucho, Chiyoda–ku, tel: 3271–4034. Phone for instructions in English on how to get there. Conveniently located near Tourist Information Center. Has English speaking staff and is well–run.

Other Pharmacies are:

The Hill Pharmacy... 3583–5044
    4–1–6 Roppongi, Minato–ku.
National Azabu Supermarket Pharmacy 3442–3181
    4–5–2 Minami Azabu.

The above pharmacies have English speaking staff. Women take note that the Pill cannot be bought in Japan. Men take note that condoms are kind of small. Stock on up both if necessary.

Hospitals
Tokyo

Hospital Information on Sundays and Holidays (Day) 3216–4820
    Night 3216–4828
International Catholic Hospital (Seibo Byoin)............................... 3951–1111
    2–5–1 Naka–Ochiai, Shinjuku–ku 161.
International Clinic..3582–2646
    1–5–9 Azabaudai, Minato–ku 106.
Japan Red Cross Medical Center (Nisseki Iryou Center)................. 3400–1311
    1–22 Hiroo 4 chome Shibuya–ku Tokyo.
Jikei University School of Medicine Hospital 3433–1111
    3–19–18 Nishi–Shimbashi, Minato–ku 105.
Juntendo University Hospital..3813–3111
    3–1–3 Hongo, Bunkyo–ku 113.

Keio University Hospital (Day)...3353–1211
   Night 3353–1208
   35 Shinanomachi, Shinjuku–ku 160.
Kyorin University Hospital.............................. 0422–47–5511
   6–20–2 Shinkawa, Mitaka–shi 181.
Musashino Red Cross Hospital...................... 0422–32–3111
   1–26–1 Kyonan–cho, Musashino–shi.
National Cancer Center.....................................3542–2511
   5–1–1 Tsukiji, Chuo–ku 104.
Saiseikai Central Hospital................................3451–8211
   1–4–17 Mita, Minato–ku.
St. Luke's International Hospital–Episcopalian.................3541–5151
   (Sei Roka Byouin) 10 Akasicho 1–chome, Chuo–ku.
St. Mary's International Catholic Hospital (Seibo Byouin)..............3951–6151
   501 Naka–Ochiai 2–chome Shinjuku–ku Tokyo.
The Second Tokyo National Hospital......................3411–1181
   2–5–1 Higashigaoka, Meguro–ku 152.
Tokyo Medical and Surgical Clinic.......................3436–3026
   3–4–30, Shiba–koen, Minato–ku.
Tokyo Metropolitan Hiroo General Hospital...............3444–1181
   2–34–10 Ebisu, Shibuya–ku.
Tokyo Metropolitan Police Hospital......................3263–1371
   2–10–41 Fujimi, Chiyoda–ku 102.
Tokyo Sanitarium Hospital (Tokyo Eisei Byoin) 3392–6151
   3–17–3 Amanuma, Suginami–ku 167.
Tokyo University Hospital................................3815–5411
   7–3–1 Hongo, Bunkyo–ku 113.
Tokyo Women's Medical College Hospital..................3353–8111
   10 Ichigaya Kawada–cho, Shinjuku–ku 162.

Yokohama

Yokohama City University Hospital (Shidai Byoin) 045–261–5656
   3–46 Urafune–cho, Minami–ku, Yokohama.

Clinics
Tokyo

National Medical Clinic...3472–2057
   4–5–2 Nimami Azabu, Minato–ku 106.
Santo Clinic 3402–3151
   8–5–35 Akasaka, Minato–ku.
Tokyo Maternity Clinic...3403–1861
   1–20–8 Sendagaya, Shibuya–ku 151.
Tokyo Medical and Surgical Clinic..................................3436–3028
   3–4–30 Shiba Koen, Minato–ku 105.

Tokyo Clinic Dental Office 3431–4225
    3–4–30 Shiba Koen, Minato–ku 105.

Yokohama

The Bluff Clinic (Day)..045-641–6961
    (Night) 045–641–6964
    82 Yamate–cho, Naka–ku, Yokohama 231.

NOTE: THERE ARE COUNTLESS OTHER CLINICS AVAILABLE.
        CALL THE NTT INFORMATION LINE AT 5295-1010 FOR THE ONE NEAREST YOU.

RECREATION

GOING OUT WITH THE JAPANESE

Never let the school administration know that you are going out with students after class! This is a major error that could eventually cost you your job. They can't actually tell you who to socialize with after school hours, although many schools put this clause in their contract, but they could become picky over other things like your teaching methods or if you were late several times. Only in a few rare cases did I hear about someone getting fired in Japan, and that was usually due to their false diploma or résumé. Forgery and lying are not permitted. In any case, why alarm the school as to your activities? Keep your meetings with students a secret and tell your students not to tell the Japanese staff how much fun you were last night! Discretion is the better part of valor.

Choose a different meeting spot other than the school. A train station is a good suggestion. Tell your students not to talk about this with anyone else as it's better to be safe than sorry. The main reason schools are against you fraternizing with students is because, in effect, you are giving away free English conversation lessons, something which the school depends upon to survive. In many cases, a male teacher meets a girl who promptly quits the school, not needing to pay anymore for her lessons. In other instances, a group of people or a busy businessman might offer the teacher a sum less than they pay now at the school, but still more than the teacher's salary. Don't get caught.

When it comes time to pay the bill, if they are university students, you'll probably go Dutch. They'll order food for everyone and lots of beer. It's the custom to fill up the other person's glass and never your own. Businessmen will usually pick up the tab, as they can put it on their expense accounts which are the largest in the world. I almost always expected an executive to pay for the tab especially after an entire night of free conversation; it was only fair.

What's great about going out with students is that they'll take you to spots you'd never find on your own. Some of my best memories of Japan are when I went out to sample local cuisine and spirits with the natives! You should be warned that Japanese men love to drink and respect a teacher who can hold his liquor.

December is an especially wicked month for drinking parties. Most companies hold End of Year parties called *Bonenkai*. Even the larger English schools invite all the Japanese staff and foreign teachers to a restaurant or their meeting hall and supply beer, food and music. They are a free–for–all and a great place to meet the Japanese socially. Don't miss them!

Top 10 After Work Activities

1. Rent a video. We must have gone through over 500 movies since 1990. We've pretty well seen everything at the 3 video shops in our area, so

now we get our fix from home. My sister taped reruns of *Cheers, Cosby, Family Ties, Movies of the Week, 60 Minutes,* and documentaries. Every few months she'll send over a batch of about 10 tapes with 8 hours of shows each! Great or what?

2.   Order pizza. Expect to pay about ¥2,500 for a large sized pizza with only 3 toppings. Good for 2 gaijin.

3.   Go to an Izakaya (Japanese Pub). A big gang pig out. Everyone orders beer and small portions off the picture menus, and soon there's over 20 dishes of neat stuff to try. Sometimes between just my wife and I we manage to order around 12 different plates before we lose steam and slow down. You can order them all at once or in spurts.

4.   Read *Shogun,* by James Clavell. A **must read** for the Japan bound traveler. It is over 500 paperback pages long and I stayed up to 3 or 4am reading this sucker nightly! His latest book *Gaijin* promises to be just as good a novel. Try it, you'll like it.

5.   Call home after 11pm when rates are cheap. You'll catch your folks at the start of their day while yours is just ending.

6.   Head for Roppongi and party it up all night til the first train home at 4:30am.

7.   Belt out a few tunes at the nearest Karaoke Bar with some Japanese friends.

8.   Play poker with the boys, or Mahjong if you know how to.

9.   Study Japanese. Every little bit you learn you'll use, believe me. I started studying 3 years ago and have another 20 to go!

10.   Do nothing. Tomorrow's another day chalk full of things to do!

MAKING FRIENDS

I decided to write this special section on making friends in Japan because it's sometimes difficult for newcomers to meet Japanese people for several reasons. To begin, let me explain a bit about Japanese relationships. By no means am I an expert in this so just take it all into consideration.

The Japanese equivalents of 'friend' and 'friendship' are 'tomodachi' and 'yujo'. Tomodachi are friends made way back in elementary school, high school or university. School friends are not bound to any of the rigidity that so permeates the rest of Japanese society. This type of friendship is probably what we would call true friends back home.

After a Japanese starts work, it is almost impossible to form a true friendship due to office politics, rank, and title. All communication is now based on a ladder system; some people are low on the ladder, others are high up. To give a minor example, depending upon your status, simply saying "I" in Japanese could be the true friend level of "ore" or other forms like 'boku', 'washi', 'jibun', 'watashi' (polite) or 'watakushi'. 'You' could be your true friend 'omae' or other forms such as: 'kimi', 'anata' (polite), 'otaku', '...kun', '...san' (respect), or '...sama' (ultimate respect) as in Markkun, Marksan or Marksama.

Friendship levels of *ore-omae* ultimately command life long support and responsibility for those involved: gifts at the appropriate times, visits, and letters. Therefore, most Japanese do not have too many *true* or *real* friends because it's basically too mentally and too financially taxing. Enter you–the 'outsider', the 'gaijin', the 'foreigner'. You, who's stay will only be a short term duration of one or two years or maybe more, but never permanent. You, the teacher who enters a company on a 'temporary basis'. You, who is 'too friendly', 'too fast'. You, who cannot speak Japanese, thus making the other person ill at ease in English. Frankly speaking, for many Japanese, you're not worth the hassle now nor in the future.

Now the good news. Every foreigner I have ever met has said that the Japanese have treated them with great hospitality, whether it was a free dinner, a free movie, a gift, a lift in a car or whatever. Everyone has found someone to help them get through the occasional difficulty and the ever frequent language barrier. With an increasing number of Japanese traveling overseas, it's becoming easier to meet them on a casual basis especially through teaching English. In fact, many students will be honored you asked them for help and will jump at the chance to practice their English outside the classroom with you. You'll know who to ask just by teaching them a few times. They're the friendly ones always asking you how you're adjusting to your new life in Japan.

To start up a friendship, be prepared to at least make the initial introduction or invitation. After awhile your social calendar can be as full as you like with new found Japanese 'friends'. They may never become lifelong, but they'll be honest, respectful, inquisitive, pleasant and very helpful during your stay in Japan. Who knows, you just might end up developing that rare charisma with someone and turn it into something permanent!

NOTE: LOVER'S LANGUAGE SECTION ON PAGE 112 COULD BE HELPFUL AT THIS STAGE.

Helpful Points to Remember

1. Try to be knowledgeable about Japan. With all the Japan bashing going on, even rudimentary understanding lifts you above the pack. Japanese love those who make an effort to understand their culture or language. However, don't push for total comprehension or you'll be blacklisted as too nosy.
2. Don't rush a Japanese; trust is utmost. Build up a relationship–call, write, or whatever. Develop good long term contacts.
3. The Japanese are sometimes in awe of foreigners. Take the stares in stride and never become angry because of them. There's no way around it: we look different.
4. We were not colonizers in Japan as in many other parts of the world. Japanese know Westerners only as leaders, teachers, and businessmen. Usually, nine times out of ten, this respect will be demonstrated to you to the point of embarrassment. After a while, you'll come to believe that there is such a thing as being too polite.

Top 10 Questions Japanese Ask Foreigners

1. Where are you from?
2. How tall are you?
3. How old are you?
4. What's your blood type? (Just like Zodiac signs carry certain personality traits, so does your blood type. A kind of fortune telling.)
5. Are you married? Is your husband/wife Japanese?
6. Do you like Japanese food?
7. Do you like Japan?
8. Why did you come to Japan?
9. How long are you going to stay in Japan?
10. Can you use chopsticks?

Of course, I left out a few, but I guarantee you'll be asked every one of these questions if you stay in Japan for about a year. And not just once, but by most Japanese you will meet during your stay! I always had several answers to each question just to spice things up a little and keep from getting bored.

Top 10 Questions Foreigners Ask Each Other

1. How long have you been in Japan?
2. Where are you from?
3. Where do you work?
4. How much money do you make?
5. How many hours a week do you teach?
6. Where do you live?
7. How much does your place cost per month?
8. What kind of visa do you have?
9. How long are you going to stay?
10. Do you speak Japanese?

Japanese Girls and Their Boyfriends

A recent phenomenon in Japan is taking place due to the fact that there are more males than females. Males have always been favored over girls throughout history and Asia is no exception. Birthrates are down to around 1.4 children per couple so if a couple only wants one child, and it's a baby boy, they stop. What this now means for single girls is there's an abundant supply of bachelors out there. Also, combined to this fact is that the average age for marriage has shot up to around thirty! Thus, many pretty girls have several young men on the line. It's become so popular that they've come up with their own lingo. Boyfriends now fall into four categories:

Ashikun: Like a chauffeur. When a girl needs a lift somewhere, the ol' Ashikun gets a call.

Mitsugukun: Gift boy. Birthdays, Christmas, White Day (opposite of Valentine's Day). In Japan, women give chocolate to men on Valentine's Day. Men respond in kind one month later on White Day, March 14th. These are all special days together. Basically, he's rich and she strings him along just for the gift bonanza.

Keepukun: Stand–by squeeze. Second string quarterback, if you will. Close, but just not good enough.

Koibito or **Kareshi:** Sweetheart. The real thing. A keeper. The main man. Oh, what a lucky guy. First prize!

Of course this is just a simplified account of the actual situation in Japan, but these words do exist and many girls have several guys in certain categories. No different than two–timing back home except that in Japan you've gotta have classifications and labels for each situation. There's no winging it here.

Also of note are the new **Oyaji Girls.** A term to describe **O.L.'s** (Office Ladies) who enjoy all the activities that businessmen do: golf, pachinko, after–work drinking and so on. Everyone and everything *must* have a label in Japan!

Lover's Language

While the intention of this book is to help the newcomer learn the ropes of working in Japan–all work and no play makes Jack a dull boy, or so the saying goes. I think it's always fun to learn a little of the language especially the romantic stuff.

Here's the top 10:
1. I love you.
   Aishiteru.
2. You're beautiful.
   Kirei desu.
3. You're really sexy.
   Iroppoi.
4. May I kiss you?
   Kisu shite–mo ii desu ka?
5. Kiss me.
   Kisu shite kudasai.
6. Can we make love?
   Aishite mo ii desu ka?
7. Let's meet again.
   Moichido aimasho–ka?
8. Will you marry me?
   Kekkon shite kureru?
9. You have beautiful eyes.
   Kirei na hitomi desu neh!

10 Are you on the pill?
    Piru nonderu?
11 Do you have any condoms?
    Kondomu motteru?

Slang

For a complete listing of all the really good stuff, buy *Making Out in Japanese* One and Two found in any English bookstore or by ordering from the back of this book. They've got all the romantic, bad and everyday stuff you'll need.

Cultural Clubs

Amanda Marga (Yoga and Meditation).. 3383–6322
America Japan Society 3201–0780
Asiatic Society of Japan 3586–1548
Buddhist English Academy 3342–6605
    Lectures Friday at 7pm; ¥500 at Joenji near Shinjuku.
Ikebana International (flower arrangement)..................................... 3295–0720
International Friends of Kabuki 3724–5858
Japan Afro–American Friendship .... 3557–2383 or 3225–1962
Japan Friendship–library, classes, newsletters, etc. 3951–9043
Sakura Harikai (Washi crafts).. 3624–1365
Sakura Kai (tea ceremony) 3951–9043
Sho International (calligraphy) 3234–8757
St. Andrews Society (Scottish)... 0282–22–5019

Friendship Clubs

There are numerous friendship clubs in Tokyo. So many in fact you might wonder if they are trying for a world record. I've also listed all of the professional ones, along with the special interest clubs and a section on networking. Here are a few of the purely friendship–oriented clubs that operate in a relaxed Western–style environment.

Corn Popper 3715–4473
    (for monthly schedule and map, fax 3715–4759) Friendship club with non-
    smoking, Western–style, English–speaking environment. Coffee, tea, beer,
    popcorn, pizza, and a paperback book exchange. Free of charge for
    foreigners on Mondays and Tuesdays; ¥500 on Wednesdays and
    Thursdays. Mexican Taco Party every Friday and Saturday night from 7pm
    to midnight. All–you–can–eat. ¥1,500 Advance Tickets. ¥2,000 at–the–door.
    Yamanote line or Hibiya line to Ebisu Station. If you don't have a fax, call
    and they'll mail you the directions.
Setagaya International Beer Bash... 3414–2807
    Held every month from 6pm. Very casual and informal. Drinks and

munchies. ¥1,000 each time. Call Shin'ichi Kaneko in the evenings for all the particulars. Over 100 people join every month or so the ad says.

New clubs are popping up all the time, so it's best to check the current listings in two excellent magazines dedicated to leisure: *The Tokyo Journal*, and *The Hiragana Times* . Both are available at major English language bookstores, or you can subscribe to them even before your departure.

Here's how:

The Hiragana Times

Send an overseas remittance. The best is an International Postal Money Order. Checks or other money orders are not accepted. Send money order by *Yubin–Furikae* (Postal Direct Deposit) to: Hiragana Times, Tokyo 2–1456. Asia, Oceana: ¥7,500 (1 year), ¥3,750 (6 months). North and South America: ¥9,000 (1 year), ¥4,500 (6 months). Europe, Africa, The Near and Middle East: ¥10,000 (1 year), ¥5,000 (6 months).

To subscribe from the U.S. or Canada, send a check for US$76 to the address below:

Hiragana Times, North American Subscription Office,
P.O. Box 11806
Birmingham, AL
35202 U.S.A.
Phone: 1–800–633–4931 or (205)991–6920 fax: (205)995–1588.

To subscribe from Australia or New Zealand, send a check for A$82 to :
Intext Book Company Pty. Ltd.
412 Heidelberg Road,
Fairfield, Vic.
3078 Australia
tel: (03)486–1755 fax:(03)486–1235.

NOTE: IN JAPAN, CALL 3341–8989 FOR DETAILS.

Also a good source of friendship clubs, and free Japanese lessons are the Foreign Affairs Sections located at every *Shiyakusho* (City Hall). The City Hall in Funabashi had an International Relations Association that sponsored parties, games, events and even a 'Free call for Foreigners' day where 200 people got to call home once for as long as they liked!

International Friendship Club

Full year's membership costs ¥6,000/person or ¥10,000/family. Then you pay as you play. Previous events included:
• 	a Swiss Dinner Party ¥3,800
• 	a Latin American music and dinner party ¥4,300

- Hakone (near Mt. Fuji) Outdoor Hot Spring Tour. All day ¥9,800 all–included
- Thanksgiving, Christmas dinner parties
- Bonenkai (Year End) Party ¥2,000
- Ski Trips
- Trips to Shrines and Festivals

The center is open to everyone including children. IFC is a non–profit organization. As a regular member, you get the monthly programs in English outlining coming events and fees, meeting places and deadlines. You make reservations by telephone or mail. Contact: 3479–8038/8047. Office Hours Mon–Sat 10:30am–8pm, Sun 10:30–4pm. Second Sun of every month closed. Tomita House 1F 4–13–16, Minami–Aoyama Minato–ku, Tokyo 107.

NOTE: REFER TO LEISURE AND CULTURE CLUB SECTION LISTED FURTHER ON FOR MORE LISTINGS.

Other Clubs in Tokyo

Foreign Correspondent's Club of Japan 3211–3161
Yurakucho Denki Bldg., 20th Floor, Kita–Kan,
1–1–7 Yurakucho, Chiyoda–ku 100.
Entrance ¥75,000, monthly ¥8,600, Deposit ¥40,000.

Kiwanis Club of Tokyo 3242–0637
7th Floor, Sankei Bldg.,
1–7–2 Otemachi, Chiyoda–ku 100.

Lions Club International 3494–2931
TOC Building,
7–22–1 Nishi Gotanda, Shinagawa–ku 141.

A.C.C.J. Toastmasters Club 3432–1701
fax 3433–3395
Meets at the Tokyo American Club.
Entrance ¥10,000; biannually ¥10,000.

Breakfast Toastmasters Club .... 3263–4801 and 3234–9942
Also meets at the Tokyo American Club.

Tokyo American Club 3583–8381
2–1–2 Azabudai, Minato–ku 106.
¥1.2 million to join.

Tokyo British Club 3443–9082
3–28–4 Ebisu, Shibuya–ku.
Also of interest to Brits is the *News From Home* program. Using the
Yomiuri Telephone News service, the latest news in English of
developments in Japan reported by *The Yomiuri Shimbun* can be obtained
by dialing
(Tokyo) 0990–30–4311
(Osaka) 0990–32–4311
Charge: ¥30 per minute plus the usual telephone charge.

Tokyo Canadian Club 3475-1063

Meets first Thursday of every month.
Tokyo Lawn and Tennis Club 3473–1545
    5–6–41 Minami Azabu, Minato–ku 106.
Tokyo Rotary Club 3201–3888
    Marunouchi Building
    2–4–1 Marunouchi, Chiyoda–ku 100.

NOTE: THERE ARE OVER 10 OTHER TOASTMASTER CLUBS IN TOKYO AND YOKOHAMA.
             CALL TO FIND OUT COMPLETE LIST AS THEY'RE ALL AFFILIATED.

Women's Clubs

Asian Ladies Friend Society...3725–0963
Association of Foreign Wives of Japanese 3877–6986
Canadian Women's Club...3478–3516
College Women's Association of Japan 5232–0613
Franciscan Women's Chapel 3400–2559
Japan Australian–New Zealand Women's Group 3446–4632
Japan Israel Women's Welfare Organization...........................3400–2559
Swedish Women's Educational Association.............................3403–9438
Tokyo Christian Women's Club 048–645–1343
Tokyo Union Church Women's Society 3400–0492
Women's Meditation Center 3806–5686
Women of Tokyo Baptist Church.................................... 0429–49–8328
Yokohama International Women's Group 045–641–3671
International Women's Club (IWC).......................................3773–6501

NOTE: SHOULD ANY OF THESE NUMBERS CHANGE, CALL T.E.L.L. AT 5481–4455 FOR
             THE LATEST CONTACT.

Professional Associations

Association of English Teachers of Children 0422–53–0024
Association of Foreign Teachers in Japan 045–323–3548
American Chamber of Commerce in Japan (ACCJ) 3433–5381
Amiga Users Association Tokyo 0422–55–8801
Australia–Japan Foundation 5232–4063
British Chamber of Commerce in Japan (BCCJ).........................3505–1734
Canadian Chamber of Commerce in Japan (CCCJ)....................3408–4311
Foreign Executive Women 3403–7516
Foreign Nurses Association in Japan 3405–1233
IBM PC Tokyo Users Group 5706–0057
International Computer Association..3353–6091
International Young Executives Club 3247–2303
Japan Association of Translators (fax) 3385–5180
Mac Tokyo Macintosh Users Group...3708–7961
Roppongi Bar Association (foreign lawyers)...............................3213–0034

SWET (Society of Writers, Editors and Translators) 045–314–0324

Leisure Clubs

Friends of the Vine–wine tasting.. 3370–9656
Harley Davidson Motorcycle Riders Group (fax)............................ 3709–5220
International Adventure Club 3327–2905
    fax.. 3333–0419
    Monthly meetings ¥5,000 annually; spouses free.
International Club (days).. 3715–9252
    (after 5pm) 3715–4473
    fax..3713–4759
    Parties every Friday and Saturday Night 5pm to midnight.
International Community Circle Cultural Exchange
    after 3pm 3423–0660
Japan International Friendship Club (3F Club) 3341–9061
Narita International Friendship Club English........................... 0476–24–1734
    Japanese... 0476–24–3198
Oikaze Cycling Info Newsletter.. 3485–0471
Renaissance Artists and Writers Association 3383–6322
    Concerts every Saturday near Nakano Fujimicho Station.
Setagaya International Club (Shinichi Kaneko) 3414–2807
    Parties every month. Participants in their 20's. Informal.
    Fee ¥1,000. Usually held on a Saturday night in Sangenjaya.
Shinagawa International Civil Friendships Association............... 3450–5315
    Japanese lessons, flower arrangement, advice on Japan, slide shows of
    foreign countries, etc. Mon–Fri 9am–4:30pm. Sat 9–12pm.
Tokyo International Singers (Classical)...................................... 044–833–9258
Tokyo Weekend Motorcycle Riders Group (fax Bob Dean)
   3709–5220

EATING AND DRINKING

    Restaurants are everywhere in Japan, but it will take some time to get used
to them all and what they sell. I recommend you buy the book *Eating Cheap in
Japan* as it's a must read for newly arrived Gaijin. It lists almost every food
you'll come across and lists average prices too. It shows a real picture of the
food as well, which is handy to compare with the plastic replicas that most
restaurants display outside in their windows. In and around train and subway
stations there are always inexpensive, good restaurants. Department stores also
have a dining floor (usually at the top) open until 9 or 10pm. Many major
office buildings have a restaurant floor in the basement which is reasonably
priced at around ¥1,000 for a lunch special.

    Lunch specials are good from around 11:30am to 1:30 or 2pm which is
great for us English teachers who usually start work at 1pm. They have the set
course displayed outside ranging in price from ¥700 to about ¥1,200. A set is
usually coffee, soup or salad, rice or bread and the main meal. Just ask the

waitress to come outside so you can point to what you want, or try to write down the Chinese characters (Kanji) the best you can and show it to her inside. If you go there often memorize how to pronounce it or you'll get tired of dragging the waitress out every time you need to order.

If you find a good restaurant near your home but don't feel like walking there all the time, ask if they have 'demae' which means home delivery service. Draw them a map to your apartment and once you know what you like, call them with an order and a guy on a little motor scooter rushes over with the hot meal in a matter of minutes. The dishes may be left by your doorstep or by the roadside depending on your surroundings for pick–up.

I must add that I've never experienced such rapid service in restaurants as I have in Japan. Compared to everywhere else I've traveled, Japan takes first prize. They'll bring the food to you in minutes after you order and will leave you to eat it in peace as well, never bothering you with useless chit chat. All this and you don't even have to leave a tip! Unfortunately, they don't refill your coffee, except in some American franchise restaurants.

Top 10 Wierd Foods I've Eaten in Japan

1. Live fish on a plate in an Izakaya. It was actually still squirming around. Ikizukuri in Japanese.
2. Raw Beef. Gyuniku Tataki in Japanese.
3. Broiled Eel on a stick(unagi).
4. Raw Octopus with Sake (Rice Wine).
5. Cow Tongue grilled in front of me at my table.
6. Fermented sticky beans. Natto in Japanese.
7. Raw Globefish or Blowfish. Fugu in Japanese. Every year a few Japanese people die of poisoning if this fish is not cut in a certain way. All sushi chefs have studied their trade, but I guess some of them were absent the day the teacher taught Fugu.
8. Cooked Squid. Ika in Japanese.
9. Konnyaku. Devil's Tongue in English. An ingredient served in Oden, a unique Japanese stew, reported to have virtually zero calories.
10. Rice, broiled fish, fermented beans and bean paste soup (Miso Shiru in Japanese) for breakfast.

Useful Phrases

1. Onegai shimasu.
   Asking for service (from a waitress).
2. Sumimasen.
   Waiter/waitress (Literally means excuse me. Used to call their attention and come to your table).
3. O–mizu kudasai.
   Water, please.
4. O–hashi kudasai.
   Chopsticks, please.

5. Supun, hoku, naifu.
   Spoon, fork, knife.
6. Koppu, napukin.
   Cup, napkin.

Restaurants

Just ask battle–hardened gaijin who've been around here for a while and they'll tell you some good spots to go. Your students or office staff should know of some great deals. You can find anything and everything in Tokyo: Cambodian, Vietnamese, Chinese, Korean, Thai, Pakistani, Indian, Indonesian, French, Italian, German and so on. I won't bother writing them all down because I couldn't recommend all of them and restaurants change so frequently. However, I have listed some of our favorites where you can really get your money's worth.

All You Can Eat

All–You–Can–Eat restaurants (*Tabe Hodai*) in Japan are rare. The high cost of food, different customs, and smaller body sizes all contribute to this scarcity. They are not to be found all over as in North America.

I weigh about 80 kilograms, and usually the servings in normal places are just a little bit too small for me so I decided to add this piece. If you find anymore, send me the info and I'll print it in my next edition.

Restaurants With All–You–Can–Eat Service

Blue Sky Lounge 3265-1111
  All you can eat Chinese buffet at the Hotel New Otani 17F.
Karubi Kyouwakoku 3402-2901
  Korean Yakiniku. Near Jingumae station, Shibuya-ku.
Kujakucho Ginza 3451-2411
  Chinese food in the Tokyu Hotel. Stuff your face as much as you want.
Manten Shibuya 3463-8989
  All you can eat Korean Bar B Que (Yakiniku).
Rarusu Akasaka 3588-1836
  Great Japanese Shabushabu.
Shakey's Pizza, Harajuku Branch 3409–2405
  All the pizza, fried potatoes and spaghetti you can eat from 11am–2pm
  (only Mon–Sat). Adults ¥600, children ¥350. Branches in Shibuya,
  Takadanobaba, Ikebukuro, Shinjuku, Tamachi, Kamata, Ochanomizu,
  Oimachi, Ginza, Hiroo, Jiyugaoka, Seijo–gakuenmae, and elsewhere. A
  great filling of food just like back home and what a bargain!
Takeya 3836–3679
  All the sukiyaki or shabushabu you can eat. ¥1,800 for women, ¥2,000 for
  men. Ueno station. Hirokoji or Shinobazu exit. Sukiyaki 11:30am–9pm,

Shabushabu 5–9pm. Open every day. Belitas Bldg. 6F, 6–14–7 Ueno, Taito–ku.

Tokaien 3200–2924
All the grilled (Korean BBQ style) beef you can eat for ¥2,500. Shinjuku. E exit. Open Mon–Fri 5–11pm, Sat, Sun and holidays 11am–11pm. 1–6–3 Kabukicho, Shinjuku–ku.

Top of the Tower 3238-0023
Western buffet at the Hotel New Otani 40F.

Restaurants With Big–Sized Portions

Western Steak Cowboy 3419–6929
Jumbo hamburgers and big steaks. Odakyu line or Inokashira line to Shimokitazawa. S exit. Open 5–11pm. Closed Mon.

Ristorante Italiano Caprichoza, Roppongi Branch 3423–1711
Hibiya line to Roppongi. Open daily 11:45am–2:30pm, 5–10pm. Nakano Bldg. B1, 5–8–3 Roppongi, Minato–ku. Other branches in Shibuya, Shimokitazawa, Yotsuya, Jiyugaoka, Kichijoji and elsewhere. Huge portions, good prices. Share your stuff with a friend. Our personal favorite and highly recommended! Other branches are:
Yotsuya Branch 3358–5817
Kashiwa 0471–67–6755
Jiyugaoka 3725–0546
Kichijoji 0422–21–7881
Shimokitazawa (two locations) 3487–0461
Umeda (Osaka) ....(06) 376–0855
Ichijoji (Kyoto) ....(075) 723–8055
Call in Japanese to get directions from the train station. All within 10 minutes walk. You won't be disappointed with this one, trust me.

The Old Spaghetti Factory 5386–0511
Pasta and all the bread you can eat. Yamanote line, Tozai line, or Seibu Shinjuku line to Takadanobaba. Open Mon–Sat 11:30am–2pm, 5–10pm, Sun and holidays 11:30am–10pm.

Top 10 Restaurants I've Eaten at in Japan

1. Tom Collins, Inage, Chiba. Best fried chicken with a cold Heartland beer on the side.
2. McDonald's. Good for a piece of home. Try the *Teriyaki Burger*, the *Curry Rice Platter*, or the *Chinese Dumplings Set*.
3. Any Caprichoza restaurant. See Restaurants With Big Portions Section.
4. Tsubohachi Izakaya. A huge franchise. Great for their low prices, lively crowds, and best of all, PICTURE menus.

5. Hard Rock Cafe, Roppongi, Tokyo. American beer, huge burgers and fries, Hot Fudge Brownies, and Babes for you single guys.
6. Johnny Rocket's, Roppongi. 1950's style Hamburger joint.
7. Victoria Station. All you can eat salad bar with lunch for ¥1,200. Great steaks too. Roppongi's branch - 3479-4601. 15 other locations.
8. Samrat Indian Food. Lunch for ¥850. Located in Shinjuku, Shibuya, and Roppongi (3478-5877).
9. Mossburger. A McDonald's clone. They've got some interesting combinations too.
10. El Torito, Nishi Kasai Station, 3804-0704. The best, cheapest Mexican food with atmosphere in Japan.

Calorie Counting

In the previous section, I mentioned where to get food and roughly how much it would cost. In this brief section, I'll list (for those who are counting) the calorie content of most foods available in Japan.

Healthy foods like sushi, tofu and *sashimi* (raw fish) are great and contain few calories. Of course, calories mentioned here are approximate due to different sized portions, but you'll soon see that there's some kind of restaurant conspiracy going on to keep all dishes exactly the same size no matter where you go. If you don't know some of the names of these foods, don't despair; neither do I after three years!

If you want to know what everything means, get a copy of the *Tourist's Handbook* from the T.I.C. which lists most Japanese foods and their English equivalents. They keep it behind the counter. It's the size of a small paperback and has a red cover. The book, *Eating Cheap in Japan*, has the same information as well as pictures of most dishes.

Most likely you will have tried a lot of these foods within the first couple of months after having gotten sick of McDonald's, KFC and Pizza Hut.

Good Eating!

NOTE: I PURPOSELY LEFT OUT THE ENGLISH TRANSLATIONS SO YOU'LL GET USED TO USING THE JAPANESE WORDS.

Alcohol .... Calories
    beer (large bottle) 250
    beer (mid–sized) 200
    chu–hai (400ml) 200
    sake (1 flask) 200
    sour (250ml) 100
Bento Boxes
    kara–age 760
    shake.. 560
    yaki–niku 620
Chinese
    age shumai 75

gomoku yaki–soba 620
harumaki (1) 170
hiyashi chuka 540
kata–yaki soba 670
sara udon 810
shumai (1) 60
sui–gyoza (1) 50
yaki–gyoza(1) 80
yaki–soba 590

Curry Rice

beef curry rice 800
chicken curry rice 890
dry curry rice 750
ebi curry rice 710
hayashi rice 640
katsu–curry 830

Donburi

chuka–don 750
curry–don 550
gyu–don 690
katsu–don 780
mabo–don 850
niku–don 510
oyako–don 710
una–ju 730

Izakaya Food (Get to know this list for sure. Popular food with students. These places have picture menus too!)

age–dashi tofu 260
asari no sakamushi 150
chikuzen ni 250
daikon no aradaki 110
ebi no shio–yaki (1) 20
eda mame (200g) 80
gyu tataki 200
hotate no butter–yaki (1) 30
ika no shiokara (50g) 50
ika no sugata–yaki (1) 90
kaiso salad 60
karei no karaage 180
ko–mochi shishamo(1) 30
niku–jaga (like stew) 210
nishin no shio–yaki 360
sanma no shio–yaki 190
Satsuma age 130
stamina tofu 210
tofu salad 180

ebi cha–han 780
gomoku cha–han 760
omuraisu 830
rice, chawan 230
rice, donburi 410

Soba and Udon

chikara udon.. 580
curry nanban soba.. 580
curry udon 610
hiya mugi 490
kake soba... 320
kake udon 310
kitsune udon 400
mori soba 340
nabeyaki udon... 590
niku nanban soba 550
oroshi soba 390
ten–zaru soba 640
tenpura soba.. 630
tori nanban 340
tsukimi soba 370
wakame soba.. 370
zaru soba... 320

Soups

daikon no abura–age miso shiru 60
kimosui 20
nameko no miso shiru 20
shijimi no miso shiru.. 30
wakame to tofu no miso shiru 40

Sushi (per piece)

aji 60
akagai 30
amaebi 30
anago.. 50
aoyagi 30
awabi 30
ebi 35
hirame 35
hotate 35
ika 30
ikura 65
iwashi 65
kanigo 55
kappa–maki 20
kazunoko 40
ko–mochi konbu 25

kohada 40
madai 35
shako 25
tako 30
tamago–maki 65
tekka–maki 25
torigai 30
uni 40

Sweets and Senbei (rice crackers)
karinto (20g).. 100
rakugan (20g)...80
kawara senbei (1) 20
okoshi (20g) 80
shio–senbei (5cm dia.) 60
geppei 160
yokan (20g)..60

Teishoku (Chinese)
butaniku nasu miso itame 730
happo sai.. 720
mabo–dofu 750
niku nira itame... 680
niku yasai itame 680
subuta 650
toriniku piiman itame 910
yasai itame.. 550

Teishoku (Japanese)
kaiseki course... 990
shabu–shabu 790

Tempura
anago 120
ebi..80
ika 70
kaki–age.. 180
kisu 70
ninjin (1)...20
okura (1)..10
piiman 30
renkon 30
Satsuma imo 40
shiitake 25
shishito (2)..20
shungiku...80

Yakitori Shops (per skewer)
asupara 10
ginnan..20
gyutan..15

hasami–yaki 30
hearts 40
kashira 25
kawa 110
liver 60
momo–yaki 40
negi–yaki 10
okura–maki 20
piiman–yaki 5
shiitake 5
shishito 5
shiso–maki 40
sunagimo 30
tongue 30
tsukune 70

Coffee Shops

Coffee shops are good places to teach private lessons. You pay for one cup at ¥300 to ¥500 and can stay as long as you want. Easy to spot as they're everywhere. Some coffee shops are free to foreigners where you are expected to talk to the Japanese while sipping your cup of java. Don't bother though as you'll be busy enough and will need that quiet relaxation time to yourself.

WASHROOMS AND RESTROOMS

Japanese–style toilets are to be found throughout the country. When I write Japanese–style, I mean the squat type; whereas, Western–style is of the sit–down variety. The best places to find Western washrooms are in department stores, modern office buildings, and fast food restaurants like McDonald's. JR and most public restrooms will be the Japanese–style toilets where you have to crouch down, squat and face the higher end. Smaller shops will have one washroom for both sexes. People will knock on the door before entering to see if someone's already in there. If you are in there, just knock back and they'll leave you alone.

In public areas, it's a good idea to buy tissue paper from a kiosk or the automatic dispenser in the restroom for ¥50 to ¥100, because they don't supply toilet paper. Check first: If you want to wash your hands, you should buy and carry around a small handkerchief to dry them with as they don't have the paper towel rolls like back home. A handkerchief is also very useful during the hot, humid days of Tokyo's summer which lasts July through to September.

NOTE: WHENEVER YOU HAVE THE OPPORTUNITY, GRAB THE TISSUE PAPER FREEBIES
             THAT YOUNG GIRLS HAND OUT REGULARLY IN FRONT OF THE TRAIN STATIONS AS
             PROMOTIONAL GIFTS.

BARS/DISCOS/CLUBS/BEER HALLS

Tokyo lacks nothing in the way of high tech, blasting clubs found back home on campus or downtown. Most discos and theme clubs are located in Roppongi, but Shibuya, Shinjuku and Shibaura (Tokyo Bay Area) are hip places too. They're expensive at around ¥4,000 to ¥5,000 on weekends for men, and ¥3,000 to ¥4,000 for women. For this price, they'll give you some drink tickets and food tickets which helps take some of the sting out. Call for directions before you head out.

Drinking

A big plus to being foreign is when you ask your students to recommend a good sushi, noodle, or spaghetti restaurant, they will usually want to take you there as their guest. When I say 'student', I am referring to all ages, but in this case I mean businessmen who are on expense accounts and therefore can afford an evening out. University students will most likely go dutch with you. Both are great times and you'll always be the guest of honor. Do your best to try everything, but don't worry if you don't–they don't expect you to like it all. Just like back home the Japanese have their likes and dislikes too. They just order octopus, seaweed and live fish to impress you–their honored guest.

After much food and drink, quite often they will suggest going to a Karaoke Bar to belt out a few *My Way*'s by Sinatra. A real blast with lots of beer, sake and whiskey. If you can hold your liquor, you are *tsuyoi* (strong), if you can't you are *yowai* (weak). The Japanese respect strong drinkers and consider getting loaded together a male–bonding type experience demonstrating trust in one another.

Discos, Live, and Loud Music
Roppongi/Nishi Azabu Area

Area..3479–3721
Bingo Bango Bongo..3479–5600
Cipango...3478–0039
Circus..5474–4570
Club Next..3479–0690
Droopy Drawers...3423–6028
Giza...3403–6538
Jail...3479–6473
Java Jive..3478–0088
J Trip Bar End Max..3587–0639
Lexington Queen..3401–1661
Maharaja...3584–2600
MZMZ...3423–3066
NU (Erotic Neurotic)..3479–1511
Odeon...3584–0021
Soul to Soul...3505–6573

Zipang 3586–0006

Shibuya/Shinjuku Area

The Cave 3780–0715
DJ Bar Inkstick 3496–0782
J Trip Bar Dance Factory 3780–0639
Milos Garage...3207–6953

Shibaura (Tokyo Bay Area)

Gold...3453–3545
Juliana's 5484–4000

Others

Deep...3796–0927
La Duc..3464–8699
Mix 3797–1313
Yakochu...5489–5403

Live Music (Jazz/Reggae/ Relaxed Atmosphere) Roppongi/Aoyama

Blue Note Tokyo 3407–5781
   Affiliated with New York's famous jazz club. Cover charge ¥6,000–¥12,000.
   All the big names visit here when in Japan.
Cavern Club–The Beatles Live House 3405–5207
Hot Co–rocket 3583–9409
Kento's 3401–5755

Shinjuku/Shibuya

Aspen Glow 3496–9709
Club Quattro 3477–8750
J 3354–0335

Tokyo Bay Area (The 'In' Place)

Ink Stick Suzue Factory..3434–1677
Tokyo Bay GoGo 3457–9931

Beer Halls

Great after work, beer guzzling, finger food, loud conversation–type places. A little pricey, but what isn't in Tokyo? Budget around ¥3,000 for a few cold ones. They are located literally throughout the city. Beer Halls just naturally spring up in train stations and on the roofs of department stores sometime around May. They're always crowded and pretty rowdy. I've listed just a few so you can try one out and get a feel for the culture!

Beer Terrace Sekirei (Aoyama–itchome) 3403–1171
Great German Cook (Shimbashi) 3501–3581
Hofbrauhaus Munchen in Tokyo (Shinjuku) 3207–7591
Pilsen (Ginza) 3571–3443
Sapporo Lion (The oldest in Tokyo. Opened in 1934. Ginza)
.... 3571–2590

KARAOKE

Sooner or later you'll get tricked into it. Your choice of English songs isn't expansive to say the least: *My Way, I Left My Heart in San Francisco, Yesterday, Love Me Tender*, etc. Some Japanese actually use karaoke to reduce stress, to let off steam so to speak. I doubt it will have the same effect on you, but after a few beers who cares anymore anyway?

A lot of karaoke bars serve as hostess bars for Japanese businessmen. Inside, Filipinos, Koreans and Japanese women (the most expensive) flirt, light cigarettes and dance with the boys.

Most university or high school students frequent karaoke boxes, which are separate booths or rooms containing T.V.'s, laser discs and mikes. Some serve alcohol while others allow you to bring in your own. Not expensive because you're usually with a group. There are also restaurant–lounge–type karaoke places where you belt out a few tunes between servings.

The following list shows the largest English selection available at karaoke bars. Don't worry if you can't get to one of these ones as there's tons located elsewhere in every neighborhood in Japan which will have a few in English for you to sing. The bars listed below have at least 500 English songs, and in the case of **Cream**, have over 2,500 songs!

Cream 3402–1361
J–POP 3464–4411
Roaring 20' 2nd 3423–9597
Roppongi Karaoke Max 3404–5521
Smash Hits 3444–0432

MOVIE AND CONCERT TICKETS

Every celebrity and every new movie eventually comes to Tokyo. Some stars even start their tours here due to the big paycheques in yen. The *Tokyo Journal* has the most extensive listings of anyone covering all plays, concerts, and movies. This is a monthly magazine you can buy in Tokyo at any English language bookstore.

There are three ways to get concert tickets in Japan: the promoter, the ticket agent, or scalpers.

Movie Tickets

Theatres are just like back home and you buy your ticket at the box office before you enter. Recently tickets were ¥1,800! In Canada, we have $3.50 Tuesdays, so basically you could watch 5 movies in Toronto for the price of one in Tokyo.

Four times a year all tickets are half the usual price: Sept 1st, Dec 1st, March 1st and June 1st. Ask the T.I.C. (3502–1461) or your students to verify these dates. There are also Theatre Discount shops that sell movie tickets 30% to 50% off the regular price. They're usually close to the movie theatres themselves so ask a friend to point one out for you or visit one of those listed in this book. If you want to see a particular movie, ask a friend to call first to see if they carry that film.

Arch Ginza Ten 3563–0851
    3–3–12, Ginza Chuo–ku.
    Mon–Sat 9:30am–7pm. Closed every 2nd and 3rd Saturday.
    Ginza has lots of movie theatres, so it's a good spot to go.
Mr. Ticket 3986–0355
    1–13–8 Nishi Ikebukuro Toshima–ku.
    Mon–Sat 9:30am–6:45pm.
    Located in the Futaba Building, 5th floor.
    They've got a lot of stuff here: museum tickets, baseball and occasionally
    sumo tickets.
Ticket Funaki 3350–7656
    3–37–17 Shinjuku, Shinjuku–ku.
    Mon–Sat 10am–7pm, Sundays and Holidays 10am–6pm.
    Good prices and open on Sunday too!
Wealth 3980–2029
    1–20–7 Nishi Ikebukuro, Toshima–ku.
    Mon–Sat 10:30am–7pm.
    Located in the Kaneko Building, 2nd Floor.
Wing Card System Ekimae Branch 3289–1800
    1st Floor Shimbashi Ekimae Building,
    #1, 2–20–15 Shimbashi Minato–ku.
    Mon–Fri 10am–6:30pm and Sat 10am–3pm.
    Also discount parking lot tickets.
Yuransha 3291–1833
    3–10 Kanda Ogawa–cho, Chiyoda–ku.
    Mon–Sat 10:30am–7pm.

Promoters

The two largest promoters are Udo Artists and Kyodo. They both have a similar system. First, for example, Michael Jackson comes to town and they issue *seiriken* which are sequentially numbered coupons, first come, first served. They're not the actual tickets themselves, but these coupons entitle you to come back at a later date and buy the real tickets at a specified time. There may be a limit of up to ten coupons per seiriken or no limit at all. Each seiriken is numbered, and numbers 1 to 100, for example, must go to the promoter's office at 9am and so on.

To actually get a low numbered seiriken is difficult. The promoters usually begin by advertising a date when you can come and get one. Ask a Japanese friend or secretary to keep an eye on the bottom of the inside back page of the Asahi Shimbun (newspaper) or the Yomiuri Shimbun both of which are in Japanese. The listings are in katakana (one of three of the Japanese Alphabets used mainly for foreign names and goods) in a black box with bold white lettering. For example, 'Ma–i–ke–ru Ja–ku–san' will be spelled out in Japanese Katakana. The ad will tell you where and when the seiriken will be issued.

When you return on the date specified to buy the tickets, an employee will ask you, as he works his way down the line, how many tickets you want and which dates. You cannot ask for specific seating in Japan as tickets are simply given away from the closest to the farthest.

Seiriken numbers 1 to 300 should get you a good seat. You could try to butt–in on someone else's number by asking politely if they wouldn't mind buying an extra ticket or two if they're not going to buy their full allotment. A free hour or two of English conversation might do it. Only for the daring who are prepared for rejection.

Udo For Seiriken Aoyama 3401–9999
  Ticket Agency near Aoyama Cemetery.
  Palace Minami Aoyama #102 4–8–4,
  Minami Aoyama Minato–ku, Tokyo.
Kyodo Tokyo 3407–7687
  Kyodo Building, 10th Floor, 3–6–18, Kita Aoyama, Minato–ku, Tokyo.
  On Aoyama Dori near Kinokuniya Supermarket and above the Health Mart Store.

NOTE: THIS SYSTEM I'VE DESCRIBED IS FOR SERIOUS CONCERT GOERS ONLY. TICKET
         AGENTS ARE WHERE MOST PEOPLE BUY THEIR TICKETS WHICH IS DESCRIBED
         NEXT.

Ticket Agents

Promoters turn tickets over to the Agents to sell. The tickets are not as good as the seiriken tickets mentioned above, but they're less hassle as you can reserve by phone and receive them by mail. Two major ticket agents are Pia and Ticket Saison.

Pia

Ginza Branch, 7 days, 10am–6pm 5237–9999
  Pia is where most foreigners buy their tickets. As I mentioned, you call them or drop by at any one of their 200 locations called Pia Stations or Spots.

You can't miss them. They also have a membership club which costs ¥1,200/year entitling you to have the purchase price automatically withdrawn from your bank account and have the tickets mailed to you directly. You get points each time you buy tickets applicable toward a free ticket in the future. In addition, they'll give you advance notice by mail of all upcoming events.

Pia also publishes PIA Magazine (in Japanese, but at least there are pictures) every week which lists almost every event in Tokyo. Ask a Japanese student or friend where to buy it.

Ticket Saison
English, 10am–7pm 3462–3848

Ticket Saison, while not as big as Pia, offers pretty much the same listings but with a slight bent towards classical music and theatre. They have a Foreign Customer Service counter at Seibu Department Store near JR Yurakucho Station if you want to speak in English. Call 3286–5482.

Scalpers/Ticket Touts

Don't bother. Too expensive. More than 10 times the price of the ticket. Up to 20 times for a good seat. An average concert ticket costs around ¥6,000, so you do the math. I don't know about you, but I don't need to see *Twisted Sister* for $500 bucks that bad!

CHURCHES

Every denomination and language seems to be well represented here in Japan, so no need to worry about not being able to go to mass if you so desire. At some point you might need a church; some people every week or others once a year. At any rate it's nice to have the information for the future or even for a newly arrived friend.

If you can't find anything on the list to suit you, call TELL (Tokyo English Lifeline) at 5481–4455 open Mon–Fri 9am–4pm and 7–11pm. They have a complete list of everything available in Tokyo and would be pleased to help. Also the Saturday Edition of the Japan Times publishes a comprehensive listing of churches in the Narita, Tokyo, Yokohama and Kansai areas. Call the numbers listed here for exact location and mass times.

Tokyo Metropolitan Area
Adventist, Seventh Day 3401–1171
Tokyo Central Church
1–11–1 Jingumae, Shibuya–ku
Ahamadiyya Moslem Center 3849–7899
404–7–25–13 Umeda, Adachi–ku
Arabic Islamic Institute 3370–5995
4–27–25 Yoyogi, Toshin Bldg., Shibuya–ku

Asia Evangelical Mission 3399–8451
1–16–16 Zenpukuji, Suginami–ku
Assemblies of God 0425–51–0966
1437 Kumagawa, Fussa
Atonement Evangelical Lutheran Church 0424–71–1855
3–2–17 Saiwai–cho, Higashi Kurume
Bahá'í Faith 3209–7521
7–2–13 Shinjuku, Shinjuku–ku
Buddhism, Tokyo Honganji Temple 3843–9511
1–1–5 Nishi Akasaka
Buddhism, Tsukjii Honganji Temple 3943–9511
Tsukjii
Chinese Christian Church 3314–6794
5–13–4 Koenji–Minami, Suginami–ku
Church of Christ, Ochanomizu 3291–0478
2–5 Kanda Surugadai, Chiyoda–ku
Church of Christ, Tachikawa 0425–36–5667
1–1–9 Kashiwa–cho, Tachikawa
Church of Jesus Christ of Latter–Day Saints 3496–6337
5–8–10 Azabu, Minato–ku
Church of Saint Mary's 3396–0305
2–31–25 Igusa, Suginami–ku
Denenchofu Lutheran Church 3721–4716
2–37–25 Denenchofu, Ota–ku
Franciscan Chapel Center 3401–2141
4–2–37 Roppongi, Minato–ku
French Speaking Catholic Community 3263–1928
1–2–5 Fujimi–cho, Chiyoda–ku
Full Gospel Tokyo Church 3357–2106
5th Floor, Yatushashi Bldg. 2–10 Yotsuya, Shinjuku–ku
German Speaking Catholic Community 3263–1928
3–18–17 Naka Meguro, Meguro–ku
German Speaking Evangelical Church 3441–0673
6–5–26 Kita
International Christian Assembly 3940–6691
1–9–1 Izumi–cho, Kanda, Chiyoda–ku
International Christian University Church 0422–33–3323
3–10–2 Osawa, Mitaka–shi
Islamic Center Japan 3460–6169
1–16–11 Ohara, Setagaya–ku
Japan Lutheran Church 3261–5266
1–2–32 Fujimi, Chiyoda–ku
Jewish Community of Japan 3400–2559
3–8–8 Hiroo, Shibuya–ku
Kanto Plains Baptist Church 0425–51–1915
1181 Musashino, Kawasaki, Hamura–machi Nishi Tama–gun

Musashino Chapel Center 0422–21–6458
1–10–21 Higashi–cho, Kichijoji
Musashino City
New Apostolic Church 0423–74–0070
1320, Kotta, Tama City
Salvation Army 3237–0881
2–17 Kanda Jimbo–cho, Chiyoda–ku
Shalom Church Shinjuku 3371–7558
7–9–7 Nishi Shinjuku, Shinjuku–ku
Shibuya Catholic Church 3463–5881
18–13 Nampeidai, Shibuya–ku
St. Alban's Anglican Episcopal Church 3431–8534
3–6–25 Shiba Koen, Minato–ku
St. Andrew's Church 3431–2822
3–6–18 Shiba Koen, Minato–ku
St. Augustine Kasai Catholic Church 3689–0014
1–10–15 Naka–Kasai, Edogawa–ku
St. Ignatius Church 3263–4584
6–5 Koji–machi, Chiyoda–ku
St. Luke's Chapel 3541–5151
10–1, Akashi–cho, Chuo–ku
St. Patrick's Catholic Church 3957–2540
1–28–22 Nagasaki, Toshima–ku
St. Paul Evangelical Lutheran Church 3261–3740
1–2–32 Fujimi, Chiyoda–ku
Scot Presbyterian Church 3401–8704
5–6–15 Roppongi, Minato–ku
Tachikawa Chinese Christian Fellowship 0425–43–1474
1–1 Showa–machi, Akishima–shi
Yokota Baptist Church 0425–53–2577
Yokota Air Base, Fussa
Yokota Church of Christ 0425–52–7964
3 Musashino Kumagawa, Fussa–shi

Kanagawa Area and Yokohama
Anglican Episcopal Service 0468–26–1911
Yokosuka Naval Base, Yokosuka
Church of Jesus Christ of Latter–Day Saints 045–401–8772
6028 Shinohara Nishi–machi, Kohoku–ku
Circulo Hispano Hablante de Kanagawa 045–894–5559
85 Yamate–cho, Naka–ku
Sacred Heart of Jesus 045–641–0735
44 Yamate–cho, Naka–ku
St. Michael's Kamakura 0467–22–3090
2–7–24 Komachi–dori, Kamakura

World Council Orth. Episcopal Churches 0464–23–0263
1387, Yamanouchi, Kamakura
Yokohama Chapel Center 0464–23–0263
Yokohama Koen, Naka–ku
Yokohama Christian Center 045–314–9676
65 Satawatari, Kangawa–ku
Yokohama International Baptist Church 045–621–6431
60 Nakaodai, Naka–ku
Yokohama Union Church 045–781–2486
66 Yamate–cho, Naka–ku
Yukinoshita Catholic Church 0467–22–2064
2–14–4 Komachi, Kamakura
Zama Baptist Church 0427–46–6879
3–5–1 Higashi Rinkan, Sagamihara
Zushi Catholic Church 0468–71–2009
6–8–47 Zushi, Zushi

SPORTS
Baseball Tickets

In 1991, major leaguers from the States participated in a three game series against the Japanese all–stars. The Japanese won. Personally, I think the boys came over here to have some fun and then play a little ball, so their minds weren't too focused. Plus, there were no finesse players. Since the Japanese think all foreign players are huge, long–ball hitters.

In 1992, they kicked ass and avenged their previous humiliation. Incidentally, Cecil Fielder ironed out the bugs in his swing here in Japan before going on to make $4.5 million per year with the Tigers. Anyway, you've got to go see a game to see the fans more than the game itself.

There are only twelve teams, six of which play near or in Tokyo. The most popular team is The Yomiuri Giants who play at the Tokyo Dome. The Nippon Ham Fighters also play at the Dome but with a name like that who knows what you're in for. Just kidding.

You've got three options if you want tickets:
1. Buy advance tickets from the stadium. Two weeks before the game, call and reserve seats. Use numbers shown below.
2. Buy advance tickets from the agencies listed under the Concert Tickets section. (Ticket PIA 5237-9999 or Ticket Saison 3286-5482/3).
3. Go Game Day. Big line–ups. Take a chance to buy a ticket. Giants usually sold out.

The two best stadiums are The Tokyo Dome and the Seibu Lions Stadium. The Dome, because games are never rained out, and Seibu Stadium for the plush greenery surrounding the outfield bleachers.

Tokyo Dome (Tokyo Yomiuri Giants and Nippon Ham Fighters)

....5800–9999
Sobu line to Suidobashi. W exit. Or Marunouchi line to Korakuen.
Jingu Stadium (Yakult Swallows) 3404–8999
Sobu line to Shinanomachi. Or Ginza line to Gaienmae.
Seibu Lions Stadium (Seibu Lions).................................. 0429–25–1151
Seibu Ikebukuro line to Seibu–kyujomae.
Chiba Marine Stadium (Lotte Orions)...........................043–296–8989
JR Keiyo line to Keihin–Makuhari.
Yokohama Stadium (Yokohama Bay Stars)...................045–661–1251
Keihin Tohoku line to Kannai.

Cycling Courses

There aren't many options if you're a keen cyclist. However, there are a few courses open to the public in the Tokyo area if you want a close–to–home workout.

If you've got more time, there are lots of cycling tours of rural Japan, some over a month long. Call the T.I.C. or domestic travel agencies for more information. If nothing here suits your needs, call the Bicycle Culture Center, 3584–4530 in English, which will provide you with alternatives. Contact the JR English info line at 3423–0111 to find out which train or subway line and the exact station and exit to use.

There's also an English cycling magazine which should be useful. Contact:

Oikaze
No. 206 2–24–3 Tomigaya
Shibuya–ku
Tokyo 151
fax: 3481–0497

There's a nice course that goes around the Imperial Palace, and another located near Meiji Jingu Shrine. Call the above numbers for more info.

NOTE: YOU SHOULD BRING YOUR PASSPORT OR ALIEN REGISTRATION CARD TO ANY OF THESE COURSES IF YOU PLAN ON GETTING A BIKE. YOU CAN ORDER **CYCLING IN JAPAN** AT THE BACK OF THE BOOK

Jogging

It stands to reason that you could go jogging on any one of these cycling paths or in your own neighborhood. However, if you don't want to dodge heavy traffic, here are two jogging courses open to everyone:

Imperial Palace course .... (5km) Chiyoda line to Nijubashimae
Yoyogi Park course .... (2.4km) JR lines to Harajuku

Call NTT or T.I.C for exact locations if you have any doubts.

Pool (Billiards)

This isn't the swimming pool section but the kind you play for money. If you want to shoot some stick with a friend or just go for a game alone, there are a few pool halls in town including a 65–table monster hall. This is huge considering Japan's lack of affordable real estate.

Several years ago, a lot of people played billiards but it's a dying trend. At least they shouldn't be too crowded for you. Here's the list in descending order of size. Prices hover around ¥750/hour. Call NTT for more listings in your area. Make sure you call to find out if these places are still in business or not before you go!

Pool Hall Cue 3409–2451
Shibuya. E exit. 65 tables.
Chuo–guchi Sportsland Billiard 3352–7501
Shinjuku. E exit.19 tables.
Billiard ACB 3209–0085
Shinjuku. E exit.17 tables.
Brunswick Sports Garden 3988–7221
Ikebukuro. E exit.17 tables.

SPORTS FACILITIES

If you like to work out, you've got tons of options in Japan. However, where and the amount of space you have is limited. It's expensive if you go to a Gold's Gym–type place, but cheap if you use your Ward sports center. Tokyo is divided into 23 wards.

Fitness centers are clean and modern just like back home. They offer aerobics, swimming, golf lessons, tennis lessons, squash, nautilus (weight training machines), free weights, yoga, jogging, and rowing machines, sauna, showers, and suntanning. Near our apartment we joined Renaissance Fitness Center which cost us ¥10,000 per month. There was also a one–time sign up fee of ¥10,000. It was open Monday to Saturday from 10am to 10pm, and Sunday from 10am to 6pm. When I checked around all the other clubs in our area, they had best prices. They have several locations and their number is 043–273–3011. Have a Japanese friend call and find out the other locations near you. Fitness centers are usually near the station. One other popular sports club in Tokyo is called Tipness.

Tipness Sports Clubs (Shibuya) 3770–3531
Facilities: Offers over 100 aerobics classes/week from 7:15am to 9:30pm.
Price: ¥20,000 sign up and ¥10,000/month after.
Locations: Also in Akasaka 3589–3531, and Shimokitazawa 3487–3531.

Ward facilities don't offer all the extras like the clubs do, but they've got the basics and they're really inexpensive. A one–day pass costs around ¥300. Also, they sometimes offer Karate, Judo, Kendo, and other Japanese sports for low fees. Have a friend call your ward to see what's available and when they're open.(see page 87). Here's just a sample of what you might find there.

NOTE: MONTHLY FEES CAN BE CHEAPER IF YOU ONLY GO IN THE MORNING, OR NOT ON
         THE WEEKENDS. CHECK INTO DISCOUNTS THAT FIT WITH YOUR WORK SCHEDULE.

Major Public Sports Facilities by Ward (Ku)

Adachi Ward Sports Center...3859–8211
Address: 2–27–1 Adachi–ku.
Facilities: Swimming pool and gymnasium.
Location: Hibiya line or Tobu Isezaki line to Takenozuka. E exit.
                        Bus for Sogo Sports Center stop.

Arakawa Ward Sports Center...3802–3901
Address: 6–45–5 Minami–senju, Arakawa–ku.
Facilities: Training room, gym, table tennis, air rifle, budo, kyudo
                        and swimming pool.
Location: Minami–Senju (JR and Chiyoda Lines) JR lines to
                        Minami–Senju. Or Hibiya line to Minowa.

Chiyoda–ku Ward Gymnasium...3256–8444
                        (Residents and non–residents)
Address: 2–1–8 Uchi–Kanda.
Facilities: Swimming pool, weight–training room, ping–pong,
                        volleyball, sumo ring, martial arts room.
Location: Near Kanda station.

Edogawa Ward Gymnasium 3653–7441
Address: 1–35–1 Matsumoto, Edogawa–ku.
Facilities: Training room, indoor pool, gym, table tennis, archery,
                        air rifle, budo.
Location: Bus from Shin–koiwa (JR) Sobu line to Shin–Koiwa. Bus
                        for Mizue–eki to Sugawarabashi stop.

Itabashi Ward Azusawa Gymnasium 3969–4166
Address: 3–1–1 Azusawa, Itabashi–ku.
Location: Shimurasakaue (Mita Line) .

Katsushika Ward Sports Center 3691–7111

Address:	7–17–1 Okudo, Katsushika–ku.
Facilities:	Training room, running track, indoor pool, gym, archery, air rifle, budo, kyudo, sumo ring,
Location:	Aoto (Keisei Line)Keisei line to Keisei–Aoto.

Kita Ward Kirigaoka Gymnasium 3908–2316
Address: 3–17–57 Akabanedai, Kita–ku.
Location: Akabane (JR).

Komaba Pool 3485–7761
Address: 2–19–39 Komaba.
Location: Inokashira Line's Komaba Todaimae station.
Note: Swimming caps required.

Koto Ward Sports Building 3649–1701
Address: 1–2–9 Kitaisago, Koto–ku.
Location: Toyocho (Tozai Line).

Meguro Civic Center (Residents and non–residents)........................ 3711–1121
Address: 1–4–36 Meguro.
Facilities: Swimming pools, bowling alley, training room, archery range, tennis courts, gym.
Location: JR Meguro station.
Note: Tennis Courts (residents only) must be reserved by post card.

Minato Ward Sports Center 3452–4151
Address: 3–1–19 Shibaura.
Facilities: 8 badminton courts, 160–meter track, ping–pong tables, 2 swimming pools, athletic gym, martial arts gym.
Location: In front of JR Tamachi station.
Note: Free facility use (residents only) on the first and third Monday of each month. Non–residents cannot come on these days.

Ota Ward Gymnasium 3733–8311
Address: 1–11–1 Higashi–kamata, Ota–ku.
Location: Umeyashiki (Keihin Kyuko Line).

Setagaya Ward Sports Field 3417–4276
Address: 4–6–1 Okura, Setagaya–ku.
Location: Bus from Seijogakuenmae (Odakyu Line).

Shibuya Ward Sports Center (Residents only)........................ 3468–9051
Address: 1–40–18 Nishihara.

| *Facilities:* | Athletic gym, swimming pool, tennis courts, baseball diamond, martial arts rooms. |
| *Location:* | Hatagaya station on Keio Line. |

Shinagawa Ward Consolidated Gym (Residents only) 3449–3011
Address:	5–6–11 Kita Shinagawa.
Facilities:	Pool, gym, training room, sauna.
Location:	JR Osaki station.

Shinjuku Ward Sports Center 3232–7701
(Residents and non–residents)
Address:	3–5–1 Okubo.
Facilities:	Swimming pool, training center, volleyball, badminton courts, table tennis, martial arts rooms. Good restaurant for lunch.
Location:	JR Takadanobaba, in Toyama Park.

Sugamo Gymnasium 3918–7101
| *Address:* | 3–8–7 Sugamo. |
| *Location:* | JR Yamanote Line's Sugamo or Otsuka station. |

Sumida Ward Gymnasium 3624–4483
| *Address:* | 4–15–1 Kinshi, Sumida–ku. |
| *Location:* | Kinshicho (JR). |

Tokyo YMCA Gymnasium 3293–7011
| *Address:* | 7 Kanda–mitoshirocho, Chiyoda–ku. |
| *Note:* | The Tokyo YMCA was established in 1917. It has a variety of facilities. Ballroom dancing used to be popular in Japan and formal lessons are available. |

Toshima–ku Zoshigaya Gymnasium 3590–1252
| *Address:* | 3–1–7 Zoshigaya. |
| *Location:* | JR Yamanote Line's Mejiro station. |

Yaguchi Kumin Center Heated Pool 3758–2941
| *Address:* | 2–21–14 Yaguchi. |
| *Location:* | Mekama Line's Musashinitta station. |

Sports Fair

A real worthwhile event is the annual University Olympic Games. University and Japanese language students participate in a one–day Olympic Games featuring volleyball, a marathon, 400 meter relays, and a tug of war. Usually held in October. Call or write for more information.

c/o Cultural Affairs, Sedion, ALC Press,
2–5412 Eifuku, Suginami–ku,
Tokyo 168.
Phone: 3323–0021

Squash and Racquetball

Only for the rich or those with a sports entertainment allowance. Expect a high entrance fee of roughly ¥40,000 and a high hourly rate of about ¥1,500. As mentioned previously, check out the sports clubs as some of them have squash courts, but usually no racquetball courts. Call NTT at 5295-1010 to get a few numbers of the bigger clubs if you're still interested.

Swimming

Bring that swimming cap if you want to get wet. No dice without it. Public pools are cheaper than private pools, but check to see if you have to live in the area to use the public one. Summer time is a madhouse as people flock to the pools and beaches to beat the high humidity. Check the Fitness Centers also before you join as some clubs have their own pool so you could combine everything into one. Call the numbers below for times and prices and location.

Public Pools

Chitose Onsui Pool 3482–4401
Chiyoda–kuritsu Sogo Tai–ikukan (indoor)................................3256–8444
Inokashira Park (outdoor) 0422–47–6900
Itabashi Ward Takashimadaira Onsui Pool 3932–5348
Joto Swimming Pool..3646–8083
Kamakura Park Swimming Pool...3673–5508
Koiwa Swimming Pool 3658–6112
Meiji Jingu Pool (indoor and outdoor).....................................3403–3456
Nerima Ward Shakujii Swimming Pool...................................3997–6131
Ota Ward Heiwajima Swimming Pool....................................3764–1414
Setagaya Koen (outdoor) 3411–6519
Tokyo Metropolitan Gymnasium (indoor) 5474–2111
Yoyogi National Stadium..3468–1171
     1st pool (outdoor), 2nd pool (indoor)

Private Pools

Ikebukuro Mammoth Pool (indoor)...3916–7171
Big Box Seibu Sports Plaza (indoor)...3208–7171
Kyobashi Kaikan (indoor) 3564–0888

Tennis Courts

Tennis is immensely popular now in Japan. Unfortunately, there aren't a lot of courts like the free ones back home at schools and Universities. Expect to pay ¥1,500/hour. Weekday mornings are the easiest time to get a reservation so most of us English teachers are all set. Some courts are so busy that you can only get a booking by winning a lottery! Definitely get a Japanese person to call and find out the procedure and to get directions.

Ariake Tennis–no–Mori (48 courts) 3529–3301
Hibiya Koen (5 courts) 3501–6428
Hikarigaoka Koen Tennis Court (8 courts) 3977–7433
Komozawa Olympic Koen (8 courts)...3421–6121
National Stadium Tennis Court (20 courts) 3408–4495
Nogawa Koen (8 courts) 0422-31-6457
Oifuto Chuo Kaihin Koen (14 courts)..3790–2378
Sarue Onshi Koen Tennis Court (8 courts) 3631–9732
Setagaya–kuritsu Sogo Undojo Tennis Court (12 courts)...............3417–4276
Shiba Koen (6 courts) 3431-4363
Takanawa Tennis Center (19 courts) 3440-1111
Tamagawa Ryokuchi Hiroba (17 courts) 3701–1679

TRADITIONAL SPORTS

Many people come to Japan to study Martial Arts. The following is a list of sports, a brief history, and their main federation's address and number. If you want to study somewhere else, write to: The Japan Martial Arts Society (JMAS) at P.O. Box 270 Tokyo 100, Japan. For a yearly fee of ¥4,000 they'll send you more precise info in English. Once in Japan you can attend lectures with demonstrations and films.

Aikido

Aikido originated in Japan and was created by Moukei Ueshiba (1883–1970). There are many *dojos* (drill halls) in wards, towns and prefectures that give lessons. Aikido incorporates psychology, philosophy and dynamics. It's considered to be a sport and a religion which combines traditional physical arts and spiritual martial arts together at the same time. It's more of a self defense sport borrowing techniques from judo, karate and kendo. Aikido teaches more throwing exercises and holding techniques designed to keep an opponent off balance and unable to mount an effective attack. No weapons are allowed unless your adversary is armed. Masters of Aikido say they have the ability to control an opponent's *ki* and thus throw him with very little effort, sometimes without even touching him. *Ki* has no English equivalent but can be roughly translated as a combination of force, energy, spirit and power. Dress is either a white *judogi* (judo outfit) or a Japanese *hakama* (split–skirt). Monthly tuition is about ¥10,000 for three or four classes per week with a one-time registration fee of around ¥5,000. Classes are offered throughout the day beginning early in the morning and continuing until late evening.

International Aikido Federation 3203–9236

| *Address:* | 17–18, Wakamatsucho, Shinjuku–ku, Tokyo. |
| *Location:* | About 10 min. by bus from Shinjuku Station, W exit. |

Aikikai Hombu Dojo..3203–9236
| *Address:* | 17–18, Wakamatsucho, Shinjuku–ku, Tokyo. |
| *Location:* | About 10 min by bus from Shinjuku Station, W exit. |

Ki–no–Kenkyukai Headquarters 3353–3461
| *Address:* | Ushigome Heim No. 101, 2–30, Haramachi, Shinjuku–ku, Tokyo. |
| *Location:* | About 15 min by bus from Shinjuku Station, W exit. |

Tenshin Dojo   .... (06) 304–8710
| *Address:* | 1–10–8, Juso Higashi, Yodogawa–ku, Osaka. |
| *Location:* | 5 min walk from Juso Station. |

Seibukan Dojo   .... (075) 701–3121
| *Address:* | 60, Izumigawacho, Shimogamo, Sakyo–ku, Kyoto. |
| *Location:* | Near Shin–Aoibashi–Katei–Saibansho–mae bus stop. |

Sobukan Hombu Dojo..3468–3944
| *Address:* | 1–36–2, Uehara, Shibuya–ku, Tokyo. |
| *Location:* | Near Yoyogi–Uehara Station on the Odakyu Line. |

Judo

Judo is another unique sport of self–defense developed in Japan several hundred years ago. *Jujutsu* was popular during the Edo Period (1603 to 1867) and was organized into modern Judo by Dr. Jigoro Kano (1860–1938). Judo was banned by the Americans after WWII, but was later reinstated under the control of Kano's son.

The basic Judo technique is to grasp and grapple with your opponent, and to defeat him by using his strength to your advantage. Beginners first study how to fall, throw, then strangle or hold down an opponent. Dress is a plain white *judogi* which consists of pants, a jacket and an *obi* (belt). Today Judo is practiced by over 6,000,000 people in roughly 70 countries. Japanese take their Judo seriously and have been bemoaning the fact that *foreigners* have been beating them up in all the major international competitions. Unfortunately, Barcelona was no exception. They don't even have Sumo anymore as the sport's highest rank of *Yokozuna* is held by a Hawaiian. C'est la vie!

All–Japan Judo Federation 3561–8251
c/o Kodokan, 1–16–30, Kasuga, Bunkyo–ku, Tokyo.
Near Kasuga or Korakuen Subway Station.

Kodokan   3818–4172
Address: 1–16–30, Kasuga, Bunkyo–ku, Tokyo.

Prices:	Registration fee:	¥4,000
	Monthly Tuition:	¥7,000
	Locker rental:	¥2,000 monthly.

Hours: 3:30–8pm, Mon through Sat. Closed Sun and national holidays.

Location: Near Kasuga or Korakuen Subway Station.

Note: Kodokan Judo Hall has a spectators' gallery which is open to visitors, free of charge, during practice hours.

Kodokan Hostel (NTT)..5295-1010

Address: 3rd floor of the Kodokan Building.

Prices: ¥2,500/person/night.
¥1,200 for a common room (capacity: 20 persons)/person/night.

Note: Conditions for staying at the Kodokan Hostel:
1) "The students are guaranteed by an approved Japanese sponsor in Japan for his conducts and payments during the stay." Basically, someone to foot the bill if you skip town.
2) "They are recommended (or introduced) by an authorized Judo body or Judo Federation that they belong to."

Nippon Budokan 3213–3534

Address: 2–3 Kitanomaru–koen, Chiyoda–ku, Tokyo.

Prices: Examination fee: ¥1,000
Registration fee: ¥2,000
Yearly tuition: ¥48,000 or ¥54,000.

Hours: 5–8pm, Mon through Sat.

Location: Near Kudanshita Subway Station.

Note: Japanese Guarantor is required.

Seibukan–Dojo ....(075) 701–3121

Address: 60, Izumigawacho, Shimogamo, Sakyo–ku, Kyoto.

Prices: Registration fee: ¥11,000
Monthly tuition: ¥5,000.

Hours: 6–7:30pm on Tue, Thu and Sat; 10am–12pm on Sun.

Location: Near Shin–Aoibashi–Katei–Saibansho–mae bus stop (25 min. ride from Kyoto Station).

Karate

Karate has about 70 styles found all over the world. It originally developed in China. However, the most popular *karatedo* comes from Okinawa, Japan formed by Gichin Funakoshi (a la *Karate Kid*). The kanji (Chinese character) for *kara* means sky or void, *te* means hand. No weapons are involved and training consists mainly of hitting, jabbing and kicking.

World Union of Karate–do Organization 3530–6637
4th floor of the Sempaku Shinkokai Building, 1–15–16, Toranomon, Minato–ku, Tokyo.
Near Toranomon Subway Station.

Headquarters and Dojos (training schools)

Japan Karate Association 3436–4567
International Headquarters (JKA)

Address:	1–6–1, Ebisu–Nishi, Shibuya–ku, Tokyo.
Prices:	1 hr for each lesson
	Registration fee: ¥3,000
	Initiation fee: ¥10,000
	Monthly tuition: ¥7,000 or ¥9,000
	Karate Wear: ¥6,000.
Hours:	Mon through Sat.
	Classes daily: 10:30–11:30am, 4–5pm, 6–7pm, 7–8pm.
Closed:	Sun and national holidays.
Location:	Near Ebisu Station.

Shotokan Karate International 3359–6614

Address:	B1, Suzuden Building, 1–10, Yotsuya Shinjuku–ku, Tokyo.
Prices:	Registration: ¥8,000
	Monthly tuition: ¥5,000 (twice a week ¥10,000 (at anytime unlimited hours)
	Annual dues: ¥10,000.
Hours:	Mon and Wed 6:30–7:30am and 10:30am–12pm. Mon–Thur 6–7:30pm and 7:30–9pm. Sat 4–5:30pm, and 6–7:30pm. Closed Fri, Sun and national holidays.
Location:	Near Yotsuya Station.

Karate–do Gojukan .... 3395–2311/2 or 3390–2929

Address:	1–16–23, Zempukuji, Suginami–ku, Tokyo.
Prices:	Registration fee: ¥10,000
	Monthly tuition: ¥6,000
Hours:	7:30–9:30pm, on Mon Wed and Fri.
Location:	Near Nishi–Ogikubo Station.

Seibukan Dojo .... (075) 701–3121

Address:	60, Izumigawacho, Shimogamo, Sakyo–ku, Kyoto.
Price:	Registration fee: ¥10,000
	Monthly tuition: ¥5,000.
Hours:	7–9pm on Tue, Thur and Sat.

Location: Near Shin–Aoibashi–Katei–Saibansho–mae bus stop.

Goju–ryu Yoyogi Karatedo Kyokai Hombu Ryu–shinkai
....3402–0123
Address: 4–30–3, Sendagaya, Shibuya–ku, Tokyo.
Prices: Registration fee: ¥15,000
                              Monthly tuition: ¥8,000
Hours: 2 hrs for each lesson, on Mon, Wed, and Fri.
Location: Near Yoyogi Station.

Kyokunshin–kai Hombu Dojo...3984–7421
Address: Kyokushin Kaikan, 3–3–9, Nishi–Ikebukuro, Toshima-
                              ku, Tokyo.
Prices: Registration fee: ¥10,000
                              Monthly tuition: ¥7,000.
Hours: 10am–12pm, 4–6pm, 7–9pm, every day, 1–3pm, Sat.
Location: Near Ikebukuro Station.

International Karate League 3984–7421
Address: c/o Kyokushin–kaikan Hombu Dojo, 3–3–9, Nishi–
                              Ikebukuro, Toshima–ku, Tokyo.
Location: Near Ikebukuro Station.

Kendo

Kendo is Japanese fencing with a long *katana* (sword) made of *shinai* (bamboo). It's the oldest of the modern disciplines. Presently, kendo is practiced by over 8 million people around the world.

Japan Kendo Federation... 3211–5804/5
c/o Nippon Budokan, 2–3 Kitanomaru–koen, Chiyoda–ku, Tokyo.
Near Kudanshita Subway Station.

Nippon Budokan Kendo School 3216–0781
Address: 2–3, Kitanomaru–koen, Chiyoda–ku, Tokyo.
Prices: Examination fee: ¥1,000
                              Registration fee: ¥2,000
                              Yearly tuition: ¥48,000
                              Term: 1 year (April–March each year).
Hours: 6–7pm, Mon through Sat.
Location: Near Kudanshita subway station.
Note: Japanese guarantor is necessary.

Kyumeikan Dojo 3930–4636
Address: 2–1–7, Akatsuka–Shinmachi, Itabashi–ku, Tokyo.

Prices:	Registration fee: ¥10,000
	Monthly tuition: ¥4,000
	Kendo Wear: ¥25,000.
Hours:	4–9pm Mon to Sat.
Location:	Near Tobu Tojo Line Shimo Akatsuka Station.
Note:	Dormitory is available. Up to one week, ¥1,500 a day.
	More than one week, ¥1,000 a day.
	Aikido and judo lessons are also available.

Kyudo

Kyudo literally means 'the Way of Archery' and is closely related with Zen. It is thought to be a very graceful exercise. It is equally pursued by as many women as men. High schools, Universities, shrines and temples all have clubs.

The *kyu* or *yumi* (bow) is 2.25 m long and made with strips of bamboo and lacquered mulberry wood. It is a very regimented sport which dictates all physical movements from beginning to end. Sometimes guys do it on horseback, which is called 'Yabusame'. The best festival is held at the Tsurugaoka Hachimangu Shrine in Kamakura on September 16th, every year.

Amateur Archery Federation of Japan 3467–7949
Kishi Memorial Hall, 4th floor, 1–1–1, Jinnan, Shibuya–ku, Tokyo.
Near Harajuku Station.

Ranges in Tokyo

Shinjuku–ku Taiikukan (Shinjuku Ward Gymnasium) 3232–7701
Address:	3–5–1, Okubo, Shinjuku–ku, Tokyo.
Price:	¥300
Hours:	9–12:30pm, 1–4:30pm on Mon, Wed, and Fri.
Location:	Takadanobaba Station.
Note:	English is not spoken.
	The range is open to those who live or work in
	Shinjuku Ward.

Minato–ku Sports Center 3452–4151
Address:	3–1–19, Shibaura, Minato–ku, Tokyo.
Prices:	¥200 (for those who work or live in Minato Ward)
	¥400 (for others).
Hours:	1–5:30pm on Tue, 1–5:30pm on Thur.
Location:	Tamachi Station.

The other ward offices give Kyudo lessons from time to time. Contact directly for further information. Some of them in Tokyo are:

Bunkyo Sogo Taiikukan..3944–2271
3–29–2 Otsuka, Bunkyo–ku, Tokyo.

Chiyoda Sogo Taiikukan 3256–8444
2–1–8, Uchi–Kanda, Chiyoda–ku, Tokyo.

Other Martial Arts

There are literally hundreds of other clubs and gymnasiums, and forms of martial arts so check around. The organizations I've listed will give you practically everything you'll need to know to get started, but if you want more info, go to an English language bookstore and buy the appropriate book or order it from us at the back.

Sumo

This section is designed to tell you how to see a tournament, rather than dwell on the techniques of current champions or the history of Sumo. There are several good books, the best being *Sumo, A Pocket Guide*, by Walter Long. There are six tournaments held each year which last for 15 days, starting and ending on a Sunday. They are:

January	Tokyo
March	Osaka
May	Tokyo
July	Nagoya
September	Tokyo
November	Fukuoka

Matches begin at 10am with the best stuff (senior wrestlers) starting at 3pm. Television coverage starts at 4pm and finishes with the last bout at 6pm. If you miss it live, there are replays of the day's most important bouts on Sumo Digest at 11:15pm.

Tickets can be bought any day of the tournament for the unreserved section. Prices range from ¥1,500 to ¥10,000. Get to the stadium really early, buy your ticket, then go in later if you want. For early matches, you'll be able to sneak down to the better seats because most people arrive later in the day. There are about 400 same day tickets to be had first come, first served.

In Tokyo, the Sumo Hall (Kokugikan) is located near JR Ryogoku Station on the Sobu line. The telephone number is 3623–5111 (Japanese only). It's open from 9:30am–5pm, Monday to Saturday. Since I began this book Sumo has enjoyed a huge surge in popularity due to a young rising star named Takanohana. Tickets have become really scarce and are sold out in hours. Ask businessmen if their companies have any free tickets to hand out.

You've gotta go at least once while you're in Japan. Just like you have to go see or climb Mt. Fuji, if you don't do these things you just haven't experienced Japan. What else are you gonna tell your friends back home? You slept on a straw–mat floor all the time and ate raw octopus and seaweed?

Are Sumo Wrestlers Rich?

Exactly how much do sumo wrestlers make? Their main source of income is their monthly salary and prize money. Prize money is paid per match by various company sponsors in ¥30,000 lump sums. In other words, if one match has ten prizes attached, the winner receives ¥300,000. Watch on TV at the end of the bout as the referee hands a stack of envelopes to the winner; the thicker the stack the richer it is. Sumo wrestlers also receive aid from their supporters (called 'tanimachi' in sumo jargon).

The monthly salary of each sumo wrestler is as follows:

Yokozuna	¥1,800,000
Ozeki	¥1,497,000
Sekiwake, Komusubi	¥1,077,000
Makuuchi	¥829,000
Juryo	¥654,000

There is no salary for those below juryo.

Sumo wrestlers' main diet consists of beer and *Chanko Nabe* which is a big pot full of meat and fish and vegetables. There are many chanko nabe restaurants near the Sumo Hall in Tokyo. Most are run by former wrestlers. Get a friend to call to make a reservation. Then you've done it all except for beat up that big, fat guy Konishiki who weighs 254kg!.

Chanko–nabe Restaurants

Japanese eat Chanko–nabe all year round, but is really good on cold winter evenings.

Ichinotani 3251–8500
    2–10–2 Soto–Kanda, Chiyoda–ku
Naruyama 3261–1632
    3–9–2 Kudan Minami, Chiyoda–ku
Hamariki 3200–2901
    2–14–5 Takadanobaba, Shinjuku–ku
Daikirin 3823–5998
    1–1–11 Nezu, Bunkyo–ku
Kawasaki 3631–2519
    2–13–1 Ryogoku, Sumida–ku
Kiyokuni 3816–5544
    2–24–13 Koishikawa, Bunkyo–ku
Kitaseumi 3672–7393
    1–21–22 Nishi–Koiwa, Edogawa–ku
Yoshiba 3567–4481
    4–8–11 Ginza, Chuo–ku
Tomoegata 3632–5600
    2–17–6 Ryogoku, Sumida–ku

Futagodake 3336–7527
    3–58–1 Minami–Asagaya, Suginami–ku
Tamakatsu 3872–8712
    3–2–12 Negishi, Taito–ku
Furiwake 3836–5888
    3–35–15 Yushima, Bunkyo–ku

Sumo Stables

You can visit a Sumo Stable (Sumo Beya) before or after the tournaments. Call to find out the where and the when. The T.I.C. in Tokyo (3502–1461) will also have further info. I've also listed famous sumo wrestlers' names after the Tokyo address. I've given a little description if the wrestlers are worth seeing, while I just wrote their name and nothing else if they're not so popular.

Ajigawa 3634–5514
    1–7–4 Mori
    Koto–ku, Tokyo 135
Asahiyama 3687–8321
    4–14–21 Kita–Kasai
    Edogawa–ku, Tokyo 134
Azumazeki 3621–4676
    4–6–4 Higashi–Komagata
    Sumida–ku, Tokyo 130. Famous due to newly promoted Yokuzuna
    Akebono. An american who has stunned the sumo world by becoming the
    first foreign born wrestler to achieve sumo's highest rank.
Dewanoumi 3631–0090
    2–3–15 Ryogoku
    Sumida–ku, Tokyo 130. Wrestlers such as Kushimaumi, Mainoumi (sumo's
    smallest wrestler), and Oginohana.
Futagoyama 3316–5939
    3–25–10 Narita–Higashi
    Suginami–ku, Tokyo 166. Huge stable with the famouse brother pair of
    Takanohana and Wakanohana. Also contains Akinoshima and Takatoriki.
Hanaregoma 3392–5010
    3–12–7 Asagaya–Minami
    Suginami–ku, Tokyo 166
Isegahama 3947–8389
    5–7–14 Hakusan
    Bunkyo–ku, Tokyo 112
Isenoumi 3676–3386
    3–17–6 Harue–cho
    Edogawa–ku, Tokyo 132. Kitakachidoki.
Izutsu 3634–9827
    2–2–7 Ryogoku
    Sumida–ku, Tokyo 130. Heart throb Terao's home stable.

Kagamiyama 3673–5358
   8–16–1 Kita–Koiwa
   Edogawa–ku, Tokyo 133. Kirinishiki.
Kasugano 3631–1871
   1–7–11 Ryogoku
   Sumida–ku, Tokyo 130. Tochinowaka.
Kasugayama 3630–4322
   1–10–14 Saga
   Koto–ku, Tokyo 135
Kataonami 3625–6087
   1–33–9 Ishiwara
   Sumida–ku, Tokyo 130. Tamakairiki.
Kise 3815–2771
   2–35–21 Hongo
   Bunkyo–ku, Tokyo 113
Kitanoumi 3463–9796
   2910–11 Kiyosumi
   Koto–ku, Tokyo 135
Kokonoe 3621–0404
   1–16–1 Kamezawa
   Sumida–ku, Tokyo 130. Popular wrestler Tomoefuji works out here.
Kumagatani 3658–2465
   1–6–28 Minami–Koiwa
   Edogawa–ku, Tokyo 133
Magaki 3623–8865
   3–8–1–Kamezawa
   Sumida–ku, Tokyo 130
Mihogaseki 3631–3067
   3–2–12 Chitose
   Sumida–ku, Tokyo 130
Minato 048–266–0015
   2–20–10 Shibanakata
   Kawaguchi–shi, Saitama–ken 333
Miyagino 3634–6291
   4–16–3 Midori
   Sumida–ku, Tokyo 130
Musashigawa 3802–6333
   4–27–1 Higashi–Nippori
   Arakawa–ku, Tokyo 116. Hawaiian born Musashimaru practices here.
Nishonoseki 3631–0179
   4–17–1 Ryogoku
   Sumida–ku, Tokyo 130. Daizen.
Onaruto 0473–35–3169
   2–22–14 Kitakata
   Ichikawa–shi
   Chiba–ken 272

Oshima 3632–0240
   3–5–3 Ryogoku
   Sumida–ku, Tokyo 130. Kyokudozan.
Oshiogawa 3643–9797
   2–17–7 Kiba
   Koto–ku, Tokyo 135
Sadogatake 3626–2875
   4–18–13 Taihei
   Sumida–ku, Tokyo 130. Kotonishiki and Kotonowaka's home.
Taiho 3641–0027
   2–8–3 Kiyosumi
   Koto–ku, Tokyo 135
Takadagawa 3656–0015
   2–1–15 Ichinoe
   Edogawa–ku, Tokyo 132. Kiraiho.
Takasago 3656–7770
   1–16–5 Hashiba, Taito–ku, Tokyo 111
   Konishiki's Stable. He's the largest wrestler whose weight was listed at
   260kg for the March 1993 Tournament. Also home to Mitoizumi.
Tatsunami 3624–4448
   3–26–2 Ryogoku
   Sumida–ku, Tokyo 130
Tatsutagawa 3222–0128
   3–2–10 Iidabashi
   Chiyoda–ku, Tokyo 102
Tokitsukaze 3635–0015
   3–15–3 Ryogoku
   Sumida–ku, Tokyo 130. Tokitunada
Tomozuna 3631–0135
   1–20–7 Mori
   Koto–ku, Tokyo 135
Wakamatsu 5608–3223
   3–5–4 Honjo
   Sumida–ku, Tokyo 130

NOTE: THERE'S ALSO A MUSEUM OF SUMO FOR THOSE REALLY INTERESTED.

Museum of Sumo 3622–0366
   1–3–28, Yokoami, Sumida–ku, Tokyo.
   Near JR Ryogoku Station.
   Hours: 9:30am–4:30pm. Closed on Sat, Sun and national holidays.
   Admission: Free.

MEDIA

   TV news is readily available in English as are magazines. I've given a list of
newspapers should you care to subscribe to one. *The Japan Times* and *The*

Daily Yomiuri being the most popular and useful (*Japan Times* for Jobs; *Daily Yomiuri* for Classified Section: Articles for Sale on Sundays). The *Tokyo Journal* has the best events listings and some interesting articles from time to time.

Television shows are sometimes bilingual. This is astounding considering the work involved. It works like this: new TV sets come with a button for the following: (1) Japanese; (2) English; (3) Japanese/English. You press the desired language or listen to both simultaneously. TV shows are listed daily in the English language newspapers. If the show has a '**B**' beside it, it means its a bilingual broadcast. Most western movies which start at 9pm are bilingual. The news is also bilingual, produced simultaneously by English translators (usually at 7 and 10pm).

I repeat, though, your T.V. or VCR must have the special tuner or you won't be able to get the English, only the Japanese.

Video shops are all over the place, if you have a VCR. All the releases eventually come to Japan following a couple months lag time. A rental runs ¥300 to ¥400 and is due the next day. Each shop has different rental periods. For example, some start the moment you rent them and go for 24 hours. Others are due back the next day at 10am. Any late charge is enforced strictly no matter what time you signed them out, believe I know!

Magazines

Business Tokyo	3423–8500
fax	3423–8505
2–13–18 Minami Aoyama, Minato–ku 107.	
City Life News	3457–7541
fax	3457–7544
2–8–13 Shiba, Minato–ku 105.	
Nippon View	3442–0211
fax	3442–0217
2–8–6 Shiroganedai, Minato–ku 108.	
Tour Companion (Tokyo City Guide)	3542–5047
5–3–3 Tsukiji, Chuo–ku 104.	
Tokyo Journal	5379–6214
12–2 Minami Motomachi, Shinjuku–ku.	
Tokyo Time Out	3589–0309
7–6–52–401 Akasaka, Minato–ku.	
Tokyo Weekender	5689–2471
fax	5689–2474
1–2–6 Suido, Bunkyo–ku.	
Yokohama Echo	045–671–7128
Tokyo City Guide	3542–5027
Free. Available at T.I.C.	
Hiragana Times	3341–8989
Monthly ¥250; Bilingual magazine.	

Newspapers

Asahi Evening News 3546–7181
    7–8–5 Tsukiji, Chuo–ku, Tokyo 104.

Daily Yomiuri, The 3242–1111
    1–7–1 Otemachi, Chiyoda–ku, Tokyo 100–55.

Financial Times 3241–2920
    1–9–5 Otemachi, Chiyoda–ku, Tokyo.

International Herald Tribune 3201–0205
    1–1–1 Hitotsubashi, Chiyoda–ku, Tokyo.

Japan Times, The 3453–5311
    4–5–4 Shibaura, Minato–ku, Tokyo 108.

Mainichi Daily News, The..3212–0321
    1–1–1–Hitotsubashi, Chiyoda–ku, Tokyo 100–51.

Nikkei Weekly, The (Business)...3219–6588

Radio

Far East Network (FEN) 0425–52–2511
    Yokota Air Base, Fussa City.

NHK.. 3465-1111
    2-2-1 Jun'nan, Shibuya-ku, Tokyo.

RF Radio Nippon 3582-2351
    Azabudai Bldg, 2-2-1 Azabudai, Minato-ku, Tokyo.

TBS Tokyo Broadcasting Systems 3584-3111
    5-3-6 Akasaka, Minato-ku, Tokyo.

Tokyo FM Broadcasting 3221-0080
    1-7-1 Kojimachi, Chiyoda-ku, Tokyo 102-80.

FM Japan (J Wave) 3797–1111
    4–17–30 Nishi Azabu, Minato–ku, Tokyo 106-88.

Television

Fuji Television Network..3353–1111
    3–1 Kawadacho, Shinjuku–ku, Tokyo 162-88.

NHK...3465–1111
    2–2–1 Jinnan, Shibuya–ku, Tokyo 150-01.

Nippon Television Network 5275–1111
    14 Nibancho, Chiyoda–ku, Tokyo 102-40.

Television Tokyo Channel 12 3432–1212
    4–3–12 Toranomon, Minato–ku, Tokyo 105-12.

TV Asahi 3587–5111
    1–1–1 Roppongi, Minato–ku, Tokyo 106-10.

TV, CABLE, SATELLITE, SHORTWAVE RADIOS AND VCRS

At first, we said to ourselves, "We don't need a T.V." We came to Japan to study Japanese culture and language, but after awhile, there's only so much culture a guy can take before he'll go crazy for lack of excitement. You just gotta have a *Terminator II* or *Hook* in there somewhere. Plus, T.V. is a good way to study culture, we reasoned. We needed to witness Japanese humor and drama in action.

Let's take a brief look at what's available to you and for how much.

Shortwave Radios

A good idea for receiving world–wide coverage from Voice of America, BBC World Service, and Radio Canada International. The first year I had one I listened every night at 10pm to catch the hockey scores during the playoffs. It also came in handy during the Gulf War to find out what Canada was doing, since the American media, namely CNN, dominated just about everything that came out. America did this, America did that. Nothing ever about Canada or the other countries participating in the war.

You can buy a shortwave radio back home for around U.S. $250. They also have cheaper models here. For example an 8 band FM/MW(AM) domestic/overseas shortwave receiver costs only around ¥10,000 in Akihabara. Even if you don't have a shortwave, you can still listen to FEN Tokyo 810AM with an ordinary radio. FEN services American Military personnel and has by far the most extensive English Language coverage available. To see what's on, check the daily newspapers or for a complete program guide, write to:

Yokota Airbase
Yokota Airbase Bldg. 3266,
Air Force Broadcast Platoon Fussa–shi
Japan

NOTE: A RADIO THAT HAS A TV/FM BAND WOULD ALSO ALLOW YOU TO WATCH BILINGUAL BROADCASTS
IF YOUR T.V. OR VCR DOES NOT HAVE THE BILINGUAL OPTION.

Televisions

Japan has a neat option for those who want to watch certain broadcasts in English rather than Japanese: bilingual television. As I mentioned in the Media section, at the push of a button you can switch to either language or hear both simultaneously. Only those programs listed in the English newspapers marked "**B**" are bilingual. For example, the news is broadcast in English and Japanese several times a day as is CNN. English movies are popular on Saturday and Sunday nights at 9pm. There are several other T.V. series like *The Incredible Hulk* and *Mission Impossible*. There must be around 20 or so of these mainly

American imports which are inevitably shown later at 2 or 3am. A bilingual T.V. will cost around ¥45,000 for a 21 inch screen. Before you buy, however, read the section on VCRs.

The latest invention of the Japanese is High Definition Television, but we're talking major dollars to buy one of these babies. Sharp has just introduced a cheaper version for ¥1,000,000 down from the original model's price of ¥10,000,000. Currently, there are 8 hours of daily HDTV programming available in Japan. Wait until there's more of them and you'll get them for next to nothing. Remember how much video cameras cost when they first came out?

With your new T.V. you can watch 8 or 9 channels in the Tokyo area. Every apartment usually has a small wall socket antenna to connect to the T.V. to get a clear reception. To get more channels you need to start paying more money. After finishing this section on home entertainment I realized how lucky we are back home in North America with anywhere from 50 to 100 channels for literally 50¢ a day.

Cable T.V.

There are several English channels available if you're willing to pay and will be here long term:

1. Subscription fees of around ¥50,000
2. Scrambler or Tuner rental deposit ¥20,000 (refundable)
3. Installation fees of roughly ¥25,000
4. Monthly charges of about ¥3,000.

Types of cable channels available are:

1. CNN–24 hour broadcasting
2. CSN Entertainment Channel–movies, dramas and documentaries
3. Japan Sports channel–broadcasts stuff produced by ESPN from the States
4. Space Vision Network–mainly sports like NFL Football
5. Star Channel–over 30 new Western movies per month. Broadcast from Hong Kong.

Now, to get one or all of these you have to contact the nearest cable television station in your area. Have a Japanese friend do this for you until you find the one that services your area.

Cable Television Tokyo (Minato–ku) 3432–0025
City Cable Television Fuchu (Fuchu–shi)....................................0423–61–7273
Hachioji Telemedia (Hachioji area) 0426–42–0260
International Cable Network (Machida–shi) 0427–22–3911
Japan Cable Television (Roppongi)..3405–3191
My TV (Tachikawa–shi) 0425–27–6666
Nippon Cable Vison (Akasaka) 3589–5135
Odakyu Joho Service (Kawasaki–shi, Yokohama–shi) 044–953–1211
Pioneer Electric Company (Meguro) 3495–9816
Suntec (Shinjuku)..3350–9585

Tokyo Cable Network, Bunkyo (Arakawa–ku)................................ 3814–2600
Tokyu Cable TV (huge area in Tokyo) 045–912–1109

Satellite T.V.

Satellite T.V. is sort of like Cable T.V., but you need more expensive equipment and the choices are fewer. Presently there are two stations broadcasting three channels by satellite:

1. NHK–BS7 and BS8
2. WowWow–BS3

NHK 3465–1111
NHK shows programs from around the world for example: ABC, CNN, BBC, NBA ball, NFL games etc. You need to buy a BS antenna and tuner at a home appliance store and have them installed. A 45cm antenna is roughly ¥43,000 and a tuner anywhere from ¥45,000 to ¥90,000 depending upon the functions available. Installation fees vary depending upon the difficulty of the set–up. Some stores offer a complete antenna tuner, installation deal so ask around. You might be able to get a cheap package deal. Plus you've still got to pay NHK ¥930 per month after all the other things are said and done.

WOWWOW (toll free) 0120–380–805
Same as NHK: BS antenna and tuner. Plus–decoder. Membership fee ¥27,810. Plus ¥2,000 monthly. You can get a slight discount for a 3, 6, or 12 month advance monthly payment similar to NHK in programming.

BOOKS
Review of Books about Japan

Your Life in Tokyo , written by *The Japan Times* is mainly for foreign nationals who are going to set up shop permanently in Japan. It deals with subjects such as: driving in Japan and all the red tape, children's educational options, adults wanting to study at a Japanese university in English, insurance (fire, theft, etc.), procedures for staying in Japan if this becomes one of your options, income tax requirements after 1 year, buying a house, a complete medical care section describing everything from childbirth to death, and an extremely useful, comprehensive guide to Japan's telephone communications systems and postal services. To be sure, the English teacher committed to only a one year stay in Japan might become somewhat overwhelmed by such minute detail, but it is there if you decide to stay on permanently, and it is written in Japanese and English.

Probably their best piece of advice regards the foreigner living in a Japanese neighborhood. They recommend that you at least say hello when the opportunity arises as the Japanese are afraid to make the first move due to the language barrier. Indeed, a Japanese proverb states that "it's better to have a neighbor close by than a relative far away." Neighbors can alleviate many a problem especially during an emergency.

John Wharton's *Jobs in Japan* is another popular book for the Japan–bound traveler. There are good points and bad points about his book. For example, his description of Japanese culture was all too brief and merely restated several outdated, armchair, psychological theories: the Japanese are leery and curious of foreigners, subservient to the W.W.II winning nations, namely the U.S., and anxious now to learn the international language of English. Surely one of several excellent books on the Japanese would serve the long–term teacher better and save him one–half hour of worthless reading.

As for his chapter on advice from people who have gone to Japan as English teachers, this is a fairly good description of daily life from the people who lived in Japan and gives the novice some insight into daily triumphs. A good chapter, probably the best of the book, although a bit uppity and overly optimistic.

His suggestion to call or write schools is totally a waste of time and money: go to Japan first then find work is this author's strongest advice. Even if you do nothing else I suggest, do yourself this one thing. Times have changed and employers can satisfy their needs strictly with local talent now. You'll waste a lot of time, paper, stamps and money.

The Visa section is totally useless to Canadians, Australians, and New Zealanders who are offered the Working Holiday Visa or 90 day Tourist Visa renewable for another 90 days. It's mainly for Americans and Britons. Also do not worry about being detected by immigration officials as to your number of teaching hours a week. It's impossible for them to locate you and not worth their effort. However, I definitely agree with Wharton's assessment that teachers with ambition will soon build up a great schedule as there are always jobs available. Opportunities for work are endless if you are motivated and have the proper Visa.

I do recommend you read his book though for these reasons:
1.   a good incentive for the undecided.
2.   a good reassurances for family and friends.
3.   a good starting point for the truly naive and uninitiated traveler.

Book Stores (All listings have an English section)

Asahiya

Ikebukuro	3986-0311
Ginza	3573-4936

Aoyama Book Center 3479–0479
Roppongi

Biblos 3200–4531
Takadanobaba

Book Center Libro 5992-8800
Ikebukuro

Isseido Booksellers 3292–0070
    Kanda Jimbocho
Jena 3571–2980
    Ginza
Kinokuniya
    Shinjuku 3354-0131
    Shibuya 3463-3241
Kitazawa 3263–0011
    Jimbocho
Kyobunkan 3561-8446
    Ginza
Kondo Bookstore 3571-2480
    Ginza
Maruzen
    Nihombashi 3272-7211
    Ochanomizu 3295-5581
National Bookstore 3442–3188
    Minami Azabu
Paperweight Books (mail order) 3498–5260
    (fax) 3498–5400
Sanseido
    Kanda Jimbocho 3233-3312
    Narita Airport Terminal 2 0476-34-6881
Tuttle Bookshop 3291–7071
    Kanda Jimbocho
Yaesu Book Center 3281–1811
    Tokyo
Yurindo
    Yokohama 045-261-1231
    Yokohama Landmark Plaza 045-222-5500

The Bookworm

This store is such a find, it deserves it's own little section. Founded in 1981 by Grace Yamakawa, it is the best used bookstore in Japan. You can also bring books back for a 75% credit towards your next purchase. Great for everyone who has to commute and needs fresh reading material daily. Over 10,000 volumes to choose from.

The bad news is that it's pretty far out on the Keio New line or the Odakyu Tama line from Shinjuku at Nagayama Station. Hours are from 11am to 6pm Tuesday to Saturday, closed Sunday and Monday.

The good news is they've started two new mail order services. The first one's for all the used books and all you have to do is send ¥250 in stamps to:

          The Bookworm
          550–8 Kaitori,
          Tama–shi, Tokyo

206
tel: 0423–71–2141

They'll send you an updated computer listing of all used books presently available. All you have to do is phone or fax your order. You pay the book price plus mailing costs, no handling fees are added. This is a great service if you're outside of Metropolitan Tokyo.

The second service is called *The Bookshelf*. It deals with new releases from the U.S. and Japan. These books are not in stock but will be ordered by Grace. Prices for Japanese books will be set by the publishers so no savings here. However, you will save money on U.S. books. Once you check out the going rate for foreign books in Japan which is usually 200% to 300% higher, the Bookworm will be able to get you a better deal due to lower overhead costs.

To join, send another ¥250 in stamps to:

The Bookshelf
Network Okinawa Bldg
6–2–13 Koremasa,
Fuchu–Shi, Tokyo 183
tel: 0243–36–0481
fax: 0423–36–0482

Second Hand Books

Bookworm 0423–71–2141
    Nagayama
The Second Story 3706–5055
    Umegaoko (Odakyu Line)

Travel Books

I'd like to repeat that the best buy on the market for getting from A to B and what to see is *Lonely Planet's Japan: A Travel Survival Kit* by Ian McQueen, a Canadian. The 1993 edition has been edited by two other writers as McQueen has changed publishers. There is no other comparable travel series available as extensive and complete for travel as the Lonely Planet series. They cover all of Asia and in the case of Japan, cover the entire country from North to South and East to West. If it's not in Lonely Planet, it's probably not worth seeing is my opinion.

I've used their books for Hong Kong, Korea, Thailand, West Africa, Canada, and Mexico. I've never been disappointed, and usually I was the one in our group making decisions based on advice in the book. They're always written by a long term resident (Japan's book 10 years) which is good, but they also incorporate other travelers' ideas and suggestions into each new edition. Therefore, they're a book for travelers written by travelers.

Other guidebooks just cover the basics like Kyoto, Mt. Fuji, Tokyo, but Lonely Planet covers all you'll need to know about travel in Japan. I could not duplicate their experience in this area, nor is this book intended to be a travel guide. Buy Lonely Planet instead.

Top 10 Books to Buy about Japan

1. Shogun, by James Clavell. Epic about the first foreigners to enter Japan in the 15th Century.
2. Gaijin, by James Clavell. Set in the 19th Century when Japan was forced to open up to the West.
3. Max Danger, The Adventures of an Expat in Tokyo, by Robert Collins. Humourously written and you'll find yourself saying, "Yeah, that's just what happened to me!"
4. Japanese for Busy People One. To get you started on the basics.
5. Making Out in Japanese. All the slang you'll ever need.
6. Japan: A Travel Survival Kit, by Lonely Planet. The only guidebook you'll need to get from A to B.
7. Remembering the Kanji, by J.W. Heisig. He also wrote guides for remembering Hiragana and Katakana. Heisig has devised neat little drawings and techniques in order to always remember the difficult Japanese written language.
8. Living for Less in Tokyo and Liking It!, by the Japan Hotline. Lots of info on all kinds of subjects.
9. Eating Cheap in Japan, by Kimiko Nagasawa. Descriptions of every type of restaurant you'll find in Japan, plus photos and suggested prices to go along.
10. You're reading it!

LIBRARIES

If you need some information from home or books on Japan in English to read for free, there are some good English libraries. Embassies usually have a host of information about their own country, plus stuff in Japanese.

The best ones are:

Asiatic Society of Japan 3586–1548
Australian–Japan Cultural Center 3498–4143
Goethe Institute..3583–7280
    18,000 German books. Ginza subway line to Aoyama Itchome. Mon–Thur 12–6pm, Fri until 8pm. Closed Aug 5 to Sept 15.
International House 3470–4611
JETRO Business Library..3582–5171
    Foreign trade, business. No sign–out privileges. Mon–Fri 9:30am–4:30pm, Sat 9:30–11:40am. Address: Near the U.S. Embassy. Call for directions. Toranomon subway station on the Ginza line.
Kanagawa Prefectural Library·..045–241–3131

Library La Maison Franco Japonaise 3291–1144
    5,000 French volumes. JR Ochanomizu Station. Open 10–12pm, 1–6pm.
    Closed Sat (July to Sept).
Metropolitan Hibiya Library 3502–0101
Shibuya–ku Central Library 3403–2591
The American Center Library 3436–0901
    800 volumes over 200 subscriptions to magazines and journals. Mon–Fri
    10:30am–6:30pm. Address: 2–6–3 Shiba koen, Minato–ku.
The British Council Library 3235–8031
    English literature, ESL materials, children's books and books on Japan.
    Mon–Fri 10am–8pm. Address: 1–2 Kagurazaka, Shinjuku–ku. Near JR
    Iidabashi station. ¥3,500/year to join. West Exit (B2 B3 for subways).
The Japan Foundation Library 3263–4505
    30,000 volumes. 200 periodicals. Emphasis on Japan. Apply for a free
    courtesy card and you have unlimited access. Tue–Fri 10am–5pm, Sat 9–
    12pm (on 1st, 3rd and 5th Sat). Address: 3–6 Kioi Cho, Chiyoda–ku.
    Yurakucho subway line to Kojimachi.
The National Diet Library 3581–2331/2341
    (Kokuritsu Kokkai Toshokan) Japan's largest library. Must be a university
    or college graduate to check–out books. Four–million volumes of which
    close to 1,000,000 are in English. Nearly 40,000 English periodicals and
    5,400 newspaper subscriptions. Mon–Sat 9:30am–5pm. Closed 4th Sat and
    Wed. Address: 1–10–1 Nagatacho, Chiyoda–ku. Yurakucho line to
    Nagatacho. Exit 1.
Tokyo Baptist Church Library 3461–8439
Tokyo Metropolitan Central Library 3442–8451
    (Tokyo Toritsu Chuo Toshokan) One million books, 1,500 periodicals, 700
    films, slides, videotapes, cassettes and records. No sign–out privileges.
    Monday 1–8pm, Tue–Fri 9:30am–8pm, Sat/Sun/holidays 9:30am–5pm.
    Closed 1st Thur and 3rd Sun. Address: 5–7–13 Minami Azabu, Minato–ku.
    Near Hiroo subway station.
World Magazine Gallery 3545–7227
    Over 1,300 magazines in 50 languages. No sign–out privileges. Must be
    read there. Specializing in foreign magazines. Mon–Sat 11am–7pm.
    Address: 3–13–10 Ginza Chuo–ku. Hibiya subway line to Higashi Ginza
    Station.
Yokohama Municipal Library 045–231–1304

NOTE: TO JOIN ANY LIBRARY, BRING YOUR ALIEN REGISTRATION CARD OR PASSPORT.
            BOOKS ARE EXPENSIVE IN JAPAN SO IT'S NICE TO HAVE AN ALTERNATIVE.

THE WORLD OF FAXES

    The technology is there, so use it. I used to write a letter to Canada, send
it, wait for a reply, and get roughly three–week old news. Then I got smart. A
fax sent at 11pm Tokyo time arrives 9am E.S.T. 14 hours earlier. Your friends or
family pick it up at a fax store or at home, read it, write a reply and send it to

you that night after 11pm when rates are cheaper. You receive it the next day in the afternoon at 1pm, 14 hours later. Fantastic or what? It costs just a little more than an international letter and really keeps you up to date. It's almost as good as a phone call.

A one page fax costs about ¥250 to send from Japan to North America. If you use a Fax/Computer store in North America that allows you to send and receive faxes, the cost is about $3.50 for pick up and $5 to send to Japan. In Canada, their names are Kinko's , Kwik Copy, and Pak Mail. Check the yellow pages or ask the operator for more information. In addition, a lot of schools are now accepting faxed résumés only, as a source of introduction, due to the sheer number of applicants. This way they just screen the good applicants based on experience and education. Lastly, if you plan to do any business here, a fax is absolutely essential for success.

Sending A Domestic Fax In Japan

You can send a fax in just about any chain convenience store like Lawson's or 7–11. Also a lot of the train stations such as Tokyo, Shinjuku, Sibuya, and Chiba have coin–operated domestic fax machines for ¥100. Just ask a clerk or JR worker for help. Write the telephone number on the back of the fax and then point to it and just say "FAX PLEASE". No problems.

Sending and Receiving a Fax From Abroad

Take your fax directly to a KDD branch office, or send the message to KDD by fax. You must be registered before–hand and it's free. They charge you about ¥300, plus the long distance charges. To receive from other countries, call KDD Teleserve at 3347–9236 to apply.

KDD Branch Offices
Shinjuku Branch 3347–5000
Otemachi Branch 3275–4343

Also, some of the major hotels and Kimi Information Center have the same services.

Alpha Corporation 3343–2575
Tokyo Hilton International Hotel, 1F, Business Center
Shinjuku. W exit. Open 9am–6pm Mon to Fri.
Kimi Information Center 3986–1604
Ikebukuro. W exit. Open Mon–Fri. 10am–7pm. Sat until 4pm.

NOTE: ALL OF THE ABOVE PLACES SPEAK ENGLISH AND YOU SHOULD HAVE NO PROBLEM
        GETTING DIRECTIONS, REGISTERING OR GATHERING INFORMATION.

Buying A Fax Machine

The Akihabara district of Tokyo and your local appliance store all have fax machines for sale. Expect to spend about ¥70,000. Other options are:

1. buying one back home and carrying it over.
2. buying a computer fax card which fits into an empty slot in your computer. However, only good for what you type in , not handwritten letters.
3. buy used out of The Daily Yomiuri for around ¥40,000.

Otherwise you can try to buy from small import companies selling new faxes at bargain prices.

Steve Hauser 3984–5200
    fax 3986–6850
    Call for price and details.
GSC Ltd (Harvinder Johar – English O.K.). 3332–0098
    fax 3331–5984
    I bought one from him, had no problems and received great service. Prices start at ¥63,000 for a fax plus answering machine. It has an automatic tel/fax switcher built in.

Advice From the Pros

1. Buy new, not used. Imagine calling a repair shop in Japanese, sending the machine in, and paying for the bill if it's no longer under warranty.
2. Buy a machine with a paper cutter option. Your machine will jam if you're not home to make sure the flow of faxes doesn't become weighted down.
3. Get speed dial and memory dial. It's a minimum of 15 digits to call home so it's easier to press just one pre–set button.
4. Whenever possible, buy a second phone line (see section on buying a telephone line from NTT) rather than a fax/phone switcher. A fax/phone switcher asks the caller to specify what type of call he's making. Unfortunately, half the time people can't understand your message and they get it wrong. It's frustrating and could be costly. Do yourself a favor in the beginning and consider shelling out the extra cash to have two lines installed.

EXPLORE JAPANESE CULTURE

Culture opportunities abound here in Japan–just choose it and go for it. The Tourist Information Center (T.I.C.) has information on any subject you want. Call them at 3502–1461.

1. Acupuncture
2. Aikido
3. Calligraphy
4. Cooking
5. Ikebana–flower arranging
6. Go
7. Judo
8. Karate
9. Kendo
10. Meditation
11. Tea Ceremony
12. Japanese Language Study
13. Yoga
14. Zen

The *Yellow Pages* in *NTT's City Source English Telephone Directory* are also useful. You can buy this for about ¥2,000 at any of the English language bookstores previously mentioned, or obtain it free from an NTT office near your home. The new issue is published sometime in March every year. They usually keep copies all year round however if you arrive before or after March. For information, call NTT's English Hotline at 5295–1010.

A pamphlet, available at the T.I.C. called *Explore Japanese Culture* has a large list of free cultural study opportunities. If you don't know what some of these subjects below mean, look them up when you get here. Tokyo's list is quite impressive. For example, they have a home visit system where you register to visit a Japanese home. We did it when we first came and still keep in contact with our host family. Usually in the evening you'll have supper, talk, take pictures, and the like. Etiquette is to bring a small gift to the home you're visiting. Something from your home country would be preferable.

From a person's home you could study:

1. Suibokuga
2. Shodo
3. Kimono Dyeing
4. Origami
5. Koto
6. Shakuhachi
7. Shamisen
8. Dance
9. Sado

10. Ikebana
11. Cooking
12. Kimono Dressing

They also have a list of public facilities where you can try other subjects such as:

1. Doll Making
2. Crystal
3. Gagaku
4. Aikido
5. Iaido
6. Kendo
7. Gardening
8. Go
9. Zazen
10. Kaiseki

Pick up their brochure which has pictures and descriptions of everything. A Japanese proverb states "one view is worth more than a thousand listenings".

Even if you just mention to your students that you're interested in something, chances are they know where to get some information for you.

Study Opportunities

Try to study something while you're here. It'll help you to:
1. get out of your teaching routine.
2. meet other Japanese besides your students.
3. experience a small part of culture unavailable in your home country.
4. give you something new and fresh to write home about and discuss with your students.

Newcomers are pretty busy the first couple of months but say after 5 or 6 months when you're dreading going to work the next day and your classes have lost a little pizzazz–take up something like karate or origami to pump some freshness into your daily life. Even Tokyo can be boring unless you keep expanding your horizons.

Acupuncture Treatment Centers

Baba Kaiseido Acupuncture Clinic 3432–0260
Near Hamamatsucho station. World Trade Center is close. Weekdays 10am–6:30pm. Saturdays 10am–4pm. Mr. Baba speaks very good English. I've gone to see him twice and found him to be excellent. Very friendly.

Calligraphy (Shuji)

Koyo Calligraphy Art School..3941–3809
Monthly fee (4 times) around ¥5,000. Around ¥10,000 for calligraphy tools. Otsuka, Yamanote line or Shin-otsuka, Marunouchi line.

Tokyo Masuda College 3685-8555
 Hirai station, Sobu line. Also has Ikebana, and Tea Ceremony.

Cooking
Akasaka B Cooking School 3582–9074
 3–21–14 Akasaka, Minato–ku, Tokyo.
Cookie Cooking School 3779–8884
 1–28–3 Nishi Gotanda, Shinagawa–ku, Tokyo.
Egami Cooking School..3269–0281
 Ichigaya, Sanai–cho, Shinjuku–ku, Tokyo.
Tokyo Masuda College 3685–8555
 4–13–4 Hirai, Edogawa–ku, Tokyo.
Yoshii Cooking...3451–1695
 5–14–2 Mita, Minato–ku, Tokyo.

Go
Nihon Kiin 3262–6161
 7–2 Goban–cho, Chiyoda–ku.

Flower Arranging (Ikebana)
 I'm told that flower arranging has a few different methods: Ikenobo, Ohara
and Sogetsu. Each has its own designs and arrangements. If you really want to
learn this art, try some different schools to see which one you like the best.
Most of the main branches have English lessons. Expect to pay at least ¥3,000
up to ¥5,000 for a one-time shot. You have to reserve lessons at least one day
in advance. Call below for times, locations and exact costs.

Ecole Printemps Ginza 3567–7235
Ichiyo School of Ikebana 3388–0141
Kenkyusha Eigo Center 5261–8940
Kokusai Ikebana School 3406–7001
Ohara School..3499–1200
Sogetsu School 3408–1126
Yamoto Gakuen...3364–0151

Japanese Water Painting (Sumie)
Tokyu Seminar BE...3477–6277
 3–month course. Shibuya. S exit. Tokyu Plaza 7F Fri 10am–1pm. Sumie
means artistic expression using Indian Ink.

Meditation
Brahma Kumaris Raja Yoga Center ....(0422) 22–8975
 12–18 Kichijoji Higashi–cho 1–chome, Musashino.

Nihon Meditation Center 3478–2681
No. 1 Aoyama Building, 2nd floor, 3–7 Kita Aoyama 3–chome, Minato–ku.

Shamisen

About ¥5,000 for a trial lesson. Call both to find out the wheres and the whens.

Gessho Osano 044-856-0081
Near Miyamaedaira Station, Shintamagawa line.
Kineya Rokuro Nagauta Shamisen Keikojo 3842–6900
Subways or Tobu Isezaki line to Asakusa. Or Ginza line to Tawaramachi.

Shiatsu Treatment

Roughly the same cost as acupuncture at about ¥5,000 per visit, with the first visit slightly more expensive due to counseling and so on.

Ichihara Shiatsu Chiryoshitsu.. 0424–84–5049
6–39–3 Jindaiji, Kitamachi, Chofu City.
Jin Acupuncture/Shiatsu Clinic... 0422–45–4911
Kichijoji Corp. 110, 1–6–15 Kichijoji Minamicho, Musashino City.
Namikosi Shiatsu Clinic... 3583-9326
Chiyoda line to Akasaka station. 4F. Yomo Bldg, 3-12-21 Akasaka, Minato-ku, Tokyo.

Tea Ceremony (Sado)

Several different methods as in Flower Arrangement. One time lessons around ¥3,000.

Dai–nihon Chado Gakkai 5379-0753
Shinjuku station.
Ecole Printemps Ginza 3567–7235
Subways to Ginza. C6 exit.
Edo Senke Iemoto 3813–9085
Nezu station on Chiyoda line.
Enshu Sado Soke 3358–6811
Near Shinanomachi station on Sobu line.
Kenkyusha Eigo Centre 5261–8940
Sobu line or subways to Iidabashi. W exit.

Yoga

Buddha Yoga Mission 3417–7882
1–30–12 Seijo, Setagaya–ku, Tokyo.

International Oki–Do Yoga Institute.. 0559–86–5655
450–1 Sawaji, Mishima City, Mishima, Shizuoka. Near Mt. Fuji. Intensive
courses available.
Tantra Yoga Center..3365–0336
Rm 202 Sasaki–so, 10–12, Kita Shinjuku 2–chome, Shinjuku–ku.
Tokyo Yoga Center 3354–4701
906, Yotsuya Gyoen Mansion, 1–26–12 Shinjuku, Shinjuku–ku, Tokyo.
Shinjuku Gyoenmae station on Marunouchi subway line. Open everyday
except Sun and Holidays from 8am–8pm. Individual lessons available.
Yoga College of India..3461–7805
New Shibuya Co–op 909, 12–3 Udagawa–cho, Shibuya–ku.

KABUKI AND NOH–JAPANESE THEATRE

There are four types of plays or theatre performed in Japan on a regular
basis. Far be it for me to describe the detailed histories of each art, so just let
me give you the facts that I gleaned from a T.I.C. brochure.

Kabuki
Facts

- established 17th century
- all male cast
- elaborate costumes and stage effects
- slow pace and difficult old–style Japanese language puts many to sleep,
  during long marathon performances
- new shows every month
- generally, plots consist of romance, family and warriors.

Where and When

Two choices:
Kabukiza 3541–3131
English Reservations. Hibiya subway line or Toei Asakusa line to Higashi
Ginza station.
Matinee at 11am. Night show at 4:30pm. Cost: ¥2,000 to ¥13,500 for entire
show. One act only ¥500 to ¥1,200. Good idea to rent an English earphone
guide for ¥600 plus a ¥1,000 refundable deposit.
National Theater of Japan 3265–7411
Subway Hanzomon line to Hanzomon station. Morning and evening
performances. Cost: ¥1,300 to ¥7,800. Entire show only. No one–act deals.
Same earphone deal as above.

Bunraku
Facts

- puppet theatre

- only 3 puppeteers, always wearing black
- shamisen music (traditional Japanese stringed instrument)
- themes of love, war and tragedy
- only one narrator for entire cast
- puppets 1/3 the size of a man.

Where and When

National Theater of Japan (see address above) 3265–7411
Performances in February, May, September and December each year.
Prices ¥4,000 to ¥4,800. Earphone guide in English ¥600 plus a ¥1,000
refundable deposit.

Noh and Kyogen
Facts

- originated in the 14th century
- oldest professional theatre in Japan
- performances usually given outside at a Shinto Shrine or Buddhist temple
- slow dance drama with precise movements
- all actors are men
- stage is always a backdrop of a single pine tree painted on the wall
- directly following a Noh play or between acts, kyogen sketches, which are like a comedy, are given to provide a breather from the more serious Noh
- main performers wear colorful masks.

Where and When

Hosho Noh Theatre..3811–4843
Sobu line or Toei Mita line to Suidobashi.
Kanze Noh Theater 3469–5241
Shibuya, Hachikoguchi exit. 1–16–4 Shoto. Shibuya–ku.
Kita Noh Gakudo Meguro 3491–7773
Occasional performances with ticket prices ranging from ¥3,000–¥10,000.
National Noh Theatre 3423–1331
Sobu line to Sendagaya.
Tessenkai Noh Butai Omotesando 3401–2285
One or two performances a month. Tickets range from ¥2,500–¥5,000.
Yarai NohGakudo 3268–7311
Tozai line to Kagurazaka. Yaraiguchi exit. 60 Yaraicho, Shinjuku–ku.

Of special interest to those who would like to see something really neat is Takigi–Noh. It is a kind of Noh play performed outdoors on an open stage lit up by flaming torches. A really exotic kind of effect and great for taking pictures of the *real* Japan to send home.

Schedules and reservations become available in May. Call the T.I.C. at 3502–1461 for further information. It's performed usually at these three spots:

1. Koganei Park
2. Kie Shrine in Akasaka
3. Zojoji Temple in Shiba

STUDYING JAPANESE

Personally, I think you're crazy to come all this way and not study at a Japanese school or privately with a tutor, even if you stay only one year. Knowing some Japanese helps enormously to facilitate not just your daily life at the Post Office, Police box, supermarket and restaurant, but with your teaching, especially children. Don't be fooled by some long term residents who profess with pride their number of years in Japan learning only enough to say "Thank you" and "Good–bye." It depends on your personality and whether you've ever studied a foreign language before, but proficiency comes fast to those who make a little effort.

Knowing Japanese will help you with your students' names, food at restaurants, and directions when you're lost. Even ordering a pizza is kind of awkward without the correct Japanese pronunciation of "ma shoe room u" (mushroom) or "tay koo out toe" (take out), not to mention your address!

Think about your future job prospects at home too. Any knowledge of the second largest economy in the world, and the Asian leader, can't hurt your résumé no matter what job you apply for. Plus, you never really know how long you'll stay in Japan, and getting started early learning Japanese won't make you regret your lost time later.

Complete mastery would take a lifetime but a couple of months of everyday study will give you the basics and an appetite to study further. Of course, any Japanese you can learn before you come is extra icing on the cake. A point to remember, as my father always told me, "education is never lost or wasted." What Japanese you learn, you'll use – believe me.

Locating a School

Finding a school is easy, but make sure it suits your needs. Most schools offer a free trial lesson, and if they don't, think to yourself, what are they hiding? Ask your fellow teachers for some school names or check *The Japan Times* Classified, *The Tokyo Journal,* or the list at the end of this section.

Some points to ponder before you plunk down your cash should be:

1. How much for tuition, registration, books, etc?
2. How far is the school from your house and your work?
3. When are the lessons? (Morning or afternoon being the easiest for you.)
4. How many students max. per class?
5. What book do they use?
6. Is it the same teacher every time?
7. Can you get credit for another lesson later if you're sick one day?
8. Do they have a language lab or tapes?
9. Do they offer visa sponsorship in case you need it now or in the future?

10. How long are classes and what days of the week?
11. How long does the course last? Is it intensive or weekly?

NOTE: ONE SCHOOL I ALWAYS SEE ADVERTISED IN THE JAPAN TIMES OFFERS
ECONOMICAL STUDY OF SEVERAL FOREIGN LANGUAGES. THEIR NAME IS SLS.
GIVE THEM A CALL TO FIND OUT WHICH DAY AND TIME THEY ARE TAUGHT.
FRENCH, GERMAN, SPANISH, AND JAPANESE LESSONS: 3 HOUR BLOCKS ONCE A
WEEK FOR ¥7,000/MONTH. CALL 3359–3661.

List of Japanese Language Schools

There must be over 500 Japanese language schools in Japan. Most are
located in Tokyo, but every city would have at least one school offering
instruction. By no means is this list complete. I can't vouch for any of these
schools except for ICT and Zeus. My wife and I study at Zeus occasionally
because the staff is very good and extremely helpful. They always go out of
their way to accommodate us, even on Sundays. They also have intensive
courses at very reasonable prices which is why we started to study there in the
first place. I study privately at ICT because the tuition is cheap and the location
convenient. Each school has its own methods and materials, so go for a free
trial lesson first and then decide later.

Academy of Language Arts 3235–0071
  Daini–Tobundo Bldg., 2–16, Ageba–cho, Shinjuku–ku, Tokyo 162
Aoyama School of Japanese 3465–9577
  1–30–17, Tomigaya, Shibuya–ku, Tokyo 151
ATI Japanese Language School 3778–1931
  3–3–4, Ohi, Shinagawa–ku, Tokyo 140
Bunka Institute of Language 3299–2014
  3–22–1, Yoyogi, Shibuya–ku, Tokyo 151
Bunsai Institute of Foreign Languages 3385–3851
  1–4–10, Koenji–Kita, Suginami–ku, Tokyo 166
East West Institute of Foreign Languages (Inage School)
 043–243–7611
  18–10, Inagedai–machi, Chiba–shi, Chiba 281
East West Japanese Language Institute 3366–4717
  2–36–9, Chuo, Nakano–ku, Tokyo 164
Fuji Academy 3203–1201
  541, Tsurumaki–cho, Waseda, Shinjuku–ku, Tokyo 162
Future Language Institute 3630–2203
  3–10–6, Kiyosumi, Koto–ku, Tokyo 135
Gateway Language School 3812–5431
  6–19–14, Hongo, Bunkyo–ku, Tokyo 113
ICT Institute of Japanese Language 3866–9461
  2–27–24, Higashi–Nihombashi, Chuo–ku, Tokyo 103
International Conversation Center Japanese Institute 3985-0423
  Shikano Bldg., 3–16–4, Takada, Toshima–ku, Tokyo 171

Japan College of Foreign Languages 3200–4011
Japanese Division, 1–28–6, Takadanobaba, Shinjuku–ku, Tokyo 169
Japanese Culture and Language Institute (JCLI) 3348–7601
2–1–1, Nishi–Shinjuku, Shinjuku–ku, Tokyo 163
Japanese Language Center 3403–3186
3–8–40, Minami–Aoyama, Minato–ku, Tokyo 107
Japanese Language School 3984–1951
3–32–7 Takada, Toshima–ku, Tokyo 171
Japanese Language School 3205–8101
(affiliated with Tokyo International University)
1–32–14, Takadanobaba, Shinjuku–ku, Tokyo 169
Japanese Language School International Students 3371–7268
3–22–7, Kita–Shinjuku, Shinjuku–ku, Tokyo 169
Japanese School Tokyo Foreign Language Academy 3966–8910
3–19–21, Ukima, Kita–ku, Tokyo 115
JET Academy 3916–2101
7–8–9, Takinogawa, Kita–ku, Tokyo 114
KAI Japanese Language School 3205–1356
1–15–18, Ookubo, Shinjuku–ku, Tokyo 169
Kanda Institute of Foreign Languages 3258–5838
2–13–13, Uchikanda, Chiyoda–ku, Tokyo 101
Kawaijuku International Education Center 3350–7681
5–2–13, Sendagaya, Shibuya–ku, Tokyo 151
Kokusai Kyoiku Gakuin Nippon–go Institute .... (0473)51–3411
1, Akemi, Urayasu–shi, Chiba 279
Kokusai Sogo Gakuin Japanese Language School 3265–2466
Haratetsu Bldg., 4–1–11, Kudan–kita, Chiyoda–ku, Tokyo 102
Kudan Institute of Language and Culture 3239–7923
Sunlight Bldg., 3–2–1, Jimbo–cho, Kanda, Chiyoda–ku, Tokyo 101
Mejiro International School of Japan 3951–0300
3–17–24, Mejiro, Toshima–ku, Tokyo 171
Musashi Language Center 3932–6144
4–25–2, Tokiwadai, Itabashi–ku, Tokyo 174
New Global Language School 3770–6071
1–7–10, Ohashi, Meguro–ku, Tokyo 153
Oji Japanese Language School 3914–5753
1–30–2, Oji, Kita–ku, Tokyo 114
Sankei International College Nihongo Center 3716–4111
2–19–17, Takaban, Meguro–ku, Tokyo 152
Shibuya Language School 3461–8854
15–15, Sakuragaoka–machi, Shibuya–ku, Tokyo 150
Shingaku International School 3461–8854
56–2, Miyamoto–cho, Itabashi–ku, Tokyo 174
Shinjuku Japanese Language Institute 5273–0044
2–9–7, Takadanobaba, Shinjuku–ku, Tokyo 169

Sony Language Laboratory Shinbashi School 3504–1356
    Kurihara Bldg., 1—6–12, Nishi–Shinbashi, Minato–ku, Tokyo 105
Sundai Japanese Language School 5259–3181
    3–28–3, Kanda–Ogawa–machi, Chiyoda–ku, Tokyo 101
Sunshine Language School 3987–1921
    Sunshine Bldg., 3–1–1, Higashi–Ikebukuro, Toshima–ku, Tokyo 170
Tokyo Central Japanese Language School 3204–6030
    Fuji Bldg., 2–7–1, Ohkubo, Shinjuku, Tokyo 169
Tokyo Foreign Language College 3367–1101
    7–3–8, Nishi–Shinjuku, Shinjuku–ku, Tokyo 160
Tokyo International Japanese School 3350–9761
    2–5–12, Shinjuku, Shinjuku–ku, Tokyo 160
Tokyo International Language College .... (0492) 61–3275
    1–5–4, Kitano, Kami–Fukuoka–shi, Saitama 356
Tokyo Language School (Ohkubo Branch) 3366–4461
    1–21–24, Hyakunin–cho, Shinjuku–ku, Tokyo 169
Tokyo Language School Shinjuku Campus 3350–0317
    5–3–19, Shinjuku, Shinjuku–ku, Tokyo 160
Tokyo School of the Japanese Language 3463–7261
    16–26, Nanpeidai–machi, Shibuya–ku, Tokyo 150
Tokyo Waseda Japanese School 3205–6021
    62, Babashita–cho, Shinjuku-ku, Tokyo 162
Tsukuba Gakuin Japanese Language School 5609–0721
    4–7–16, Hirai, Edogawa–ku, Tokyo 132
Waseda Japanese School 3318–6218
    4–45–2, Koenji–Minami, Suginami–ku, Tokyo 166
West Coast Language School 3759–5831
    35–13, Higashimine–machi, Ohta–ku, Tokyo 145
WIZ Language Institute 3779–5951
    1–20–8, Ohsaki, Shinagawa–ku, Tokyo 141
Yoshida Institute of Japanese Language 3202–0828
    1–23–14, Nishi–Waseda, Shinjuku–ku, Tokyo 169
Zeus Institute of Languages 3362–2321
    Daikan City 2F, 7–20–16 Nishi Shinjuku, Shinjuku–ku, Tokyo

NOTE: IF YOU CAN'T FIND ON ECLOSE, OR LIVE IN A DIFFERENT CITY, CALL THE TOURIST
           OFFICE NEAREST YOU. SEE LIST UNDER T.I.C.

Studying at a Japanese University

    As most people don't come to Japan to study at a university, I'll just
mention that there are English Institutions which offer everything you'd find
back home. However, Japanese university students are notorious partyers,
their four years representing the only free time they've had.
    Academically, there aren't many (if there ever were) Nobel Prize winners
coming from Japanese university programs. Students are expected to support
and verify their professors' own theses, thus discouraging personal research.

Skipping classes is rampant, especially the last year when future graduates start visiting companies as early as August to try to secure a job before graduation the following year in March. Most students also belong to several leisure clubs and hold down a part time job as well. Late night drinking parties also hinder studying.

My suggestion is if you want to make some new friends and have a good time, go for it, but your credits or degree won't cut you much prestige or even transfer credits back home unless you just concentrate on taking Japanese language courses.

Of course, there are several universities in Tokyo that teach in English and are not included in my brief summary. If I receive any positive feedback from readers who want this kind of information in my second edition, I'll definitely add it. For now, you can go to your local university and research such info yourself.

TOURS OF JAPANESE INDUSTRIES

For those of you who are curious about exactly how the Japanese have achieved their economic miracle, there are several industrial tours available to satisfy your curiosity. You can visit: a car factory, a brewery, a newspaper company, a television station, the Stock Exchange or even traditional industries such as kimono dying, silk weaving, pottery or woodblock making. The Japanese National Tourist Office (JNTO) states "while there's usually no fee or admission charge, these factories request visitors to observe certain rules and conditions," which basically means, no picture taking. Call The JNTO (3502–1461) if you have a particular interest and the business is not listed here. Again, I'd like to acknowledge the T.I.C. for a copy of their excellent pamphlet explaining how to find a tour to Japanese Industries.

Key to the Listings:
1. Name of Company
2. Address of factory
3. Access to factory
4. Hours open to visitors
5. How to apply
6. Where to apply
7. Tour length
8. English: yes or no
9. Restrictions

Automobile Manufacturing
1. **Toyota Motor Corporation**
2. Assembly Factories
   Motomachi Plant: .... 1 Motomachi, Toyota–shi, Aichi Pref.
   Takaoka Plant:......................... 1 Sanko, Honda–cho, Toyota–shi, Aichi Pref.
   Tsutsumi Plant:....... 1 Umanokashira, Tsutsumi–cho, Toyota–shi, Aichi Pref.

English Factories
Kamigo Plant: .... 1 Taise–cho,Toyota–shi, Aichi Pref.

3. 10 min walk from Mikawa Toyota station on Aichi Kanjo Railway, or 20 min by Meitetsu Bus from Meitetsu Toyota–shi station.
4. 9–12pm and 1–5pm, Mon through Fri, English tour at 1pm.
5. Apply by phone. If OK, send a letter specifying the date you want, names, nationality, number of visitors, and purpose of your visit.
6. Public relations Dept., Toyota Motor Corporation: 1 Toyota–cho, Toyota–shi, Aichi Pref.
7. 2 hrs. 30 min. (30 min for film presentation, 30 min at exhibition hall, 60 min at assembly line and 30 min flex time)
8. English speaking staff available.
9. Photography and smoking not allowed.

1. **Nissan Motor Co., Ltd.**
2. Oppama Plant: 1 Natsushima–cho, Yokosuka–shi, Kanagawa Pref.
3. 10 min by bus from Oppama station on Keihin Kyuko Line.
4. 10am–12pm and 1:30–3:30pm, Mon through Fri in Japanese. English–guided tour is at 10am–12pm on Tuesday. Except mid–August, late December to early January.
5. Apply by phone. If you want an English guided tour on another day, request by letter two months in advance.
6. International Corporate Communications Dept., Nissan Motor Co., Ltd: 6–17–1, Ginza, Chuo–ku Tokyo. Tel: 5565–2149 (direct). Fax: 3546–2669
7. 2 hrs. (30 min for introductory presentation, 60 min at assembly line, 30 min for questions and answers).
8. English speaking personnel available.
9. Children under 11, photography, smoking and high–heeled shoes are not permitted.

1. **Mazda Corporation**
2. 3–1, Shinchi, Fuchu–cho, Aki–gun, Hiroshima Pref.
3. 5 min walk from JR Mukainada station.
4. 9:30am–12pm and 1–3pm, Mon through Fri.
5. Apply by phone.
6. General Affairs Dept., Mazda Corporation: 3–1, Shinchi, Fuchu–cho, Aki gun, Hirochima Pref., Tel: (082) 286–5700 (direct).
7. 1 hr. 30 min.
8. English–guided tour is available.
9. Photography and smoking are prohibited in the plant.

Brewery

1. **KIRIN Brewery Corporated**
2. Tokyo Plant:: 4–2–51, Horifune, Kita–ku, Tokyo
   Kyoto Plant: 126, Takada–cho, Kuze, Minami–ku, Kyoto

3. Tokyo Plant:: In front of Arakawa Shakomae Sta. of Toden Arakawa line. Kyoto Plant: 15 min walk from JR Muko–machi Sta., or 5 min by taxi from Hankyu Katsura sta.
4. Tokyo Plant:: 10am–, 10:30am–, 1:30pm–, 2pm–, 2:30pm–, Mon through Fri.
   Kyoto Plant: 9am–, 10:30am, 1pm–, 2pm–, Mon through Fri.
5. Apply in Japanese by phone as soon as possible before your visit, at least, two weeks ahead of the date of your intended visit.
6. Tokyo Plant .... General Affairs Section: Tel. 3927–7287.
   Kyoto Plant .... General Affairs Section: Tel. (075) 921–8111.
7. 1 hr. 30 min. (including beer sampling)
8. No English speaking guides.
9. In both plants, photography and smoking are prohibited. In the Kyoto Plant there are tons of staircases, so get in shape.

Broadcasting

1. **NHK Broadcasting Center**
2. 2–2–1, Jinnan, Shibuya–ku, Tokyo
3. 10 min walk from JR Shibuya sta., Harajuku sta., or Meiji Jingu–mae sta.
4. 10am–4:30pm except on the 4th Mon.
5. Booking is required for a group of 20 or more.
6. Tel. 3465–1111, ext. 6981.
7. 40 min.
8. No English speaking guides.

1. **NHK Broadcasting Osaka Station**
2. 3–43, Banba–cho, Chuo–ku, Osaka.
3. 5 min walk from Tanimachi Yonchome sta., Exit No. 7, Chuo subway line.
4. 10am–5pm, Mon–Fri, 10am–12 noon on Sat.
5. Booking is required for a group of 20 or more.
6. Tel. (06) 941–0431.
7. 30 min–1 hr.
8. No English speaking guides.
9. Flash photography not permitted in the studio.

Ceramics

1. **Noritake Co., Ltd.**
2. 1–1, Noritake–Shinmachi, Nishi–ku, Nagoya.
3. 15 min, walk from JR Nagoya Sta.
4. Two tours: 10am–, 1pm–, Mon–Fri.
5. Apply by phone.
6. Welcome center, Noritake Co., Ltd., tel. (052) 562–5072 (direct).
7. 1 hr 30 min.
8. English speaking guides available.

9.   Interestingly, people employed in the same industry are not allowed in. Smoking and flash photography are prohibited.

Computer and Home Electronics

1.   **NEC Showroom C and C Plaza**
2.   Hibiya Kokusai Bldg., 2–2–3, Uchisaiwaicho, Chiyoda–ku, Tokyo 100.
3.   In front of Uchisaiwaicho Subway station on the Toei Mita Line, or 5 min walk from JR Shimbashi sta., or Shimbashi sta. on the Ginza Line or Toei Asakusa Line.
4.   10am–6pm
5.   No need for advance booking.
6.   Not applicable.
7.   30–60 min.
8.   English speaking guides are available.

1.   **Toshiba Science Institute**
2.   1 Komukai–Toshiba–cho, Saiwai–ku, Kawasaki–shi, Kanagawa Pref.
3.   10 min by bus from stop #23 or #24 in front of the east exit of JR Kawasaki station.
4.   9am–5pm, Mon–Fri.
5.   Apply by phone, preferably a few days ahead.
6.   Tel. (044) 511–2300.
7.   1 hr.
8.   English speaking guides are available.

Distillery

1.   **Suntory Ltd. Hakushu Distillery**
2.   Torihara, Hakushu–cho, Kitakoma–gun, Yamanashi Pref.
3.   20 min by taxi from JR Kobuchizawa Sta.
4.   10am–, 11am–, 1pm–, 2pm–, 3pm–, daily.
5.   Apply in Japanese by phone.
6.   PR Dept., Suntory Ltd. Hakushu Distillery: Tel. (0551) 35–2211. (direct)
7.   1 hr. 20 min. (includes a free whiskey sampling)
8.   If you reserve one month in advance, English speaking guides are available.
9.   Photography and smoking are prohibited.

Newspapers

1.   **The Asahi Shimbun**
2.   5–3–2, Tsukiji, Chuo–ku, Tokyo.
3.   10 min walk from Tsukiji Subway station. on the Hibiya subway line.
4.   Three one–hour tours daily starting at 11am, 1 and 2:30pm except 1st and 3rd Sat, Sun and National Holidays.
5.   Apply by phone at least 3 days in advance.
6.   Tel. 3545–0366.

7. 1 hr.
8. English speaking guides are available.
9. Photography in Editorial and Production Departments is not allowed.

Stock Exchange

1. **Tokyo Stock Exchange**
2. 2–1, Kabuto–cho, Nihombashi, Chuo–ku, Tokyo.
3. 5 min walk from Kayabacho subway station on the Hibiya or Tozai Line.
4. 9am–4pm, Mon–Fri except National Holidays. English guides are available at 9:30–10:30am and 1:30–2:30pm.
5. For a guided tour, call a few days in advance.
6. Office of Public Relations (Visitor's section) tel.3666–0141.
7. 1 hr.
8. English speaking personnel available.
9. Flash photography and smoking are not permitted.

Winery

1. **Suntory Yamanashi Winery**
2. 2786 Onuta, Futaba–cho, Kitakoma–gun, Yamanashi Pref., 407-01.
3. 30 min by taxi from JR Kofu Sta.
4. 9:30am–3:30pm daily.
5. Apply in Japanese by phone, 9–12pm, 1–5pm except Sun and National Holidays.
6. For reservation, tel. (0551) 28–3232.
7. 30 min in the factory.
8. No English speaking guides.
9. Photography and smoking are not permitted in the factory.

Traditional Industries

Many craftsmen's skills have been handed down through the generations. The following is a brief listing of places in Kyoto where you can catch a glimpse of artists at work.

Yuzen Cultural Hall Nishi–kyogoku station on the Hankyu Line. Demonstrations of a 300 year old Yuzen kimono dyeing technique. Open 9am–5pm (last admission, 4pm). Closed on Mon. Admission: ¥310.
Nishijin Textile Museum Horikawa–Imadegawa bus stop. Has a collection of Nishijin products and gives a demonstration of silk–weaving. Open daily 9am–5pm. Admission: free except for a kimono show (¥210).
Kyoto Handicraft Center Kumano–Jinja–mae bus stop. Retail cooperative of Kyoto's leading shops of handicrafts. You can watch artists make pottery, silks, damascene, lacquerware, woodblock prints, and dolls. Open daily from 9:30am–6pm (Mar–Nov), 9:30am–5:30pm (Dec–Feb).

Inaba Cloisonne Sanjo station on the Keihan Line. Retailer/manufacturer of cloisonne accessories and crafts. Open daily from 9am–5:30pm. Closed Sun and National Holidays.

Kyoto Municipal Museum of Traditional Industry Kyoto–Kaikan–Bijutsukan–mae bus stop. Exhibits handicrafts made of silk, bamboo, lacquer, hand–made paper, and ceramics. Open daily 9am–5pm except on Mon. Admission: Free.

SHOPPING

Department stores are open from 10am to 6 or 7pm and are closed one day of the week (see list for the exact schedule). Some stores have maps to guide you once you enter, but it's best for the first time to just go in and wander around to get a feel for all the goods they carry. Just about everything you can think of will be on one of the floors. These stores really are one–stop shopping locations. Get there at the opening and you'll be greeted by several pretty, young, bowing, Japanese ladies thanking you in advance for being their honored customer.

Food goods are always in the basement, and the bargain floor is at the top just before the restaurants and the beer gardens. Beer gardens are a great place to relax and people watch in the summer time (June, July, and August).

One small note of interest here about the plastic replicas of food you'll see in many of the restaurants around. You can buy these novelty items near Kappabashi area near Tawaramachi subway station on the Ginza line. There you will find all kinds of stores selling basically the same plastic displays.

Useful Phrases

1. Ikura desu ka?
   How much is it?
2. Kore kudasai.
   I'll take it.
3. Takai desu.
   It's expensive.
4. Sumimasen, _____ wa doko desu ka?
   Excuse me, where are the _____?

Conversion Tables

The shoe and clothing size used in Japan are sometimes different from those used in America, England and Europe. To avoid confusion, check out the following charts:

Men

Men's Suits, Overcoats and Sweaters

Japan	S		M		L		LL
USA	34	36	38	40	42	44	46
UK	34	36	38	40	42	44	46
Europe	44	46	48	50	52	54	56

Jacket

Japan	A4	A5	A6	A7	AB4	AB5	AB6	AB7
USA/UK	36ES	37S	38S	39R	38ES	39S	40S	41R
Europe	44–6	46–6	48–6	50–6	44–4	46–4	48–4	50–4

Shirts and Collars

Japan	36	37	38	39	40	41	42
USA/UK	14	14 .5	15	15.5	16	16.5	17
Europe	36	37	38	39	40	41	42

Men's Shoes

Japan	24	25	26	26.5	27.5	28	29
USA	5.5	6.5	7.5	8.5	9.5	10.5	11.5
UK	5	6	7	8	9	10	11
Europe	39	40	41	42	43	44	45

Women

Women's Dresses and Suits

Japan	9	11	13	15	17	19	21
U.S.A	10	12	14	16	18	20	22
UK	32	34	36	38	40	42	44
Europe	38	40	42	44	46	48	50

Women's Shoes

Japan	22.5	23	23.5	24	24.5	25	25.5	26
USA/UK	4.5	5.5	6	6.5	7.5	8.5	9	10
Europe	34	35	36	37	38	39	40	41

Weights and Measures

Length

cm	m	km	inch	foot	yard	mile
1	0.0100	——	0.3937	0.0328	0.0109	——
100	1	0.001	39.370	3.2808	1.0936	0.0006
100000	1000.0	1	39370	3280.8	1093.6	0.6214
2.5399	0.0254	——	1	0.0833	0.0277	——
30.479	0.3047	——	12	1	0.333	——
91.440	0.9144	——	36	3	1	——
——	1609.3	1.6093	——	——	——	1

Weight

g	kg	ounce	pound
1	0.001	0.035	0.00220
1000	1	35.274	2.205
28.35	0.028	1	0.063
453.59	0.454	16	1

Gifts

Usually, good teachers receive presents from their students during the summer gift giving season and in the winter gift giving season. They are called *Ochugen* and *Oseibo*. Don't get into the habit of gift giving as you're likely to obligate that person into reciprocating with a more expensive gift that they cannot afford. The Japanese will keep score as to who gave what and how much it might have cost.

My advice is to just accept the gift with two hands and say "Arigato." Sometimes ignorance is bliss.

If you do want to get someone something, it's a good idea to buy them some local food on one of your trips to Kyoto or elsewhere as this is very common and easy to do. Naturally, if the gift is for someone really special, gifts from your home country will be warmly received.

Souvenirs of Japanese Crafts

In case you ever need some Japanese Christmas presents or birthday gifts, you can usually get what you need at the airport for about the same price you'd pay elsewhere. However, the larger department stores do have a section devoted just to souvenirs and probably you'll find more selection there. Check out the list of Major Shopping Stores listed further on. I've listed three of the best touristy stores below:

Oriental Bazaar... 3400–3933
The best with all kinds of Asian stuff. Yamanote line to Harajuku stop, or subway to Omotesando. A1 exit. Open 9:30am–6:30pm. Closed every Thur.

Prefectural Shopping Arcade..3212–8011
9th floor of the Tokyo Daimaru Department store. They've got 11 different shops from across Japan loaded with dolls, crafts and foods. What they don't have in stock you can order through their mail–order catalogues. JR lines to Tokyo Station. Yaesu Chuo Exit. Open 9am–5pm. Closed Wed, 2nd and 4th Sat, Sun and holidays.

International Shopping Arcade 3591–9826
If you want inexpensive trinket–type stuff, go here. Subways to Ginza Station, C1 exit. Open every day 10am–6:30pm.

Tax–Free Shopping

If you plan to buy a video camera or anything else on this list, do it while you still have your tourist or working holiday visa and you'll save yourself the 3% consumption tax for purchases over ¥10,000. For us Canadians stuck with the G.S.T. and P.S.T. (a 15% or 16% tax in some provinces) it's nice to pay the sticker price for a change.

Tax–free shopping is available at any of the stores where a 'Tax–Free' sign is placed at the entrance. These include shops in hotel arcades, specialty stores and the major department stores. When you buy tax–free goods, just show your passport. You'll get a certificate entitled, *Record of Purchase of Commodities Tax–Exempt for Export*, which must be shown at the Customs Office when you leave Japan. Tax–free rates vary from 5% to 40%, depending on the item. Sample Tax Free articles are listed below:

1. Articles made of or decorated with precious stones or semiprecious stones.
2. Pearls and articles made of, or decorated, with pearls.
3. Articles made of precious metals, decorated with gold or platinum and plated or covered with precious metals.
4. Articles made of tortoise shell, coral, amber and ivory.
5. Cloisonné ware.
6. Furs.
7. Hunting guns.
8. Household implements made of fiber.
9. Portable TV sets.
10. Record players and stereo equipment.
11. Radio sets.
12. Magnetic tape recorders.
13. Cameras, movie cameras and projectors, including parts and accessories.
14. Slide projectors.
15. Watches.
16. Articles used in smoking.

NOTE: IF YOU HAVE LIVED IN JAPAN FOR A LONG TIME AND HAVE A WORK VISA, YOU ARE OUT OF LUCK.

DEPARTMENT STORES

Below I've listed the major department stores in the Tokyo and Yokohama areas. Stores are normally open from 10am until 6 or 7pm. All stores are closed one day a week. If known, the closed day appears in brackets.

Tokyo

Daimaru, Tokyo Station (Wed)..3212–8011
Hankyu, Yurakucho (Thur)..3575–2233
Isetan
    Shinjuku (Wed) 3352–1111

Kichijoji (Wed)	0422–21–1111
Foreign Customer Service	3225–2514
Keio, Shinjuku (Thur)	3342–2111
Matsuya, Ginza (Tue)	3567–1211
Matsuzakaya	
Ginza (Wed)	3572–1111
Ueno (Wed)	3832–1111
Mitsukoshi	
Nihombashi (Mon)	3241–3311
Chiba (Mon)	043–224–3131
Ginza (Mon)	3562–1111
Shinjuku (Mon)	3354–1111
Ikebukuro (Mon)	3987–1111
Odakyu, Shinjuku (Tue)	3342–1111
Seibu	
Ikebukuro (Tue)	5992–0394
Shibuya (Wed)	3462–0111
Foreign Liaison Office	3462–3848
Yurakucho (Wed)	3286–0111
Foreign Liaison Office	3286–5482
Takashimaya, Nihombashi (Wed)	3709–3111
Tokyu, Shibuya (Tue)	3477–3111
Tokyu Hands	
Shibuya (2nd and 3rd Wed)	5489–5111
Ikebukuro (2nd and 3rd Wed)	3980–6111

Yokohama

Matsuzakaya (Wed)	045–261–2121
Mitsukoshi (Mon)	045–312–1111
Sogo (Tue)	045–465–2111
Takashimaya (Wed)	045–311–1251

SHOPPING AREAS
Tokyo

Akihabara	Electronics and appliances.
Aoyama	Fashion in the medium to expensive range.
Asakusa	Traditional Japanese products. Here's where Japanese from the 'country' buy their Tokyo souvenirs.
Ginza	Expensive shopping. Major department stores and many exclusive boutiques. Outrageously expensive. Gotta see it to believe it.
Harajuku	Fashion area for the upscale 'young' set.
Kanda	Books, antiques, and old print shops. Also has lots of martial arts and sporting goods shops.

Kappabashi	Wholesale restaurant supplies. Plastic food models like in all the restaurants in Japan.
Nihombashi	Well known for its older shops which specialize in traditional crafts.
Shibuya	Fashion shopping for the 'young' set. Good 'Love Hotel' area.
Shinjuku	Cameras and electronic goods.
Ueno	Many discount shops.

Yokohama

Chinatown	Unique gift items.
Motomachi	Discount shopping area.
Yokohama Station	Major department stores.

DISCOUNT SHOPS

Most stores which carry the label 'discount' are not the same as in North America. One of the things you'll have to get used to in a hurry in Tokyo (or Japan for that matter) are the exorbitant prices. Frequently, there are sales of up to 50% off, but with your busy schedule it's hard to know when and where. By the time you find out sale–hungry, battle–hardened housewives have snapped up the best merchandise already.

SUPERMARKETS

They're everywhere and you'll recognize one when you see it. However there are some special Western supermarkets that cater to foreigners located in the Tokyo metropolitan area. They stock all your favorite goodies from home: ravioli, Swiss cheese, Canadian, American, British and Australian beer, and Oreo cookies.

There's National Azabu Supermarket located near Hiroo subway station on the Hibiya line, or Meidiya supermarket in the Ginza, Roppongi, and also in Hiroo. I recommend a trip to one of these stores after a few months just to treat yourself and also because it is such a busy, pretty area. Benten's Supermarket in Shinjuku (16–2 Wakamatsu–cho) will send you a catalogue so you can shop by phone. Call them at 3202–2421.

HEALTH FOOD
Stores

Where can I get all my natural food stuff, you ask? Look no further. Voila! If you can't get it at your local grocery store or basement department store food section, call these shops. Call the JR info line (3423–0111) on how to get to the stations listed, then ask at the Police Box once you arrive. All stores are close to the station.

Alpha 3889-2651
American Nutrition B.O. Okada Inc. (Kobe) 078-231-3464
    Over 80 general nutritional vitamins and minerals by mail order.
Green Foods 3704-5191
Horiuchi 3370-3357
Koiwa Natural Food Center (Koiwa).. 3658–2875
Natural House, Aoyama Branch (Akasaka) 3589-1070
Organic Foods Shop Yui (Asagaya)..3337–2241
Pure Foods Square, Tenmi (Shibuya) 3496–7100
Sunray 3639-2530
Tengu Natural Foods 0429-74-3036
    Western style natural foods by mail. Call for a free catalogue.
Waseda Natural Foods (Wasada).. 3202–9611

Health Food Restaurants

Not a lot to choose from, but they should be able to satisfy you. Unfortunately, if you're a confirmed vegetarian, you're out of luck because a lot of Japanese dishes use meat. Nevertheless, tofu, vegetables, salads, rice, noodles, fruit and dairy products should hold you over. To get a really good meal you just might have to cook it yourself. Check *The Tokyo Journal* for a list of all restaurants available.

Health Drinks

Small, dark colored, little bottles of potent concoctions are all the rage here in Japan. Overworked salarymen guzzle these expensive pick–me–ups to the tune of over ¥100 billion ($870 million) per year. The industry even predicts a strong 20–30% increase due to the higher number of women entering the workforce emulating their peers. The drinks are touted to cure or induce one, all, or a combination of the following:

1. tiredness
2. hangovers
3. stiff shoulders
4. stress
5. increased blood circulation.

Two famous brands contain: nicotine, cocaine, atrophine, and morphine, all derived from seed plants designed to stimulate nerves throughout your body. The best though, has got to be 'Yusugen King' which adds snake oil extract and Korean ginseng. The result is a powerful aphrodisiac (or so the company swears!) that sells for ¥3,000 per 50 ml bottle. That's just a little more than a one ounce shot of liquor.

Most of the other brands, however, are so chock full of white sugar and caffeine they'd kill a mouse. Some of the low end drinks under ¥500 contain the equivalent of five teaspoons of white sugar! Surely the health benefits of any vitamins these drinks contain are negated by all this sugar, not to mention the overload of caffeine.

Kenko Inryo (health drinks) are marketed intensively with big name Japanese celebrities. Arnold Schwarzenegger even plugs a cheap drink relentlessly on T.V. and posters. I wonder if the Fitness Council of America, of which he was president, would approve? Really, I mean, did he need this crap to become Mr. Universe five times?

Anyway, my purpose here is not to scare, only to inform you about what's inside these 'health' drinks so you're aware of what you're ingesting. Try a few out, I did, but just don't slug'em back everyday thinking you're doing your body any favors. You've gotta admit, they'll make a great conversation piece or souvenir back home!

BARGAIN FOOD BY MAIL
Foreign Buyers Club (FBC)

The ultimate in personal shopping for foreign food exists in the Foreign Buyers Club, a non profit, co–op type, California–based importer. They offer between 1,500 to 2,000 items. However, orders are by the case, so get together with friends to divide up the goods. Call Chuck or Kelly Graft to order a copy of their main, 21 page catalog. Other specialty catalogs at ¥200 a piece are (1) Baby Stuff, (2) Vegetarian and Health Nut Catalog, (3) Coffees and Teas, and (4) Vitamins.

They've got all the great stuff like Kellogg's, All Bran, Pop Tarts, Chef Boy–Ar–Dee, dried fruit, Del Monte, Green Giant, and more. Deadlines for orders are the first and third Fridays of each month. You can pay by *furikae* or *denshin furikae* (see Post Office section). With your first order, include an extra ¥1,000 to join for 12 months. Delivery to Tokyo costs ¥500 per case and it takes about six weeks to arrive. As soon as you order by phone or by fax, FBC will send you a receipt along with the expected arrival date.

FBC   tel: 078–221–2591
       fax: 078–222–3206

> FBC
> 4–20–5 Yamamoto Dori
> Chuo–ku,
> Kobe 650

USED ARTICLES

There are many ways to furnish an apartment, so always keep your eyes and ears open. A lot of stuff is just as good used as it is new, especially here in Japan. If your neighborhood "GOMI" (garbage area) doesn't prove fruitful, and you're always too late for the good articles in the Sunday edition of *The Daily Yomiuri,* try your luck at one of these used shops below. If you're looking for something in particular, have a Japanese person call ahead. You may save yourself an unnecessary trip.

Antiques

The perfect place to pick up old Japanese goods at a reduced price. Personally, this area is not my specialty, but I'm sure some readers will find this list excellent. Give them a call in Japanese for directions and commence hunting.

Antique Gallery (Meguro) 3493-1971
Antiques Twenty (Nishi Azabu) 3404-4085
Fuso Trading Co. Ltd., (Hiroo)...3442–1945
Gallery Fuso (Kamata)...3730-6530
Harumi Antiques (Roppongi)...3403–1043
Hasebe-ya Antiques (Azabu)...3401-9998
Iidabashi Antique Market (Iidabashi.)...3235–0181
Japan Sword (Toranomon)...3434-4321
Kathy Milan Antiques (Hiroo) 3408–1532
Kensington Market (Tsukishima) 3536-4431
Nakamura Antiques (Hiroo)..3486–0636
Okura Oriental Art (Azabudai) 3585-5309
Roppongi Antique Market (Roppongi)..3583–2081
Togo Antique Market (Meiji–jingumae)...3425–7965

Flea Markets

If you couldn't find what you were looking for at the Antique Markets, you might give the flea markets a try. You'd be surprised by what the Japanese consider garbage. For example, a friend of ours loves the little Japanese dolls in the glass cases and she found tons for around ¥3,000 to ¥5,000 at the Salvation Army Bazaar in Nakano. Flea Markets come and go so I can't list them all. However, the one in Yoyogi Park will always be here as it is Japan's largest. It is located on the Yamanote line at Harajuku station.

NOTE: FOR A COMPLETE LIST OF MONTHLY FLEA MARKETS, BUY A COPY OF *THE TOKYO JOURNAL* . THEY LIST THEM NEAR THE BACK OF THE MAGAZINE.

Used Bicycles

Nagata Shokai (Musashi–Koganei).. 0423–83–9068
Sankyo Ringyo (Hatagaya)...3377–0341

NOTE: ASK A JAPANESE PERSON TO CALL THE NEAREST POLICE STATION TO FIND OUT WHEN THEY HAVE THEIR LOST BICYCLE SALE. GREAT SECOND HAND BIKES WHICH WERE STOLEN, LOST OR FORGOTTEN SOLD AT BARGAIN PRICES.

Recycling Groups

The Citizen's Recycle Movement of Japan (English OK)................3226–6800
> They are the largest organization of their kind and hold markets at
> different locations usually every month from 10am–4pm. You can even sell
> all your unused stuff here when you take off by becoming a member. This
> includes the booth rental charge.

The Tokyo Metropolitan Public Sanitation Bureau 5320–5719
> They have furniture, electrical appliances and stuff from the garbage to
> give away by lottery. You have to live within each particular ward to take
> advantage of the lotteries. See individual ward phone numbers under the
> Local Government Offices section on page 87.

REPAIRS/HANDYMAN/DO–IT–YOURSELF

If you want to fix up your apartment or repair your bike or motorcycle,
there's a store called Tokyu Hands. They've got tools and materials for
everything. They also give free delivery to certain wards (areas) for purchases
over ¥3,000. Call in English to find out. There are 6 stores in the Tokyo area
and all are open from 10am–8pm.

Fujisawa Store (Fujisawa).. 0466–26–8735
Futako Tamagawa Store (Futako Tamagawaen)...............................3708–1211
Ikebukuro Store (Ikebukuro)...3980–6111
Machida Store (Machida) 0427–28–2511
Shibuya Store (Shibuya) 5489–5111
Yokohama Store (Yokohama) 045–320–0109

Two other stores which carry a wide range of goods are the Shibuya and
Ikebukuro Loft stores. Go and see if they've got what you need.

Shibuya Store (Loft) (Shibuya) 3462–0111
Ikebukuro Store (Loft) (Ikebukuro) 3981–0111

HAIRCUTS

I decided to put in just a few phrases to help you out when you get a
haircut or perm. You can get all the latest styles no problem, with a haircut
costing around ¥3,500.

The unique thing about getting a haircut in Japan is that they give you a
free neck and shoulder massage! One guy even twisted my neck like a
chiropractor, though he did stop before it cracked. Part of the price, so just
enjoy.

Another funny thing was they always washed my hair after they had cut it.
I always thought it was before, but "When in Rome...."

Guys who get a shave will be relieved to know that they will shave all that unwanted hair off your earlobes, forehead, between your eyebrows, and on the bridge of your nose. Now that's a real shave!

Useful Phrases

1. How much is it?
   Ikura desu ka?
2. What day are you closed?
   Nanyobi ga yasumi desu ka?
3. How late are you open?
   Nanji made yatte imasu ka?
4. Do you take appointments?
   Yoyaku dekimasu ka?
5. Please cut and perm my hair.
   Katto shite pama o kakete kudasai.
6. Please set my hair
   Setto shite kudasai.
7. Please shampoo and blowdry my hair.
   Shampu to buro o onegai shimasu.
8. Please give me a partial permanent.
   Bubun pama ni shite kudasai.
9. Please use conditioners on my hair.
   Toritomento o onegai shimasu.
10. Please color my hair
    Kezome dake ni shite kudasai.
11. Just a haircut, please.
    Katto dake ni shite kudasai.
12. Cut it short, please.
    Zentai ni mijikaku shite kudasai.
13. Overall trim, please.
    Zentai o soroete kudasai.
14. Cut without changing the present hairstyle, please
    Ima no sutairu no mama mijikaku shite kudasai
15. Trim my bangs, please.
    Maegami o mijikaku shite kudasai.
16. Part my hair on the right (left).
    Migi (Hidari) ni wakete kudasai.
17. Trim the back so it won't touch the collar, please.
    Ushiro wa eri ni tsukanaiyo ni shite kudasai.
18. Trim the sides so it won't cover my ears.
    Yoko wa mimi ni kakaranaiyo ni shite kudasai.
19. Please trim my sideburns.
    Momiage wa mijikaku shite kudasai.
20. Style my hair the same way as this picture.
    Kono shashin to onaji stairu ni shite kudasai.

21. A little shorter, please.
    Mo sukoshi mijikaku shite kudasai.
22. Do not cut it any shorter, please.
    Kore ijo kiranai de kudasai.
23. Please don't use any hair oil.
    Abura wa tsukenai de kudasai.
24. Please don't shave my beard.
    Hige wa soranai de kudasai.
25. Please shave off my whole beard.
    Hige o zenbu sotte kudasai.
26. Please trim my beard.
    Hige o soroete kudasai.

English Barbers and Beauty Salons

Haircuts are expensive but at least you don't have to tip. This section is mainly for those with specific styles or who want a permanent done. The local barber should be able to figure out your style even if he doesn't speak English. However, if you're trying for a new look or just would like to talk and give specific instructions, try one of these hair stylists out.

Both men and women should be accepted. Call first to see, and to make a reservation. Perms cost from ¥7,000 to ¥8,000. No cuts accepted one hour before closing; perms two hours before.

Aiko Yamano Beauty Salon (Akasaka) 3505-6707
Andre Bernard Hair International (Roppongi) 3404–0616
Arden Yamanaka (Hibiya) 3271–9316
Beauty Salon Magaret (Yurakucho) 3216-4771
Clara Bow (Roppongi) 3479-3868
Eton Crop (Omotesando) 3797-0139
Fashion Hair World (Akasaka).. 3588-5060
Hollywood Beauty Salon (Roppongi)...3408–1613
Koetsu (Ebisu)..3461–3171
Max Beauty Salon (Shinjuku)...3354–5211
New Hair Story (Nogizaka) 3403–6558
Panorama (Jingumae) 3400-3901
Shiseido Beauty Salon (Ginza)... 3571-4511
Sweden House of Beauty (Roppongi)..3404–9730
Taya Harajuku Shop (Harajuku)...5474–4510
Toni and Guy Japan (Omotesando) 3797–5790
Y. Company (Roppongi) 3423–8331/2
Yes, George Beauty Salon (Kioicho)... 3261-8665
Y.S. Park International Roppongi (Roppongi)...................................3423–2244

TRAVEL

TRAVELING IN JAPAN

I've always felt that travel offered me new opportunities and experiences in life not available at home. My desire to travel let me escape from everyday monotony and rejuvenated me. In Japan, you will acquire a new perspective of yourself and others, as well as on issues in your daily life that went unnoticed before. Travel teaches crisis management, communication skills, self reliance, perceptiveness, and tolerance of different people. Japan is no exception, and it will be a rocky ride for some. Japan can be stimulating, frustrating and infuriating all at the same time, possibly even on the same day! With that said, let's look at some specifics.

I feel travel in Japan compensates for an otherwise boring routine of trains, rice, noodles, and endless teaching hours. It's a chance to relax and forget about the daily grind. Planning is of the utmost importance, especially if you'll be traveling during one of the big three Japanese holidays: New Year's (Shogatsu), Golden Week (late April to early May) and Obon Festival (middle August).

Some full time teaching positions run on different days of the week, for example instead of the normal Monday to Friday routine, many schools have Tuesday to Saturday or Wednesday to Sunday. It's worth considering taking one of these irregular schedules as everyone else in Japan will have the weekend off, and you'll be able to travel hassle free on Monday and Tuesday. Traffic is lighter for just about every train, bus, taxi, or special event.

I highly recommend Lonely Planet's *Japan: A Travel Survival Kit* for great descriptions on all cities and points of interest. They have written many travel guidebooks for around the world, and the one on Japan is excellent. If you haven't already heard about this book, rush out and buy it. If you already have it, great.

I've also made a summary of all the most commonly mentioned holiday destinations. Take it to the Tourist Information Center (T.I.C.) in the Ginza (3502-1461) which will gladly supply you with all the corresponding free pamphlets.

1. Matsumoto
2. Kiso Region
3. Izu Peninsula
4. Okutama Cherry Blossoms
5. Chichibu
6. Kawagoe
7. Boso Hanto Peninsula
8. Nikko
9. Sendai and Matsushima Bay
10. Iwate prefecture

11. Kanazawa
12. Osaka
13. Hiroshima and Miyajima Island
14. Okinawa
15. Sand Beaches, Beppu, Kyushu

Travel in Japan is extremely expensive compared to Europe, and one thing that's never a bargain is a plane ticket bought in Japan. Buy these in Canada, the States, Hong Kong, or Bangkok if you're going to be stopping through. For example, a round trip ticket from, say, Toronto to Tokyo on Korean Airlines with one free stopover in Seoul would cost about US$1,000 or Cdn$1,250.

Also available for about US$150 to US$200 would be a return trip to say Bangkok, Taipei or Hong Kong during the major portion of your above one–year open return ticket, which you could book once you arrived in Japan. As far as I know, one–year open tickets are not available in Japan, therefore I cannot compare the first part of the ticket. However, the $200 dollar side–trip takes on astronomical value when one has to fly out of Tokyo. That same $200 dollar ticket jumps to about US$1,565 (¥180,000) during Golden Week in May or Obon Week in August!!! 'Caveat Emptor'; let the buyer beware!

Again, go to the T.I.C., and they can supply you with cheap accommodation and travel information. The best place to stay on trips within Japan will be their 'ryokans' or small inns. There is a pamphlet entitled *The Hospitable and Economical Japanese Inn Group* which has listings for every major city with an average price of ¥4,000 per person (very reasonable for Japan). You can reserve these by telephone or fax. Pick up a recent copy at the T.I.C. when you arrive, or get one from the Japanese Tourist Association in your home country. See the list further on in this section.

In addition, three times a year, Japan Railways sells a special group of tickets called *Seishun 18 Kippu* which entitles you to a set of five tickets for ¥11,300. Each ticket can be used for unlimited travel on a local or rapid train for one day. No matter what time of the day you start using a ticket, it expires at midnight. Theoretically, you could travel all the way from Tokyo to Kyoto, which is almost 600km, on local lines if you've got the stamina and want to save cash.

T.I.C. (TOURIST INFORMATION CENTER)

I've mentioned the Tourist Information Center so often throughout this book that I thought I better tell you a little more about it. They have the widest range of free material on anything you could possibly think of doing anywhere in Japan. They're staffed with bilingual Japanese who'll give you free maps and brochures. They'll even book hotels or ryokans for you, saving you the long distance telephone fee.

Arita Tourist Information Center ....(0955) 43–3942
Atami Station Travel Service Center ....(0557) 81–6002
Beppu City Tourist Information ....(0977) 24–2838

Chiba Convention Bureau Information Center .... (043) 296–0535
Ehime Prefectural International Center (EPIC) .... (0899) 43–6688
Fuji Visitor Center .... (0555) 72–0259
Fujiyoshida Tourist Information Service .... (0555) 22–7000
Fukuoka City Tourist Information .... (092) 431–3003
Fukuyama Tourist Information Center .... (0849) 22–2869
Hakodate Tourist Information Center .... (0138) 23–5440
Hida Tourist Information Office.. (0577) 32–5328
Hakone Tourist Information Center...................................... (0749) 22–2954
Himeji Tourist Information Center.. (0792) 85–3792
Hiroshima City Tourist Association .... (082) 247–6738
Imari Tourist Information Center .... (0955) 22–6820
Ito Station Travel Service Center .... (0557) 37–3291
Ito Tourist Association Information Center........................... (0557) 37–6105
Kagoshima City Tourist Service .... (0992) 53–2500
Kanagawa Prefectural Tourist Association .... (045) 681–0007
Kanazawa City Tourist Information Office............................ (0762) 31–6311
Kawaguchiko Information .... (0555) 72–0346
Kintetsu Nara Station Tourist Information Office .... (0742) 24–4858
Kita–Tohoku Sightseeing Center .... (0196) 25–2090
Kobe International Tourist Association.................................. (078) 392–0020
Kochi City Tourist Information Office .... (0888) 82–1634
Kumamoto Airport Information Office .... (096) 232–2311
Kumamoto City Tourist Office.. (096) 352–3743
Kurashiki JR Station Tourist Informaion Office .... (0849) 26–8681
Kyoto...075-371-5649
Matsue Tourist Information Center .... (0852) 27–2598
Matsumoto City Tourist Information Center .... (0263) 32–2814
Matsuyama City Tourist Information .... (0899) 31–3914
Miyazaki City Tourist Information Center .... (0985) 22–6469
Nagasaki City Tourist Information ....(0958) 230–3631
Nagoya City Tourist Information Center .... (052) 323–0161
Nagoya International Center .... (052) 581–5678
Nara City Tourist Center .... (0742) 22–3900
Narita Tourist Information Office .... (0476) 24–3198
Narita Tourist Pavilion Tourist Information Center .... (0476) 24–3232
Niigata Eki Bandaiguchi Tourist Information....................... (025) 241–7914
Nikko City Tourist Information Center .... (0288) 53–4511
Nagoya City Tourist Information... (052) 541–4301
Okayama City Tourist Information Office.............................. (0862) 22–2912
Osaka Municipal Tourist Information .... (06) 345–2189
Otsu Tourist Information Center... (0775) 22–3830
Sapporo City Tourism Department .... (011) 211–2376
Sapporo City Tourist Office , ... (011) 232–7712
Sendai Tourist Information Office .... (022) 222–4069
Shin–Onomichi Tourist Information Office .... (0848) 22–6900

Shirahama Eki Information .... (0739) 42–2900
Takamatsu Tourist Information .... (0878) 51–2009
Takeo City Tourist Information Center .... (0954) 22–2542
Tokyo 3502-1461
Toyama City Tourist Information .... (0764) 32–9751
Tsuchiura City Tourist Information .... (0298) 21–4166
Tsukuba Information Center .... (0298) 55–7155
Ureshino Onsen Tourist Information Center .... (0954) 42–0336
Utsunomiya Tourist Information Center .... (0286) 36–2177
Yamagata Airport Tourist Information Center .... (0237) 47–3111
Yamagata Tourist Information Center .... (0236) 31–7865
Yokahama Municipal Tourist Association .... (045) 473–2895
Yokohama Tourist Information .... (045) 441–7300

NOTE: THERE'S AN EASTERN JAPAN TOLL FREE NUMBER AT 0120-222-800 AND A
WESTERN JAPAN TOLL FREE AT 0120-444-800.

JNTO ABROAD

The Japan National Tourist Office has many brochures and pamphlets and can generally inform you about any questions you have, either by answering the questions themselves or directing you to the proper service. Call to find out when they're open.

They'll give you good information, for example where to find a cheap Japanese Ryokan (Inn) for your first few days in Tokyo. The pamphlet is called *Reasonable Accommodations in Japan.* Reservations can be made from abroad by phone or fax if available. Also available is the book entitled *Japan Inn Group* and is quite useful for cheap ¥3,500 to ¥5,000 accommodations across Japan. Write to the: Japanese Inn Group Tokyo Liaison Office, c/o Sawanoya Ryokan, 2–3–11, Yanaka, Taito–ku, Tokyo 110, Japan. They'll send you a free booklet listing over 90 ryokans throughout Japan.

JNTO Japan

JNTO (Tokyo) 3216–1901
JAPAN Travel Bureau (JTB) 3276–7777
Tourist Information Center (T.I.C.) 3502–1461
Teletourist Information: English 3502–2911
French 3503–2926

JNTO Offices Overseas

USA

45 Rockerfeller Plaza
New York, NY, 10020
(212) Plaza 7–5640.

333 North Michigan Ave
Chicago, Il, 60601
(312) 32–3975.

1420 Commerce St.
Dallas, TX, 75201
(214) 741–4931,

1737 Post St.
San Francisco, CA, 94115;
(415) 931–0700.

624 South Grand Ave
Los Angeles, CA, 90017
(213) 623–1952.

2270 Kalakaua Ave
Honolulu, HI, 96815
(808) 923–7631

Canada

165 University Ave , Toronto, Ontario
M5H 3B8
(416) 366–7140.

U.K.

1676 Regent St.
London W1;
(071) 734–9638.

Australia

115 Pitt St.
Sydney, NSW 2000;
(02) 232–4522.

Germany

Biebergasse 6–10, 6000 Frankfurt;
tel 292792.

Hong Kong

Peter Bldg., 58 Queen's Rd, Central
tel 5–227913.

Switzerland

Rue de Berne 13, Geneva; tel 318140.

Thailand

56 Suriwong Rd, Bangkok; tel 233–5108

JAPANESE EMBASSIES

Japanese Embassies are a good source of pamplets, information and the only place to get a visa before you leave the country. They will answer any official questions you might have, plus give you the run down about any special programs going on like JET, Work/Holiday Visa, Culture Visa and so on.

USA

Embassy of Japan,
2520 Massachusetts Ave. N.W.,
Washington D.C. 20008
(202) 234-2266

Consulate-General Of Japan
909 W. 9th Ave. #301,
Anchorage, Alaska 99501
(907) 279-8428/9

Consulate-General of Japan,
400 Colony Square Bldg. #1501,
1201 Peachtree St. N.E.,
Atlanta, Georgia 30361
(404) 892-2700/6670/7845

Consulate General of Japan
Federal Reseerve Plaza 14th Fl.,
600 Atlantic Ave.,
Boston, Massachusetts 02210
(617) 973-9772/3/4

Consulate-General of Japan
625 N. Michigan Ave.,
Chicago, Illinois 60611
(312) 280-0400

Consulate-General of Japan
1742 Nuuanu Ave.,
Honolulu, Hawaii 96817
(808) 536-2226

Consulate-General of Japan
5420 Allied Bank Plaza,
1000 Louisiana St.,
Houston, Texas 77002
(713) 652-2977/8/9

Consulate-General of Japan
Commerce Tower #2519,
911 Main St. (P.O. Box 13768),

Kansas City, Missouri 64105
(816) 471-0111/2/3

Consulate-General of Japan
250 E. 1st St. #1507,
Los Angeles, California 90012
(213) 624-8305

Consulate-General of Japan
1830 International Trade Mart Bldg.,
No. 2 Canal St.,
New Orleans, Louisiana 70130
(504) 529-2101/2

Consulate-General of Japan
299 Park Ave.,
New York City, New York 10171
(212) 371-8222

Consulate-General of Japan
2400 First Interstate Tower,
1300 S.W. 5th Ave.,
Portland, Oregon 97201
(503) 221-1811

Consulate-General of Japan
1601 Post St.,
San Francisco, California 94115
(415) 921-8000

Consulate-General of Japan
3110 Rainier Bank Tower,
1301 5th Ave.,
Seattle, Washington 98101
(206) 682-9107/8/9/10

Canada

Embassy of Japan
255 Sussex Drive,
Ottawa, Ontario
K1N 9E6
(613) 236-8541

Consulate-General of Japan
10020 100th St.,
Edmonton, Alberta

T5J 0N4
(403) 422-3752/423-4750

Consulate-General of Japan
600 Rue de Lagauchetiere Ouest, #1785,
Montreal, Quebec
H3B 4L8
(514) 866-3429/20

Consulate-General of Japan
Toronto Dominion Center #1803 (P.O. Box 10),
Toronto, Ontario
M5K 1A1
(416) 363-7038

Consulate-General of Japan
1210-1177 W. Hastings St.,
Vancouver, British Columbia
V6E 2K9
(604) 684-5868

Consulate-General of Japan
730-215 Garry St.,
Credit Union Central Plaza,
Winnipeg, Manitoba
R3C 3P3
(204) 943-5554/942-7991

U.K.

Embassy of Japan
43-46 Grosvenor St.,
London, England
W1X 0BA
01-493-6030

Australia

Embassy of Japan
112 Empire Circuit,
Yarralumla, Canberra A.C.T. 2600
733244/733686/733675/732272

Consulate-General of Japan
Brisbane Plaza 26th Fl.,
68 Queen St.,
Brisbane, Queensland 4000
(07) 31-1430/8/9

Consulate-General of Japan
Holland House 3rd Fl.,
492 St. Kildan Rd.,
Melbourne, Victoria 3004
267-3490/3244/3255

Consulate-General of Japan
CAGA Center 36th Fl.,
8-18 Bent St.,
Sydney N.S.W. 2000 (G.P.O. Box 4125, Sydney 2001)
(02) 231-3455

New Zealand

Embassy of Japan
Norwich Insurance House 7 Fl.,
3-11 Hunter St., Wellington 1,
New Zealand (P.O. Box 6340, Ya Aro, Wellington)

Consulate-General of Japan
National Mutual Center 6th Fl.,
Shortland St.,
Auckland, New Zealand

AIRLINE TICKETS

Price wars have hit Japan like everywhere else in the world. Most of their business comes only three times a year at Christmas and New Years, Golden Week in May and Obon in August, so they have begun to try to entice off–season travelers. Planes, hotels, and trains are booked sometimes to triple or quadruple capacity with huge waiting lists during the three big holidays, but comparatively dead the rest of the year.

Recently, there are some great deals to be had. Now, there are discount travel agencies in Tokyo willing to cut prices in order to secure business. Here's their latest price schedule in Yen. **A** to **I** correspond to list of Travel Agents at the end of destination list.

Asia

Bali	75,000 (D)		Hanoi	115,000 (A)
Bangkok	57,000 (A)		Hong Kong	56,000 (D)
Beijing	65,000 (D)		Jakarta	93,000 (H)
Bombay	107,000 (E)		Katmandu	115,000 (A)
Kuala Lumpur	99,000 (D)		Seoul	25,000 (A)
Manila	42,000 (D)		Singapore	54,000 (D)
Phnom Penh	145,000 (A)		Taipei	45,000 (C)
Ulan Bator	99,000 (C)			

North America

L.A.	54,000 (F)	Dallas	110,000 (D)
N.Y.	80,000 (D)	Vancouver	72,000 (I)
Honolulu	72,000 (D)	Mexico	68,000 (I)
Miami	84,000 (I)		

Europe

Berlin	103,000 (D)	London	85,000 (D)
Paris	78,000 (D)	Moscow	103,000 (D)

Australia/New Zealand

Darwin	120,000 (G)	Sydney	68,000 (F)
Melbourne	103,000 (D)	Wellington	125,000 (G)

South Pacific

Fiji	91,000 (A)	Tonga	115,000 (A)
Guam	88,000 (D)	Vanuatu	130,000 (A)
Tahiti	130,000 (A)		

Africa

Cairo	103,000 (D)	Cape Town	295,000 (A)
Nairobi	203,000 (A)		

South America

Lima	220,000 (E)	Buenos Aires	245,000 (A)
Rio de Janeiro	250,000 (H)		

Discount Agencies

A. Across Traveler's Bureau
Shinjuku 3374–8721
Ikebukuro 5391–2871
B. Flex International
Shibuya 3797–5501
Takadanobaba 3207–0128
C. GSKO Travel
Takadanobaba 5386–4880
D. Just Travel
Takadanobaba 3207–8311
E. Map International
Shinjuku 3356–9731
Takadanobaba 3207–3674

F.   No. 1. Travel
   Shinjuku.. 3366–2481
   Shibuya 3770–1381
G.   STA Travel
   Shibuya 5485–8380
   Ikebukuro... 5391–2922
H.   Summit Tour
   Nishi Kamata 3739–0981
I.   World Air Plan
   Shibuya 5466–4300

These prices are for those who didn't plan ahead and are forced to pay Tokyo prices. If, however, you're smart, you can add on stopovers or side trips for little extra cost when you purchase your original ticket to Japan from your home country.

For example, we live in Toronto, Canada and bought our first ticket in Toronto for Cdn$1,200 (US$950). That ticket was a one year, open–return ticket on Korean Airlines with a free stopover in Seoul coming or going.

On our way back we stopped in Seoul for five days for a little vacation. Our next ticket we bought from a New York agent and we added Hong Kong to our package (Toronto → Buffalo → New York → Seoul → Hong Kong → Seoul → Tokyo). The bill was Cdn$1,160 (US$920). Other friends of ours have added Bangkok, Taipei, Manila, and Singapore.

Our third trip back home we added Honolulu for Cdn$1,160 (US$920), again on Korean Airlines. Their prices can't be beat. One friend from Los Angeles got L.A. to Tokyo return plus one trip to Hong Kong and one trip to Bangkok for one year all for US$1,000! (Korean Airlines). That's the best way I know of to pick off other countries one by one. In Tokyo, to go to Bangkok and Hong Kong would have cost roughly US$1,050 (¥121,000)!

Plus, KAL has a frequent flyer club just like all the other airlines, so join up just in case you use them more than you had planned on in the beginning. Other airlines like Northwest, United, and Japan Airlines all have similar stopover routes but cannot match KAL's prices and destinations.

English Speaking Travel Agents in Japan

To help you plan a nice Hot Spring trip near Mt. Fuji, or a beautiful ski weekend in Northern Hokkaido, I wrote this section about English speaking travel agents.

Package Tours are cheaper than individual travel in Japan. I guess that explains all the Japanese tour groups invading Europe, Australia, and Hawaii. This fact took awhile to sink in for me until a friend gave me a Japan Travel Bureau (JTB) catalogue on trips to Thailand. I had just come back from a three day business trip to Bangkok that I had organized myself. Here's what I learned.

Mark's Plan	JTB Option
Ticket ¥70,000 Purchased from discount agency in Shinjuku (No. 1 Travel) About ¥13,000 more due to short notice booking.	Package Deal which included Ticket
Hotel ¥6000/night (x2)=¥12,000	Hotel *three* nights
Taxi to and from airport ¥1,500 (x2)=¥3,000	Transportation to and from airport
Food. All depends where and how much you eat.	*3 breakfasts, 1 lunch, 1 dinner*
¥85,000 + food	**¥88,000**

Only ¥3,000 more for one extra night, food, and a few tours. The tours are strictly optional and you can pass them up if you want to go it alone.

If you're planning a trip out of Tokyo, definitely check out one of these English Speaking Travel Agencies to see what's available. Personally, I'll take the tour package every time from now on.

American Express (Toranomon) 3508–2400
American Tourist Bureau (Kanda) 3233–1079
Business Travel Center (Kasumigaseki) 3504–3375
Canon Tours (Shinjuku) 3342–1911
Cosmo International (Nihombashi) 3669–8501
Global Travel Service (Akasaka) 3586–4155
Hankyu Express International (Shimbashi) 3459–9080
Isogai Travel Service (Kisarazu) 0438–25–0711
Japan Amenity Travel (Ginza) 3573–1011
Japan Soviet Tourist Bureau (Kamiyacho) 3432–6161
Japan Travel Bureau (Nihon Kotsu Kosha) 3276–7777
Joe Grace Travel Center (Kasuga) 3814–9271
Kinki Nippon Tourist (Akihabara) 3253–6131
Meitetsu World Travel (Kyobashi) 3552–1525
Nichiboku Tours (Gotanda) 3447–5361
Nippon Express (Akihabara) 5256–2351
Nippon Travel Agency (Akasaka) 3588–0373
Pacific Travel Service (Akasaka) 3586–4621
Royal Travel (Kanda) 3294–7246
Summit Tour (Kamata) 3739–0981
Times Travel (Shimbashi) 3572–1107

Tobu Travel (Tokyo).. 3272–1806
Tokyu Tourist Co. Ltd (Akasaka–mitsuke).. 3401–7131
Travel Experts (Kojimachi) 3262–9966

NOTE: ALSO, IF YOU'RE IN A HURRY, MOST MAJOR JR STATIONS HAVE TRAVEL
AGENCIES YOU COULD TRY. PROBABLY NO ENGLISH, BUT GOOD SERVICE.

Travel Agencies–The Best Around the World

Here's a list of travel companies I've personally used and strongly recommend to all my readers. I've found them to be reliable, fast, honest, and the cheapest around.

CANADA

Korea Travel
456 Bloor Street
Toronto, Ontario
M5S 1X8
tel: (416) 531–4607
fax: (416) 538–1789

Ask for Hee. Best flights on Korean Airlines. Will service any city in Canada. For example they have several packages available: T.O. → Van. → Seoul → Tokyo return for CDN $1,200. Or T.O → L.A. → Hong Kong → Tokyo → Honolulu → L.A. → T.O. return for about CDN $1,400.

USA

Travel Center
38 West 32nd St.,
10012,
New York, NY
tel: 212–947–6670
fax: 212–947–6911

For example: Buffalo (or any other U.S. city) → New York→ Seoul→ Tokyo→ Seoul→ Honolulu→ Los Angeles→ Chicago→ Buffalo. US$1,040.

JAPAN

No. 1 TRAVEL
Shinjuku Hamada Building, B1 Floor,
7–4–7 Nishi Shinjuku, Shinjuku–ku,
Tokyo 160
tel: (03) 3366–2481
fax: (03) 3366–1018

Ask for Seikesan. Best discount travel agency in Japan. Tons of agents to choose from.

THAILAND

STA TRAVEL
Thai Hotel,
78 Prachathipatal Road,
Bangkok 10200
tel: (02) 281–5315 or (02) 282–2070 or (02) 281–0731
fax: (02) 280–1388

Bangkok rivals Hong Kong for cheap tickets in Asia. When you purchase your ticket in North America, buy it all the way to Thailand with a stopover in Tokyo. That way, you'll have a free return trip to Bangkok from Tokyo any time you want. Also while in Bangkok, you can fly out to any other country cheaply because ticket prices are half that of Tokyo. It pays to plan ahead.

HONG KONG

Y and J TRAVEL SERVICES Ltd.
Front block, 4th Floor,
Wah Ying Cheong Building,
234 Nathan Road,
Kowloon, Hong Kong.
tel: (852) 368–6187/8 or 366–6877 or 739–8165
fax: (852) 739–8165

Ask for Icy Ng. Same cheap prices as Bangkok. Same scenario as above.

Frequent Flyer Programs

Anyone traveling as far away as Japan would be a fool not to consider Travel Points Programs. Most airlines now offer some kind of reward for repeat use of their airplanes. It is definitely worth investigating due to the sheer distance involved traveling to Japan. Most programs have a free sign–up and many offer a 5,000 mile starting bonus. Add this to the 11,500 miles you earn going from eastern North America return, and you are already at 16,500. Most free tickets start at 20,000 points. However, if you use the club's credit card to purchase your tickets and any other goods, you could easily earn the extra points necessary to obtain a free ticket for travel in North America or within Asia.

For example:

1.	Toronto or New York to Tokyo (11,500 miles return)	=	11,500
2.	Sign up Bonus	=	5,000
3.	Mastercard or Visa ticket purchase – about $1,500	=	1,500
4.	Other purchases with card totaling $2,000. i.e. clothes, restaurants, trips. Just put everything on the card when you arrive and you'll top $2,000 in a few weeks.	=	2,000
	free ticket!	=	20,000

Most airlines, however, have a lower or non–existent sign–up bonus, but it never hurts to ask. Others give a premium for flying within 60 days of enrollment. Always read the small print!

Many people decide to go home for awhile after one year then come back again. Here again you can only benefit from the extra points earned. Be sure to check into all plans because you never know where your travels will take you. Consider the points like money in the bank always ready for a rainy day. We fly Korean Airlines and have earned enough points for 2 free Trans–Pacific flights each!

Check with your travel agent or better yet visit the airline's office in person to receive their brochure on their frequent flyer plan. Some popular plans are: *Aeroplan*, Air Canada; *Perks*, Northwest Airlines; and *Plus*, Canadian Airlines. In some cases, you can even earn 500 points a day for car rental or one night's stay in a member hotel. Lots of airlines are connected to each other and trade miles to each other's programs. For example, Air Canada allows you to fly Cathay, Austrian Airlines, Finnair, Singapore Airlines, United Airlines and several others, while United Airlines lets you combine with Air Canada, Air France, Alitalia, British Airways, KLM, Lufthansa, Sabena, Swissair and still others.

The bottom line: enroll now, count your points and pick your destinations later.

Travel to U.S.A. and Canada for Holiday Only

Those of us who have decided to make Japan our home for a few years can take advantage of a deal offered only to those who purchase this ticket in Japan.

United Airlines

UA Friendly Pass–N.A. Economy class only. Three to 10 coupons available: ¥50,000 (3), ¥74,000 (5). ¥101,000 (8), and for ¥119,000 (10).

Wherever you land in the U.S. or Canada, if this city is serviced by UA, you then have x number of one–way tickets from that point on. Thus, with three coupons, you could go from L.A. (your landing point from Japan) to New York to Miami back to L.A. for ¥50,000 (about US$435 at ¥115 to U.S$1). This pass can be bought in Japan or the U.S., but if you buy it in Japan it is easier to get a seat once in the States as airlines set aside special seats for UA *Friendly Passes* bought abroad.

Northwest and American Airlines

Northwest and American Airlines have their *See America* pass and *Visit USA* pass, but the best deal has to be Delta Airlines which has a Eurail–type pass. For 30 days or 60 days you can buy a stand–by ticket for US$557 (¥58,500) or US$929 (¥97,500). You can fly anywhere in the U.S. on a stand–by basis. What a deal! Call the airlines for up–to–date rules, regulations and prices.

The best advantage to booking a side trip when you purchase your ticket in North America, Europe or Australia, is using your stopover within the three major peak seasons in Japan:

1. Christmas/New Year's .... December 28th–January 5th
2. Golden Week .... April 29th–May 5th
3. Obon Week .... August 9th–August 16th (approximate dates)

The airlines reserve a certain percentage for tickets purchased outside of Japan. To buy a ticket in Japan for the three peak seasons is financial suicide. Triple fares are the norm. For example Tokyo to Bangkok return would be around ¥180,000, if space is even available. Hong Kong would be about ¥150,000.

Travel agencies will not take reservations until March for May for example, so long–term planning is difficult. Even then you're not guaranteed a seat and will probably be put on a waiting list. It's obviously a seller's market during these three times. Do yourself a big favor and take care of any travel plans beforehand. The Japanese will be extremely impressed when you tell them of your $50 vacation to Seoul, Hong Kong or Bangkok. (Based on Korean Airlines regular $50 surcharge to stopovers in any of the above mentioned cities.)

FESTIVALS AND ANNUAL EVENTS IN JAPAN

Japan has many festivals. I've attempted to list all of the major ones that might be of interest to you. Of course, I couldn't list all the rural events as there's literally thousands scattered throughout the entire country. I picked up a free pamphlet from the T.I.C. and summarized their often lengthy descriptions to what you see below. Start planning now as you might only get one shot at some of these events.

Date	Event, Place	Description
January 1st	New Year's Day (national holiday)	New Year's Day, the 'Festival of Festivals' in Japan. People pay homage to shrines and visit friends and relatives.

3rd	'Tamaseseri' or Ball–Catching Festival, Hakozakigu Shrine, Fukuoka City, Kyushu	The main attraction is a struggle between two groups of youths to catch a sacred wooden ball, which brings good luck to the winner.
6th	'Dezome–shiki' or New Year Parade of Firemen, Tokyo	The parade takes place in Harumi Chuo–dori. Firemen in traditional garb perform acrobatic stunts on top of tall bamboo ladders.
7th	'Usokae' or Bullfinch Exchange Festival of Dazaifu Temmangu Shrine, Dazaifu Fukuoka Pref	Hundreds of people try to get hold of 'good luck' bullfinches made of gilt wood which are given away by priests. Passed from hand to hand in the light of a bonfire.
9th–11th	'Toka Ebisu' Festival of Imamiya Ebisu Shrine, Osaka	Thousands of people pray for successful New Year's business; 'Ebisu' is the patron deity of business and good fortune. The festival has a procession of kimonoed women, carried in palanquins, through the main streets.
15th	Grass Fire on Wakakusayama Hill, Nara	In the evening, a trumpet signals the setting ablaze of Wakakusayama Hill in Nara Park. More than ten centuries ago a long war over the boundary of two major temples in Nara ended in this manner.
15th	'Toshi–ya' or a Traditional Japanese archery contest, Sanjusangendo Temple, Kyoto	Annual archery contest is held in the rear of the 118–meter–long hall of the temple. Men in traditional attire, from different parts of Japan, draw bows and shoot the arrows into a target.
17th	'Bonten' Festival at Miyoshi Shrine, Akita City	Dozens of 'Bonten', symbol of the Creative God, are carried by young men, who fight to be the first to reach the shrine. There's a similar festival at Yokote in Akita Pref. February 17th.
February 3rd or 4th	'Setsubun' or Bean–Throwing Festival in all of Japan	According to the lunar calendar, 'Setsubun' marks the last day of winter. People go to temples to participate in the traditional ceremony of throwing beans to drive away devils, shouting 'Fortune in, Devils out!'
3rd or 4th	Lantern Festival of Kasuga Shrine, Nara	More than 3,000 lanterns, either standing in the precincts or hung from buildings are lit. A really neat sight.

5th–11th	Snow Festival at Sapporo, Hokkaido (6th–12th in case 11th falls on Sat or Sun)	Snow sculptures are lined up along the main street of Sapporo.
15th & 16th	'Kamakura' at Yokote, Akita Pref.	'Kamakura' is for children. They make snow houses called 'kamakura' in which they enshrine the God of Water.
3rd Sat	'Eyo' Festival of Saidaiji Temple, Saidaiji, Okayama Pref.	Lots of scantily clad young males elbow one another to get a pair of sacred wands thrown to them in the dark. A must see for chicks!
17th–20th	'Emburi' Festival at Hachinohe, Aomori Pref.	'Emburi' is a harvest festival. More than 50 groups of villagers of at least 30 people, get together at Shiragi Shrine on Mt. Choja. In the morning they go down into the streets in a long procession.
March 1st to 14th	'Omizutori' Water–Drawing Festival of Todaiji, Nara	In the evening, a rite is performed by the light of pine torches. Young people carry burning torches, drawing circles of fire and shaking off the burning ashes. People rush to catch them because they think the ashes have a magic power against evil.
3rd	'Hinamatsuri' Doll Festival in all Japan	Special festival for girls. A set of 'Hina' dolls and miniature household articles are arranged on a tier of shelves, covered with bright red cloth. These 'Hina' dolls consist of the Emperor and Empress in ancient costumes, their ministers and other dignitaries, court ladies and musicians. You'll have to see thin one at someone's house.
13th	'Kasuga Matsuri', Kasuga Shrine, Nara	History of 1,100 years. Classic dances called 'Yamatomai' and 'Azuma Asobi' are performed.
2nd Sat & Sun	'Sagicho' Festival, Himura Shrine, Omihachiman, Shiga Pref.	Decorated floats are carried along the streets. On the last day of the festival, these floats are burned in the shrine precincts while everyone watches.
20th or 21st	Vernal Equinox Day (National Holiday)	The week centering around this day is known as 'Higan' when all Buddhist temples throughout the country hold special services and people pray for souls of the dead.

April 2nd Sun– 3rd Sun	'Kamakura Matsuri', Tsurugaoka Hachimangu Shrine, Kamakura, Kanagawa Pref.	This festival features great characters in history, such as Yoritomo Minamoto, Yoshitsune Minamoto. Sacred dances, a mikoshi parade and 'yabusame' or horseback archery.
14th & 15th	'Takayama Matsuri', Hie Shrine, Takayama, Gifu Pref.	This festival, said to date back to the 15th century, is noted for the gala procession of gorgeous floats.
16th evening & 17th	'Yayoi Matsuri', Futarasan Shrine, Nikko, Tochigi Pref.	Many decorated floats
May 3rd–4th	'Hakata Dontaku' at Fukuoka, Fukuoka Pref.	Japanese in disguise parade through the streets, accompanied by 'samisen', flutes and drums.
3rd–5th	Kite Battles at Hamamatsu, Shizuoka Pref.	Huge kites are flown and "everyone tries to cut the strings of their opponents' kites by skillful maneuvering." This one sounds good to me!
11th & 12th	'Takigi Noh' Performance of Kofukuji Temple, Nara	Noh Plays are presented nightly on a torch–lit stage set up near the temple.
11th– (Oct. 15th)	Cormorant Fishing on the Nagara River, Gifu Pref.	Cormorant fishing is an old method of catching 'ayu' , a trout–like fish, with trained birds. A rope is placed tightly around their necks so they can't swallow this fish. This takes place at night under the light of fire torches fastened to the fishing boats.
Sat & Sun to the 15th	'Kanda Matsuri', Kanda Myojin Shrine, Tokyo (held every other year)	Dozens of mikoshi (portable shrines) are carried. A big tea ceremony is also held.
2nd Fri, Sat, & Sun	'Sanja Matsuri', Asakusa Shrine, Asakusa, Tokyo	Nearly 100 mikoshi (portable shrines), carried by men and women. Afterward there is a parade. A big pageant, with 1,000 participants in traditional garb.
15th	'Aoi Matsuri', Hollyhock Festival of Shimogamo and Kamigamo Shrines, Kyoto	The festival has a huge pageant which reproduces the Imperial procession that paid tribute to the shrines centuries ago.

17th & 18th	Grand Festival of Toshogu Shrine, Nikko, Tochigi Pref.	**This is one of the three biggest festivals in Japan**. A centuries–old festival which has a parade on the 18th with over 1,000 armor–clad people. Awesome!
3rd Sun	'Mifune Matsuri' or Boat Festival, Arashiyama, Kyoto	This festival is held on the Oi River near Arashiyama in the suburbs of Kyoto. Depicts the Heian Period (794–1192) when the Emperor and his courtiers often went on pleasure trips down the river.
June 1st & 2nd	'Takigi Noh' Performance at Heian Shrine, Kyoto	Famous 'Takigi Noh' is presented after dark on an open air stage set up in the shrine's compound. This performance is in all the tourist shots you see in travel books on Japan.
10th – 16th	Sanno Matsuri, Akasaka Hie Shrine	**One of the three biggest festivals in Japan.** Originating in the Edo Period (1603–1867), the festival has a procession of mikoshi (portable shrines) through the hub of Tokyo. This event is held every other year.
14th	Rice–Planting Festival at Sumiyoshi Shrine, Osaka	Twelve young women ceremoniously transplant rice–seedlings in the shrine's paddy field while singing traditional songs.
15th	'Chagu–Chagu Umakko' Horse Festival Morioka, Iwate Pref.	Decorated horses are led by their owners to Sozen Shrine where they pray for the longevity of their horses.
July 1st–15th	'Hakata Yamagasa' at Fukuoka, Fukuoka Pref.	This festival is highlighted on the 15th by a fleet of 'Yamagasa' floats topped by decorations representing castles, halls and dolls. They are either pulled along or shouldered by young kids through the streets.
7th	'Tanabata' or Star Festival in all Japan	As an offering to the stars, Vega and Altair, who meet across the Milky Way, children set up bamboo branches and tie their poems to them.

13th–15th	'Bon' Festival	The festival is celebrated from the 13th to the 15th either in July or August, depending on the area in Japan. Religious rites are held throughout the country in memory of the dead who, according to Buddhist belief, revisit the earth during this period.
14th	'Nachi Himatsuri' (Fire Festival of Nachi Shrine), Nachi–Katsuura, Wakayama Pref.	This festival features the lighting of 12 giant torches carried by white–robed priests.
17th	'Gion Matsuri', Yasaka Shrine, Kyoto	The festival is actually celebrated from the 1st to the 31st of July and is one of the most noted festivals in Kyoto. It dates back to the 9th century, when the head priest of the Yasaka Shrine led a large number of men and women in forming a procession to escort the decorated palanquins to protect the gods against the pestilence that was then ravaging the city. On the 17th, 'yama' and 'hoko' floats parade through the main streets. **One of the three biggest festivals in all of Japan.**
23rd & 24th	Summer Festival, Warei Shrine, Uwajima City, Ehime Pref.	The festival is highlighted by many mikoshi crossing the river accompanied by hundreds of people with torch lights in their hands. 'Togyu' or bull fighting and a fireworks display are other major events.
23rd & 25th	'Soma Nomaoi' or wild Horse Chasing, Hibarigahara, Haramachi, Fukushima Pref.	A thousand riders in ancient armor fight to get three shrine flags set–up on the plain. Men in white costumes try to catch the wild horses chased into an enclosure by the horsemen.
24th & 25th	'Tenjin Matsuri', Temmangu Shrine, Osaka	A fleet of sacred boats bearing shrine palanquins sail down the river.

Mid July	'Kangensai' or Music Festival,, Itsukushima Shrine, Miyajima, Hiroshima Pref.	The date of this festival varies every year, since it takes place on the 17th of June according to the old calendar. Sacred boats are towed from the large red-painted 'torii' gate standing in the sea to the opposite shore across the channel. On the boats classical 'gagaku' (court music and a dance) is performed.
Last Sat	Fireworks Display on the Sumida River, Asakusa, Tokyo	This is the biggest one of its kind in Tokyo. Needs no description.
August 1st–7th	'Nebuta Matsuri' at Aomori and Hirosaki, Aomori Pref.	'Nebuta' (papier-maché dummies representing men, animals and birds) are placed on carriages and pulled through the streets. The festival is held in Aomori City from the 2nd to the 7th, and in Hirosaki from the1st to the 7th.
Mid July–Early Sept	'Gujo Odori' at Gujo-gun, Gifu Pref.	'Gujo Odori' is one of the most popular folk dances in Japan. Thousands of people wearing 'yukata' dance to lively music.
5th–7th	'Kanto Matsuri', Akita Pref.	This festival is a form of 'Tanabata', which asks for "divine help for a prosperous autumnal harvest." Young men in traditional attire try their luck at balancing 'kanto', long bamboo poles hung with many lighted lanterns, on their hands, foreheads and shoulders.
6th	Peace Ceremony, Hiroshima	The ceremony held at the Peace Memorial Park in the city is in memory of the A-bomb victims. In the evening, thousands of lighted lanterns are set adrift on the Ota River, with prayers for world peace. You might have seen this one on television at home before. The Japanese think they were victims of WWII and not the aggressors. At least this is what they teach in the schools.
Fri & Sat to the 7th	'Waraku Odori', Nikko, Tochigi Pref.	This is one of the most popular folk dances performed in Japan during the 'O-Bon' season. Thousands of people dance traditional Japanese music.

6th–8th	'Tanabata' or Star Festival at Sendai, Miyagi Pref.	The festival, the largest of its kind in Japan, is observed one month later than in most parts of the country. The streets are decorated with colored paper streamers and strips.
12th–15th	'Awa Odori' at Tokushima, Tokushima Pref.	The entire city is full of singing and dancing. Day and night, groups of musicians parade through the streets.
15th & 16th	'Daimonji' bonfire on Mt. Nyoigadake, Kyoto	A great spectacular bonfire in the shape of the Chinese character 'DAI', meaning large, is lit near the summit. This is the greatest attraction of the Bon Festival in Kyoto.
16th	'Yamaga Toro' Festival, at Yamaga City, Kumamoto Pref.	A parade of 'Toro Odori' dances are performed by women wearing 'yukata'. Each has a lantern on her head that is lit as they parade through the main streets.
Late Aug	'Bon' Festival in Okinawa	The date of the festival changes every year, since it takes place on the 15th of July according to the old calendar. Bon Odori dances called 'Eisa' are performed in traditional style.
26th & 27th	Lantern Festival, Suwa Shrine, Isshiki, near Nagoya	In the evening, great paper lanterns, painted with colorful designs, are lit in the shrine compound.
September 1st–3rd	'Owara Kaze–no Bon' Festival, at Yatsuo, near Toyama	In the evening, there is an 'Owara–bushi' folk dance while 'samisen', flutes and drums are played.
16th	'Yabusame' at Tsurugaoka Hachimangu Shrine, Kamakura, Kanagawa Pref.	'Yabusame' is the sport of horseback archery, like in the feudal days when 'samurai' warriors competed to the death.
Mid Sept	'Oyama–Mairi' or a Visit to Iwaki Shrine, Iwaki, Aomori Pref.	Mt. Iwaki, known as 'Tsugaru Fuji' from its resemblance to Mt. Fuji, is considered a sacred place by the local people, who march to the shrine on the mountain reciting prayers with music.
October 7th–9th	'Okunichi' Festival, Suwa Shrine, Nagasaki	A parade of ancient Chinese floats are paraded along the city's main streets.

8th–10th	'Marimo Matsuri' on Lake Akan, Hokkaido	'Marimo' is a green weed found in Lake Akan in Hokkaido and Lake Yamanaka in Yamanashi Prefecture. The festival is held by native Ainu inhabitants. On the 9th, Ainu dances are performed on the lake shore, and on the 10th the weeds are thrown into the water. Ainu are considered Japanese, but remain fiercely independent much like the Native Indians in North America.
9th & 10th	'Takayama Matsuri' of Hachiman Shrine, Takayama	This festival, dating back to the 15th century, is noted for its huge procession of floats.
12th	'Oeshiki' Festival, Hommonji Temple, Tokyo	This festival is celebrated in commemoration of a famous Buddhist leader. People march toward the temple carrying large lanterns decorated with paper flowers.
14th & 15th	'Mega Kenka Matsuri' or Roughhouse Festival, Matsubara Shrine, Himeji, Hyogo Pref.	Shrine palanquins, each carried by several men, bump and push each other in a race through the streets.
17th	Autumn Festival, Toshogu Shrine, Nikko, Tochigi Pref.	A palanquin is carried from the main shrine to the sacred place called 'Otabisho' escorted by armor–clad participants.
22nd	'Jidai Matsuri' or Festival of Eras, Heian Shrine, Kyoto	This festival is held to commemorate the founding of the old capital city of Kyoto in 794. A procession of over 2,000 people wearing period costumes. Each group represents important milestones in the city's history.
22nd	Fire Festival of Yuki Shrine, Kurama, Kyoto	Long rows of torches are placed along the street leading to the shrine. They are set on fire by children.
November 3rd	'Daimyo Gyoretsu' at Hakone, Kanagawa Pref.	A long parade which passes along the old Tokaido Highway lined on both sides with tall cryptomeria trees.
2nd–4th	'Okunichi' Festival, Karatsu Shrine, Karatsu, Saga Pref.	This festival is highlighted by a parade of huge colorful floats pulled along the streets by young men.

15th	'Shichi–go–san–' or Childrens' Shrine Visiting Day in all Japan	'Shichi–go–san' literally means 'seven–five–three'. Children of these three years, all dressed in their best, are taken to the shrines by their parents to express their thanks for their good health and to pray for future blessings.
Dates subject to change	'Tori–no–ichi' or Rooster Fair, Tokyo	These festivals are held on 'rooster' days in November according to the oriental zodiacal calendar. You can buy 'Kumade' or bamboo rakes adorned with ornaments symbolizing good fortune. Otori Shrine at Asakusa is the best.
December 2nd & 3rd	'Chichibu Yo–matsuri' or all–night festival, Chichibu City, Saitama Pref.	The festival, counted as one of the three grandest float festivals in Japan. It is highlighted by a parade of six huge floats. On the evening of the 3rd, all the floats assemble at the Chichibu Shrine (around 7:00pm) and proceed along the city's main streets. There is a display of fireworks at Hitsujiyama Park, 8:30–10:00pm. In the daytime, there is a performance of a local Kabuki Play in front of Musashino Bank, at 1:00–3:00pm.
14th	'Gishi–sai' at Sengakuji Temple, Tokyo	'Gishi–sai' or memorial celebrations of the famous vendetta carried out by the 47 Ronin (masterless samurai) of Ako, now called Okayama Prefecture, back in 1702. It takes place near Nihombashi over Ryogoku Bridge. The costume parade by businessmen reenacting the uprising will start at 6:00pm, near Higashi–Nihombashi Sta. on the Toei Asakusa Line, crossing Ryogoku Bridge, and will arrive at the Matsuzakacho Park around 6:30pm. After a reception at Matsuzakacho Park, the warriors will proceed to Higashi–Nihombashi Sta. to catch the Toei Asakusa Subway Line to Sengakuji Sta. They are due at the Sengakuji Temple, the burial place of the 47 Ronin, at around 7:30pm, and a memorial service will be held in the worship hall.

17th–19th	'Hagoita Ichi' or battledore Fair, Asakusa, Tokyo	It is held in the compound of Asakusa Temple, Asakusa Sta. on the Ginza Subway Line, from 10am-9pm every day. Food and game stalls will be open all night.
17th	'On–Matsuri' of Kasuga Shrine, Nara	This festival has a big procession of courtiers, retainers and wrestlers.
31st	'Namahage' on Oga Peninsula, Akita Pref.	In the evening, groups of 'Namahage', men disguised as devils, make door–to–door visits, growling, "Any good–for–nothing punks around here?"
31st	'Okera Mairi' at Yasaka Shrine, Kyoto	At midnight a sacred fire is lit in the shrine and each worshiper tries to take home some of the sparks to cook the first meal of the new year.

COSTUME/FORMAL WEAR/TUXEDO RENTALS
Halloween

Every year a group of gaijin take complete control of one entire train car on the Yamanote line which does a loop around the city of Tokyo. Everyone's dressed up and the booze is flowing. Japan Railway's officials turn a blind eye in order to limit the damage I guess. Just go to any Yamanote line station(Green colored trains), get on at one end of the car and walk down until you find the party. It should be evident which train and car it is. Call up one of the shops below and reserve your costume.

Atelier Hashimoto 3496–3980
Specializes in kimono, furisode and hakama. Staff will help put on kimono. 10am–8pm, daily. 1–32–29–204 Ebisu Nishi.

Big Kids 3777–1978
Halloween costumes including Japanese, foreign national costumes and animal outfits. From ¥5,000 to ¥18,000. 10am–7pm; Sat until 5pm. Closed Sun and holidays. Sanno Urban Life 515,2–1–8 Sanno.

Nihon Geino Bijutsu 3353–2552
Shinjuku. Policemen, samurai, or sumo wrestlers. Call in advance and tell them what you want and your size. Your outfit will be ready the next day. Rates run about ¥10,000. Hours: 10am–6pm. 9–15 Wakamatsucho, Shinjuku–ku.

Renrie 3400–8799
(toll free) 0120–228799
Specialty shop renting kimono, furisode and hakama. Kimono from ¥9,000 for 2 nights. 11am–8pm. Closed Sun and holidays. Kobachi Bldg., 3F, 4–11–30 Nishi Azabu.

Tokyo Isho (Tokyo Costume) 3485–2101
    Also Yoyogi 3467–1451
    Costumes such as sumo wrestlers, monkeys and period outfits. From
    ¥8,000 (2 nights), 10am–6pm. Closed Sun and holidays. 3–21–8 Nishihara,
    Shibuya–ku.

Formal Clothing

Tuxedos and dresses are rented at a two–night, three day rate just like the
Halloween costumes. A lot of the Embassies have annual balls as do many of
the Chambers of Commerce. For these affairs it's recommended to reserve at
least 3 weeks in advance. If you're big by Japanese standards, check as far
ahead as possible so that alterations can be made. Both of the stores mentioned
here also carry the 'Black Wedding Suit' that all men must wear if invited to a
Japanese wedding.

Ricky Sarani 3587–0648
    Full range of men's formal clothing in large sizes. Tuxedos for ¥16,500 for
    2 nights. English spoken. 10am–7pm,10am–5pm on Sat. Closed Sun and
    holidays. 3–3–12 Azabu–dai.
Well Up 21st 3497–1129
    Formal clothing for women and men including tuxedos, cocktail and
    maternity dresses. Dresses ¥13,000 (2 nights). 10am–8pm; Sun and
    holidays 10am–6pm. Tulis Nishi Azabu 2F, 3–13–16 Nishi Azabu.

BED AND BREAKFAST IN JAPAN

A good deal and a great way to meet 'real' Japanese in their homes to
witness their daily life. Over fourteen cities are offered including: Tokyo, Kyoto,
Nara, Osaka, Hiroshima, Sapporo and Nagoya.

A single person would pay ¥4,000 per night which includes breakfast.
Discounts are offered for one week and one month stays for ¥25,000 and
¥60,000 respectively.

For a brochure contact:

        Bed and Breakfast Japan
        〒273,
        3–4–12 Natsumi,
        Funabashi–shi, Chiba–ken,
        tel: 0474–22–8148
        fax: 0474–26–0965

ZEN TEMPLE LODGINGS

There's an opportunity for those who would like to stay in an authentic
Japanese Zen temple. You're expected to live as the priests do, so some
Japanese knowledge would be helpful. The T.I.C. brochure that I sourced said
Japanese was a must, but I think if you have a Japanese friend call and explain

that you just came over 9,000km to experience Japan's marvelous culture, you might stand a chance. I think as long as you're willing to adapt the best you can and not rock the boat, you'll be O.K.

Try to read up on the subject beforehand so you're not offending anyone in a major way and you should be well received. I've only listed some in Tokyo and Kyoto, but I'm sure if you asked around others exist in any city you might want to try. If this is one of your goals, go for it because you won't find anything like this back home.

Shukubo (Temple Lodgings) Around Tokyo

Komyoji Temple	....(0467) 22–0603
	of the Jodo Sect in Kamakura City, Kanagawa Prefecture.
Address	6–17–19, Zaimokuza, Kamakura City, Kanagawa Pref.
Facilities:	9 rooms (capacity 80 people) on a 'sharing–room arrangement'.
Price:	¥4,500 with 2 meals each person.
Closed:	July and August.
Location:	From Kamakura Station take the Keihin Kyuko bus for Zushi–eki or Zushi Station via Kotsubo and get off at Komyoji Bus Stop. It takes about 10 min on foot.
Note:	On request, *shojin–ryori* (vegetarian fare eaten by Buddhist priest), is served — ¥3,000.
	Separate facilities for men and women.
	Reservations:
	1. Accepted for more than 2 persons by telephone in Japanese.
	2. Must be made in Japanese 10 days prior to your visit.
	3. "Foreigners are expected to have some ability in speaking and understanding Japanese."
	4. No smoking or drinking alcohol.
	5. "Before breakfast, guests at the temple must conform to the same daily schedule as the temple priests."
	6. Bath–taking is limited to 2 hours, 6pm–8pm.
	7. Gates close at 9pm and lights out at 10pm.
	8. *Zazen* (zen meditation) is not conducted since it is a Jodo Sect temple.
Kofukuji Temple	....(0492) 94–0718
	of the Soto Sect in Saitama Prefecture.
Address	117, Takinoiri, Moroyamacho, Iruma–gun, Saitama Pref.
Facilities:	3 rooms (capacity 18 persons).
Price:	¥7,000 with 2 meals for one person.
Closed:	August 27th–29th every year.

Location:	10 min walk from Moroyama Sta. on JR Hachiko line originating at Hachioji Sta.
Note:	Reservations accepted for more than 2 persons by telephone in Japanese. 1. Bring your own toiletries. 2. You have to make your own bed. 3. If you wish you can take part in the temple's functions and *zazen*.

Tenryuji Temple

.... (0429) 78–0050
of the Tendai Sect in Hanno City, Saitama Prefecture.

Address	461, Oaza Minami, Hanno City, Saitama Pref.
Facilities:	11 rooms.
Price:	¥5,000 with 2 meals for one person (supper is usually a simple Buddhist priest's meal).
Closed:	No accommodations available December–May and July–August.
Location:	From Nishi–Agano Station on Seibu Ikebukuro Line, 1 hour 30 min on foot or 15 min by taxi. The temple was originally built more than 1,000 years ago. It has been remodeled since about 100 years ago. There are hiking courses as the temple is located at the top of a 640m mountain. There is a very heavy iron *waraji* (Japanese footwear) weighing 2,000kg which is enshrined in the main sanctuary.
Note:	1. Reservations must be made at least 10 days prior by phone in Japanese. 2. Foreigners must be able to understand and speak Japanese. 3. Guests are requested to follow the rules of the temple. 4. *Zazen* can be practiced if desired.

Seichoji Temple

.... (0470) 94–0525
of the Nichiren Sect in Chiba Prefecture.

Address	Kiyosumi, Amatsu–Kominato, Awa–gun, Chiba Pref.
Facilities:	Capacity for 300 people.
Price:	¥6,000 with 2 meals for one person.
Closed:	August 11th–18th and September 20th–26th due to temple activities.
Location:	20 min walk by bus from Awamatsu Station on JR Sotobo Line.
Note:	Reservations by telephone in Japanese. 1. Foreigners are expected to have some ability in understanding and speaking Japanese.

2. It is compulsory for guests to attend a sutra recitation at 5am.

Shukubo (Temple Lodgings) In Kyoto

Myorenji Temple
in Kyoto Prefecture.....................................(075) 451–3527
Address
Teranouchi Horikawa. Kamigyo–ku, Kyoto.
Price:
¥3,000 with breakfast.
Location:
From Kyoto Station, take bus #9 (B1 Bus stop) to Horikawa Teranouchi.
Note:
No bath at the facility, but a public bath is near the temple.

Myokenji Temple
in Kyoto Prefecture................... (075) 414–0808/431–6828
Address
Teranouchi Horikawa, Kamigyo–ku, Kyoto.
Price:
¥3,500 with breakfast.
Location:
From Kyoto Sta. take bus #9 (B1Bus stop) to Horikawa Teranouchi.

Hiden–in Temple
....(075) 561–8781
Address
35, Sennyuji Sandai–cho, Higashiyama–ku, Kyoto.
Price:
¥4,000 with breakfast.
Location:
From Kyoto Sta. take bus #208 to Sennyuji–michi or take JR Nara line to Tofukuji.

HOMESTAY PROGRAMS – SERVAS

Servas' name comes from the international language of Esperanto and means "to serve". It is an international network of hosts and travelers "working to foster understanding through person–to–person contacts".

Servas began after the Second World War in Europe when most accommodation was virtually destroyed and travelers needed a place to stay. It is a non–political, non–profit organization which has roots in the philosophy of Mahatma Gandhi: an "open door hospitality system for anyone and everyone". Presently, the United States has the most number of hosts at 2,000. World–wide, there are some 9,000 hosts in over 100 countries.

The Japanese branch of Servas started in 1962 and now has about 350 members. To join, you have to pay a ¥2,000 registration fee plus a yearly fee of ¥2,400. You must pass an interview in your home country before receiving the official letter of introduction and host lists for other countries. You can write to the main office at:

U.S. Servas Committee
11 John St., Room 706
New York, NY, 10038
(212) 267–0252

You must be over 18 and may not stay more than two days with any one host. Membership costs $45/year. For that you'll receive a list of Servas members who want to host travelers. The list has information on hosts' professions, languages, hobbies, interests, telephone numbers, kinds of accommodation, amount of advance notice required and distances to public transportation. You are expected to be part of the family, even helping with chores if necessary, and to pay all phone bills and transportation costs.

A lot of people feel that it's really an awesome experience being able to view a country from the inside for a change instead of from a hotel room or tour bus. In Japan, Servas seems like a great way to see some of the remote areas of the countryside away from over–crowded Tokyo. Considering the Japanese propensity for generosity towards foreigners, you will probably be treated with great hospitality. Once invited into their home, you'll never forget it.

> Japan Regional Director
> Mr. Kunio Tanaka
> 3–13–15 Den Enchofu
> Ohta–ku
> Tokyo–145
> 3721–1607 Home
> 3263–7676 Office

If they have changed the director in Japan, call NTT at 5295–1010 or the T.I.C. at 3502–1461 to get the current director.

Other Organizations Offering Homestay Programs

AFS Intercultural Programs Inc. They arrange homestays with families for three months to a year for high school students, teachers and adults. Contact:

> AFS
> 313E 43rd St.
> New York, NY. 10017.
> Phone # (800) AFS–INFO.

Experiment in International Living. Homestay from one week to four weeks. Write to:

> Experiment in International Living
> Box 595,
> Putney, Vermont,
> 05346
> (802) 387–4210.

LOVE HOTELS

There are close to 40,000 'love hotels' in Japan averaging around 15 rooms each. The average stay is only a few hours for ¥3,500, or ¥7,000 for the entire night. You do the math–it's a big business! Most clients are young and go around 8pm. The 18 to 21 year old market dominates the industry using roughly 66% of all available rooms. Love hotels open around 11am starting probably with housewives looking for an illicit thrill with a secret lover. 'Theme' rooms are very popular: S & M, swimming pools, merry–go–rounds, and even a Nintendo Game Room. The list goes on.

Rooms are rented in two–hour shots, but if it's late enough, sometimes you can get them all night. There's no regular reception desk, but rather a small hole where you pass the money through. In the lobby, they have picture menus of the theme rooms available. You'll also find vending machines supplying last–minute sexual aids.

In Shibuya, Erotic Hill is lined on either side with castle–like neon love hotels. More couples than you could imagine walk up and down before choosing from the Swimming Pool room, the SM torture chamber, or the Hot Spring room.

Definitely, take advantage of this unique cultural opportunity when the situation arises.

Useful Phrases

1. Are there any rooms?
    Oheya wa arimasu ka?
2. How much is it?
    Oheya wa ikura desa ka?
3. How much is it per night?
    Ippaku ikura desu ka?
4. Is room service available?
    Rumu sabisu wa arimasa ka?
5. Please give me a wake–up call at ___o'clock.
    ___–ji ni moningu koru o onegai shimasu.

CAPSULE HOTELS

Capsule hotels are those neat coffin–like sleeping boxes you've seen on T.V. They do exist just like the guys with white gloves who push you into the train during rush hour. You've got to try one once just to say you've done it. You also might want to use one after a late drinking night if you've missed the last train.

I used one once to get a jump on the next day's travel from Shinjuku to the Mt. Fuji area. I lived about an hour from Shinjuku so it saved some time in the morning and I didn't have to worry about having a good time the night before.

Usually an all–male businessman's enclave, capsule hotels run around ¥4,000/night per person. No couples allowed. Bathrooms and toilets are shared. Some hotels have a small gym, sauna, bar, or restaurant.

Some accept reservations while others do not. If you phone, have a Japanese friend phone for you to smooth out the reservation and to prepare the staff in advance for a foreigner. All are located within a 5 minute walk from the station. Another "you'll–never–believe–what–they–do–in–Japan" story for only ¥4,000 per night.

Akihabara Capsule Inn Akihabara 3251-0841
A special four–person capsule is available for Mah–Jong players, with a Mah–Jong table in the center. It costs ¥20,000. Free satellite television is available in every capsule. Reservations accepted. Check–in: 5pm. Check–out: 10am. Men only. Akihabara Stn, Showa Dori Exit.

Asakusa Capsule Hotel Asakusa...3847-4477
This capsule hotel is the only one with a Ladies Only Floor (the 5th,–all 36 capsules). Special coded doors keep men out. No restaurants. Reservations accepted. Check–in: 4:30pm. Check–out: 9:30am. Men's capsules available. Tawara–machi Sta.

Asakusabashi Sauna Hotel Sekitei 3663-8911
There is a large communal bath, big bathroom, suntan salon and bar. Off-hour rates cost ¥1,500 for three hours. No reservations. Check–in: 6pm. Check–out: 10am. Men only. Asakusabashi Sta.

Business Inn Shimbashi 3431-1391
Capsule Hotel Kawase 3843-4910
Capsule Hotel Shimbashi 3434-0022
Capsule Inn Akasaka 3588-1811
Central Inn Shibuya 3770-5255
Ebisu Blue Train Ebisu 3440–3445
Large bathroom, sauna, shower but no restaurant. No reservations. Check–in: 5pm. Check–out: 10pm. Men only. Ebisu Sta. Convenient if you've been partying it up at the Tokyo British Club which is very near.

Ikebukuro Ikebukuro Plaza 3590–7770
Bathroom as well as sauna. No reservations accepted. Check–in: 4pm. Check–out: 10am. Men only. Ikebukuro Sta.

Kinshicho Wing..3846–1311
Mini–pool, electric chair massage, and a Japanese restaurant. Stay 10 times and the 11th one will be free. Reservations accepted. Check–in: 4pm. Check–out: 10am. Men only. Kinshicho Sta.

Ochanomizu Ochanomizu Cock Pit Inn 3253–1631
Office–like room is available with desk, sofa, and television. Reservations accepted. Check–in: 5pm. Check–out: 10am. Men only. Nearest stations are Ochanomizu and Akihabara.

Ryogoku Midori Hotel...3635–2626
Reservations accepted. Check–in: 6pm. Check–out: 9am. Men only for the capsules, either sex for the regular hotel rooms. Near Ryogoku Sta.

Shibuya Capsule Inn Shibuya 3462–0300
Looks like a real hotel and not like a bee hive. Reservations accepted.
Check–in: 5pm, Check–out: 10am. Men only. Shibuya Sta.
Shinjuku Green Plaza Shinjuku 3207–4923
Free weight training room, sauna, suntan salon and 3–hour dry cleaning
service. Restaurant. No reservations accepted. Check–in: 5pm. Check–out:
10am. Men only. Seibu Shinjuku Sta.
Space Inn Shinjuku 3232–9456
Ueno Capsule and Sauna Century Hotel 3836–3436
Afternoon rentals are ¥1,500 per eight hours. Sauna and restaurant also
available. Reservations accepted. Check–in: 12pm. Check–out: 10am. Men
only. Ueno Sta.
Yushima Kiosk Inn Yushima..5688–0728
Sauna is available. Reservations accepted. Check–in: 5pm. Check–out:
10am. Men only. Yushima Sta.

SNAPPY COMEBACKS FROM VETERANS

Sometimes life isn't fair and those of us brave enough to travel to foreign
lands experience criticism, racism and downright discrimination. The following
is a list of complaints, rebuffs and stinging criticisms from veterans who at
some point during their stay have felt anger or frustrations toward the Japanese.
These questions were complied on an informal basis over a few beers with
friends in a Japan bashing mood. Believe me, these are by no means a
complete list and some would even argue that they are quite mild. Having said
that, read the list objectively now, then again after a year or two in Japan.
Everyone likes to let off steam now and then, and all I'm stating here is that
you'll probably do it too. Don't feel that you're alone in your dislike when it
happens. Just get it off your chest and accept that Japan has it's shortcomings
just like everywhere else in the world.

1. Do you kill whales?
2. Did you start W.W.II with the Americans?
3. Is the Stock Market controlled by the Yakuza?
4. Do students commit suicide over exams and pressure?
5. Do you live in Rabbit Hutches?
6. Can you get a seat on the train?
7. Do you stare at non–Japanese?
8. Does rice cost 10 times more than everywhere else in the world?
9. Are women treated fairly?
10. Can everyone buy a house in Japan?
11. Do you have lots of free time and participate in all kinds of leisure
    activities?
12. Do you have a free society, one in which people speak honestly and
    directly?
13. Why do you think you're the best? History has proven that each race has
    it's day of glory.

14. Did you know that psychologically speaking, only an insecure individual resorts to discrimination in order to assert his supremacy?
15. Is it normal for a new employee to work 6 days or 7 days a week 12 to 14 hours a day? Is it normal for long–standing employees to have to do the same?
16. Why do you refuse to admit all races are equal?
17. Why do you borrow so many cultural aspects from other countries if your race is so great?

NOTE: SEND ME IN SOME OF YOUR OWN COMPLAINTS AND I'LL MAKE SURE THEY GET PRINTED UP IN THE NEXT EDITION.

THOUGHTS AFTER THE FIRST YEAR

Below are some of my thoughts expressed to friends and family after some pondering of my future:

"It's funny. Sometimes I think I could really like this Japanese lifestyle. Good pay, but long hours. At least I don't have too much free time to go out and spend all my money. This way I really appreciate my free time. This is a great experience for me to prove to myself that I can really work hard at something I like."

"I could really build up a nest egg if I stayed another year. Two months were lost just setting up and paying back start up costs. Plus airfare! Then again, nothing is as exciting or daring the second time around. I'd no longer be the cute foreigner who's experiencing everything for the first time. However, my Japanese would improve. There's a possibility too of getting private lessons going. I'm really torn. My parents back home would like me to come back soon too."

"It is great traveling though. Some of my best memories are of traveling. It's so easy too to travel around to other countries using Japan as a base. Bangkok, Seoul, Hong Kong, Manila, Guam, Singapore, China–even Australia is close."

"A certain melancholy set in after a year or so that's easy to explain; the newness of Japan has worn off and life has become a routine. I mastered the transit system, haven't been lost in ages, and have been invited out several times by my students to bars, restaurants and even some Japanese homes. I have witnessed the complete cultural calendar of festivals and events and have read several books unraveling some of the Japanese psyche. Food has ceased to be a problem after discovering by trial and error my likes and dislikes. Money worries that I had at the beginning are no longer a concern, and I have amassed a small fortune."

"In short, I have become accustomed to living and working in Japan and now consider it to be home. I'll start planning social events, going to movies, sightseeing and enjoying life to the fullest."

CONCLUSION

No one has ever mentioned before that Japan is addictive. If you follow all my advice, by that I mean dress, conduct and how to take care of problems, you'll enjoy being a guest and treated as such.

Forget the stares people will give you or the school kids screaming "GAIJIN!!!" in remoter parts of the country. Just relax and go about achieving your goals as planned. My philosophy always was and is, **"There's no sense complaining about what you can't change; Act instead of React"**. If your job, apartment, city or whatever bothers you, take immediate steps to rectify the situation.

Problems seem to magnify while overseas. Get a support group of friends built up, people you can count on, especially Japanese friends. Memorize all useful English Help Lines or write them down in your wallet. USE THEM TOO! It never ceases to amaze me that gaijin miss a train or plane because they were too disorganized to find out the correct departure times.

Above all, be adaptive and open to new sights, sounds and ideas. You'll certainly get your fill in Japan. My last words to you are 'Think Positive'. In a country with such a diverse culture from our own and with such an emphasis on group harmony, there is no room for negativism. BON VOYAGE!

ORDERING JAPANESE BOOKS

If you want to get a jump on your reading but can't find many books on Japan at home, send us an order and we'll mail you the selections. This is an awesome service, by the way, you won't find anywhere else in Japan. I wish I would have been able to do this before I had left Canada.

We will buy your books, pack them in a box and send them off by seamail. Allow 6 to 8 weeks for delivery. If you're really in a hurry, open up a Federal Express account, send along your account number and you'll receive the books within 2 days by C.O.D.

The cost of mailing will be set as follows:

Up to 5 books ¥800
5 to 10 books ¥1,100
10 to 15 books ¥1,750
15 to 20 books ¥2,250

Orders will be processed right away. This is not a charity service, so I have added on a profit to cover my transportation, and time. If you are like most foreigners who come to Japan, you'll acquire a huge library in no time. Having advanced knowledge of Japanese etiquette, cultural nuances, and opportunities would be invaluable to make a smooth transition. I still buy all the new releases even to this day to keep up with the latest trends.

Thus, choose your books, send us a certified check or money order in any currency to **Mark Gauthier**, specify what method of transport then sit back and wait for the goods. Call the bank to find out the exact exchange rate for your particular currency. I guarantee you won't regret spending $150 to $200 dollars on some great guide books. That money by the way would be equal to one day's teaching salary once in Japan.

I will be using my parent's home in Canada as a base as we might change apartments in the future. They have lived at the same address for the last 35 years! As soon as they receive your order, they will fax it to me in Japan and we'll get to work immediately.

Write or fax to:

Mark Gauthier
59 Maywood Road,
Kitchener, Ontario
N2C 2A2
Fax: (519) 893-6128

Books About Kids

A Parent's Guide to Japan...¥3,000
Japan for Kids ¥4,000

Business and the Japanese Economy

Competing With Japan ¥2,300
Gaijin Kaisha ¥2,300
How to Do Business With the Japanese ¥2,800
Inside Corporate Japan ¥2,400
Intelligent Businessman's Guide to Japan ¥2,500
Japan as Number One ¥2,700
Setting Up & Operating a Business in Japan ¥3,000
Sogo Shosha, Japan's Multinational Traders ¥2,800
The House of Nomura ¥2,200
The Japanese Company ¥2,600
The Japanese Negociator ¥5,600
The Salaryman in Japan ¥2,000
1001 Teaching, Modeling, Editing and Hostessing Jobs in Japan ¥3,000

Culture

Experiencing Japanese Culture ¥3,300
Invitation to Practice Zen ¥2,000
Japanese Art of Miniature Trees ¥4,600
Kabuki: A Pocket Guide ¥2,200
Mah Jong for Beginners ¥2,000
Origami: Japanese Paper-Folding ¥1,300
Sho: Japanese Calligraphy ¥4,000
Zen and Japanese Culture ¥3,500

Eating and Food

Diner's Guide to Japan ¥1,500
Eating in Japan ¥2,000
Guide to Food Buying in Japan ¥2,500
Japanese Recipes ¥1,100
Reading Japanese Menus ¥2,000

General Books

283 Useful Ideas from Japan ¥4,000
Chrysanthemum and the Sword ¥2,500
"Even Monkeys Fall From Trees" and Other Japanese
   Proverbs ¥2,200
Japanese Secrets of Beautiful Skin & Weight ¥4,000
Max Danger: The Adventures of an Expat in Tokyo ¥2,500
More Max Danger: The Continuing Adventures ¥2,500
The Japanese Mind ¥2,500
The Japanese ¥2,700

History

Daily Life in Japan at the Time of the Samurai	¥2,500
Everyday Life in Traditional Japan	¥2,200
History of Japan	¥2,700
Japan: The Story of a Nation	¥2,900
Legends of Japan	¥1,700
Who's Who of Japan	¥2,000

Japanese Language and Dictionaries

All-Romanized English-Japanese Dictionary	¥2,400
Basic Japanese Conversation Dictionary	¥1,600
Basic Japanese Grammar	¥1,700
Colloquial Japanese	¥3,800
Complete Japanese Verb Guide	¥3,100
Guide to Reading and Writing Japanese	¥3,700
Guide to Witing Kanji & Kana	¥4,700
Japanese Business Dictionary	¥1,500
Japanese for Busy People Level II	¥7,500
Japanese for Busy People	¥6,200
Making Out in Japanese	¥1,500
Making Out in Japanese: the Cassette	¥2,700
More Making Out in Japanese	¥1,500
Outrageous Japanese	¥1,500
Reading and Writing Japanese	¥5,200
Remembering the Kanji	¥7,500

Living Japanese Style

Code of the Samurai	¥2,700
Etiquette Guide to Japan	¥2,000
Glimpses of Unfamiliar Japan	¥3,100
Japan Today	¥3,300
Japan Unmasked	¥2,100
Japanese Homes and Their Surroundings	¥2,300
Japanese: How They Live and Work	¥2,500
Living for Less in Tokyo	¥4,000
Living Japanese Style	¥2,000
Shopper's Guide to Japan	¥1,300
The Japan Experience: Coping and Beyond	¥2,300
The Kimono Mind	¥2,000
Winning Pachinko	¥2,000

Nightlife

Bachelor's Japan	¥2,500

Lover's Guide to Japan ¥1,500
The Japanese Mistress ¥1,700
Tokyo After Dark ¥2,600
Women of the Orient ¥1,500

Sports

Aikido and the Dynamic Sphere ¥6,000
Black Belt Karate ¥6,000
Cycling in Japan ¥4,500
Japanese Baseball ¥2,000
Karate: The Art of "Empty-Hand" Fighting ¥3,000
Karate's History and Traditions ¥3,000
Ninja and Their Secret Fighting Art ¥2,700
Ninjutsu: The Art of Invisibility ¥1,200
Secret Joys of Judo ¥2,500
Tae-Kwon Do ¥4,000
The Joy of Sumo ¥2,300

Studying in Japan

ABC's of Study in Japan ¥2,000
Japanese Language School Guide ¥2,000

Travel and Guide Books

A Guide to Japanese Hot Springs ¥4,000
Day Walks Near Tokyo ¥4,000
Festivals of Japan ¥2,000
Guide to Japanese Inns in Japan ¥2,000
Japan - A Travel Survival Kit by Lonely Planet ¥8,000
Must See in Kyoto ¥2,000
Must See in Nikko ¥2,000
Tokyo: A Bilingual Map ¥1,700
Unbeaten Tracks in Japan ¥2,500

1993 年 10 月 15 日 　発　　　　行

Making It in Japan
Work, Life, Leisure and Beyond

1993 年 10 月 15 日 　第 1 刷発行

著　者　Mark Gauthier

発行者　　株式会社 三省堂　代表者 守屋眞明

発行所　　株式会社 三省堂
　〒101 東京都千代田区三崎町二丁目 22 番 14 号
　　　　　　　　　電 話 編集　(03) 3230-9411
　　　　　　　　　　　　販 売　(03) 3230-9412
　　　　　振替口座　東京 6-54300

〈Making It in Japan・256 pp.〉